Brian J. Robb is the *New York Times* and *Sunday Times* best-selling biographer of Leonardo DiCaprio, Johnny Depp and Brad Pitt. He has also written acclaimed pop culture books on silent cinema, the films of Philip K. Dick, Wes Craven and Laurel and Hardy, TV series *Doctor Who* and *Star Trek*, Steampunk and J. R. R. Tolkien. He is co-editor of the popular website Sci-Fi Bulletin and lives in Edinburgh.

D1099616

A BRIEF HISTORY OF

WALT DISNEY

Brian J. Robb

ROBINSON   RUNNING PRESS
PHILADELPHIA · LONDON

ROBINSON

First published in Great Britain in 2014 by Robinson

Copyright © Brian J. Robb, 2014

A CIP catalogue record for this book
is available from the British Library.

ISBN: 978-1-47211-056-5 (paperback)
ISBN: 978-1-47211-072-5 (ebook)

Typeset by TW Typesetting, Plymouth, Devon

Printed and bound by CPI Group (UK) Ltd, Croydon, CR0 4YY

Robinson
An imprint of
Little, Brown Book Group
100 Victoria Embankment
London EC4Y 0DY

An Hachette UK Company
www.hachette.co.uk

www.littlebrown.co.uk

First published in the United States in 2014 by Running Press Book Publishers,
A Member of the Perseus Books Group

Books published by Running Press are available at special discounts for bulk purchases
in the United States by corporations, institutions, and other organizations. For more
information, please contact the Special Markets Department at the Perseus Books
Group, 2300 Chestnut Street, Suite 200, Philadelphia, PA 19103, or call (800) 810-4145,
ext. 5000, or e-mail
special.markets@perseusbooks.com.

US ISBN: 978-0-7624-5475-4

US Library of Congress Control Number: 2014937837

9 8 7 6 5 4 3 2 1

Digit on the right indicates the number of this printing

Running Press Book Publishers
2300 Chestnut Street
Philadelphia, PA 19103-4371

Visit us on the web!
www.runningpress.com
Printed and bound by CPI Group
(UK) Ltd, Croydon, CR0 4YY

CONTENTS

INTRODUCTION: THE KING OF CARTOONS

In December 2013 – as part of the launch of the new films *Saving Mr Banks* (2013), which chronicled the struggle of Walt Disney to make *Mary Poppins* (1964), and the new animated feature film, *Frozen* (2013) – the Disney studio threw a party celebrating nine decades of animation. The event took place at the appropriately named Legends Plaza, located on the Burbank studio lot in Los Angeles. At the gathering were some of the remaining Disney legends of animation who had worked for the pioneering studio from its earliest days.

Attending that day were 103-year-old Ruthie Thompson, an 'inker' who'd worked at Disney for forty years; 100-year-old Milton Quon, an artist who'd contributed to *Fantasia* (1940) and *Dumbo* (1941); and (the youngster among them) seventy-eight-year-old Burnett 'Burny' Mattinson, who'd shortly before celebrated his sixtieth year working for Disney and was the last person then working at the studio who had worked personally with Walt Disney. It's clear to see why Disney studio executives felt they couldn't wait another decade to celebrate the studio's centenary of animation, as it was unlikely there'd be anyone still around from the earliest days to participate.

The cocktail reception was hosted by Disney's Chairman and Chief Executive Officer Bob Iger and its Chief Creative Officer John Lasseter, the men who'd been in charge of the company since 2006. Iger had climbed to the top of the corporate ladder at Disney after his time at ABC television, and was seen as a new hope for the ever-expanding business after the twenty years of growth and turbulence under previous head, Michael Eisner. Lasseter was an ex-Disney animator who'd left the studio in the mid-1980s, sensing a downturn in its creative output, and keen to explore new avenues for animation that Disney was more or less ignoring. With Apple's Steve Jobs, he'd gone on to launch Pixar, dominate the world of computer-generated animated movies with the *Toy Story* series (released through Disney) and others, and eventually lead a reverse creative takeover of the Disney studio when it bought Pixar in 2006.

These two men – one in charge of finance and business, the other the creative driving force behind the studio's movies – uncannily echoed the founding figures of the studio they now led: the brothers Walt and Roy Disney. Roy was the older brother, the one who ran the business side and found the finance to pay for his younger sibling's creative schemes. Walt Disney was the dreamer, the founder of the Disney studio and the creative driving force not only behind a stream of ground-breaking hit animated movies such as *Snow White and the Seven Dwarfs* (1937), *Pinocchio* (1940) and *Dumbo* (1941), but also much-loved television series, a collection of real-world theme parks and a host of technological developments.

The Disney studio was established in 1923 when Walt arrived in Los Angeles and began to build an empire. He'd left behind him in Kansas City a bankrupt company and a group of friends and colleagues who'd helped him learn the basics of cinema animation – some of them would eventually join him in Los Angeles at the new studio. Walt arrived in

Hollywood, the American home of movies, with little more than $40 in his pocket and an unfinished cartoon film in his shabby suitcase. There was one person already in town he knew could help him realize his dreams: his older brother Roy, who'd relocated to California to recover from tuberculosis. Over the next four decades, Roy would be Walt's secret weapon, repeatedly finding sources of finance for his little brother's latest scheme, whether it be a full-length animated feature film, a brand new studio complex or a unique idea in movie-based theme parks.

From the creation of such enduring cartoon characters as Mickey Mouse, Donald Duck, Pluto and Goofy, through a series of animated fairy-tale feature films (including *Cinderella*, 1950, and *Sleeping Beauty*, 1959), trend-setting wildlife documentaries in the *True-Life Adventures* series, to live-action filmmaking that stretches from *20,000 Leagues Under the Sea* (1954) to *Mary Poppins* (1964), from *Swiss Family Robinson* (1960) to *The Incredible Journey* (1963), Walt Disney masterminded a new form of family entertainment.

From the Depression of the 1930s, that gave birth to the Mickey Mouse craze, to wartime propaganda, such as *Der Fuehrer's Face* (1943), in which Donald Duck satirizes Hitler, Walt was a representative of the American character. However, a 1941 animators' strike at his studio saw him develop an obsession with communists infiltrating his company and possibly led to him becoming an informer for the FBI in the 1950s. The decade of conformity saw his studio contribute heavily to mass media depictions of the perfect family life. Through his animated films, live-action features and television persona as friendly 'Uncle Walt', Walt Disney came to epitomize a certain innocent, family-friendly form of entertainment. At the same time, his company was accused of appropriating other countries' folklore and fairy tales and putting them through an American filter to produce homogenized entertainment that appealed to the lowest common denominator in audiences.

Very little of what went out under the Disney banner was actually created by Walt – even the origins of the symbol of the Disney studio, Mickey Mouse, and the graphic of the distinctive 'Walt Disney' signature are disputed. Walt Disney was an indifferent artist, a poor communicator and a barely competent animator, as shown by the earliest silent works that he did create almost entirely alone. He became a figurehead for the creative work of others – the 'story men', artists, animators and creators who toiled under the Disney name. Walt was involved in originating many of the original Disney projects, and heavily involved himself in story-development sessions before the war, but the bulk of the creativity that made up the output of the Disney studio came from others. Despite that, 'Disney' became a powerful brand name, especially for a certain type of entertainment.

Walt Disney hated to repeat himself – once he'd mastered or created something that had never been done before, he wanted to move on to something new. After the first feature-length American animated movie, *Snow White and the Seven Dwarfs*, Walt all but lost interest in his company's animated feature films. During the war he devoted himself to training and propaganda films, pioneering a new form of campaigning movie with the polemical *Victory Through Air Power* (1943). After the war, his creative energies were poured into television, with the launches of the television shows *Disneyland* (1954–2008, under various titles) and *The Mickey Mouse Club* (1955–9, during its first run). Then came developments in animatronic technology and theme parks that dominated Walt's final years, until his death aged sixty-five in December 1966.

Following Disney's death, the Disney studio faced several challenges. Those left in charge struggled to maintain the same level of quality output without Walt's 'magic touch'. After fifteen years of decline and the exodus of a group of unhappy animators led by Don Bluth, Walt's nephew Roy E. Disney championed change at the studio, bringing in experienced studio executives Michael Eisner, Jeffrey Katzenberg and Frank Wells. Together, and with Roy Disney in charge of animation, they revitalized and expanded the Disney studio, resulting in the 'Disney renaissance' in movies such as *The Little Mermaid* (1989), *Beauty and the Beast* (1991) and *The Lion King* (1994).

However, all was not well behind the scenes with a series of personality clashes resulting in Katzenberg's departure, the threat of hostile takeovers and plans to split the company up, and the return of the crusading Roy E. Disney – this time to save his uncle's company from the man he'd put in charge, Michael Eisner. In 2005–6, Disney was saved once more with the arrival of Bob Iger and Pixar's John Lasseter as the latest knights in white armour.

This book is a chronicle of the life and times of Walt Disney. It's not simply a biography of the man who created Mickey Mouse: it is also a history of the company that bore his name and the cultural products – films, television, theme parks and technology – it created. Inevitably, Walt Disney himself dominates the first two-thirds, and the book has a strong focus on Disney's animated films, as they are the studio's defining achievements. Think Disney, and it's animated movies that come to mind.

However, the Disney studio continued long after Walt himself was gone, through tough times and prosperous times. It has been expanded hugely to become one of the biggest multimedia entertainment corporations of the twenty-first century. This process began with Eisner and Katzenberg, but it kicked into a higher gear with the arrival of Bob Iger. In recent years, the Disney behemoth has swallowed up not only Jim Henson's Muppets, but Marvel comics and Lucasfilm's *Star Wars* franchise as well. Each of these companies comes with countless unique characters to be exploited in movies and tie-in merchandise for decades to come, ensuring that the studio Walt Disney built will continue to thrive. There's plenty of life left yet in what Hollywood trade paper *Variety* dubbed the 'Mouse House'.

At that celebration of ninety years of Disney animation, John Lasseter said: 'There is something special and unique about the kind of entertainment that Walt Disney created that no one has ever been able to reproduce – that warmth he puts in your heart . . . the humour, the beauty. It's why I chose this life's work and why all the artists here at Disney chose it. At one point, Walt Disney touched all our lives.'

A Brief History of Walt Disney explores the man, the films he created and the company he built, with a special emphasis on animation. After all, as Bob Iger said at that same celebration: 'Animation really has been the heart and the soul of this company.'

PART ONE: BUILDING THE 'MOUSE HOUSE'

I

FROM CHICAGO TO HOLLYWOOD

[Marceline, Missouri] must have made a deep impression on me. I can clearly remember every detail. Those were the happiest days of my life. Maybe that's why I go for country cartoons . . .

Walt Disney, *Family Circle*, 24 June 1938

The roots of the success of Walt Disney and the company that he built (and named after himself) are to be found in his rural childhood, his love of fairy tales and fables, and his early business failure in the new world of film animation. His first twenty years laid down much of the character that he would later display, both privately in his creative roles and publicly as the man who became known universally – thanks to television – as 'Uncle Walt'.

The twentieth century had just begun when the man who would do much to shape and influence the entertainment that defined that century was born. Walter Elias Disney – known to everyone as Walt – was born on 5 December 1901 in Chicago,

Illinois. His work, and that of those he employed in developing the art form of animation, would make its mark on the history of cinema. Moving pictures themselves were barely twenty years old at the time of Disney's birth. The first practical motion-picture cameras had been invented in the late 1880s, just shortly after Walt's pious father, Elias Disney, had arrived in the United States from Canada.

Disney's great-grandfather, Arundel Elias Disney, had been born in Gowran, County Kilkenny, Ireland, a full century earlier in 1801. He claimed ancestry back to Frenchman Robert D'Isigny of D'Isigny-sur-Mer on the coast of Normandy, who had travelled to England with William the Conqueror in 1066, although later researchers could find no definite family connections going back that far. The D'Isigny family name was soon anglicized to 'Disney', and became the name of their village of Norton Disney, south of the city of Lincoln. The family branched out to Ireland and then, with the emigration of Arundel and his brother Robert and their families, to the United States. They arrived in New York on 3 October 1834 and went their separate ways, with Robert heading to the Midwest to take up farming and Arundel heading north to the Goderich township in Ontario, Canada.

The North American gold rush of the late 1800s brought Arundel's son Kepple Disney and his grandson Elias Disney (the oldest of Kepple's eleven children) back to the United States, heading for the California gold fields. En route, convinced that land was perhaps a more sound investment than panning for gold, Kepple bought 200 acres of Union Pacific Railroad land near Ellis, Kansas, and established a farm. Farm life didn't suit young Elias and he spent some time working on the railroad, before returning to the Kansas family farm thanks to the attractive charms of their near neighbour, Flora Call.

Flora's family, of Scottish and English descent, had also pursued the riches promised by the gold rush, only – like the Disneys – to end up as Kansas farmers and landowners, a much more reliable lifestyle. Neither family liked the Kansas weather, however, so the Disney and the Call families moved together to Florida in 1884, where Elias bought a forty-acre farm and Flora became a schoolteacher. The pair finally married on New Year's Day in 1888 at Flora's parents' home in Acron, Florida (just forty miles from the eventual site of the Walt Disney World Resort). Elias Disney was twenty-eight and Flora Call was just nineteen.

By 1890 Elias and Flora had moved once again, to Chicago, where his brother Robert now lived. It was there, three weeks before Christmas, that Walt Disney was born, joining his three older brothers, Herbert (b. 1888), Raymond (b. 1890) and Roy (b. 1893). One longstanding fabrication had Walt Disney adopted by Elias and Flora, as he was supposedly really the son of a Spanish nobleman and a washerwoman, and had been born in Mojacar, southeast Spain. The absence of a birth certificate (there was only a baptismal certificate dated 8 June 1902 for Walt) helped to fuel such rumours, which were traced to a false story in a 1940 Spanish movie magazine, *Primer Plano* (although this didn't stop the fanciful tale forming the basis of at least one Walt Disney biography, *Hollywood's Dark Prince*, in 1993).

Although a successful housebuilder (he'd also constructed a church in Chicago in 1898), Elias Disney took a dislike to city life in Chicago and decided he would prefer his family to live in the kind of rural environment in which he'd first met Flora. In 1906, when Walt was just four years old, the Disney family were on the move again, this time to Marceline, Missouri, where Elias's ever-supportive brother Robert had already bought some farmland.

Walt Disney's earliest childhood memories were not of city life in Chicago, but of the countryside of Missouri, and they would help shape his future creative life. The charms of the traditional Marceline main street would remain with him his entire life (and would form the basis for the romanticized Main Street of the Disneyland parks), as would his happy memories of life

on the family farm. It was there he first developed his artistic skills, taking up drawing as a hobby, with a horse named
Rupert that belonged to a local retired doctor a favourite illustration subject for the young Disney. At the age of seven, young
Walt was selling his sketches and drawings to neighbours. He
started school that same year, having been held back by his
parents until his younger sister Ruth (b. 1903) was old enough
to attend with him. He'd rather spend his time drawing pictures of animals and nature – things he was close to around the
farm – than doing his school work, where his grades were little
better than fair.

Young Walt also became obsessed with the railroad and
trains, as the Atchison, Topeka and Santa Fe Railway ran
right through Marceline and came close to the Disney family
property. Walt liked nothing better than to put his ear to the
thrumming railroad tracks, listening for the telltale signs of
distant approaching trains. Trains and the railroad would
become another lifelong obsession for him.

The trains were left behind when the Disney family moved
120 miles to Kansas City in 1911, this time because life on
the farm was much tougher after the two elder Disney boys,
Herbert and Raymond, fled their domineering father to move
to Chicago. Although he thought of his time on the farm as
the best years of his life, Walt was largely unaware of the hard-
scrabble existence endured by his devout parents and older
brothers. Young Walt was terribly upset when the farm animals
were auctioned off to nearby neighbours and other farmers as
the property was sold off.

Settled in Kansas City, Walt, now aged ten, attended Benton
Grammar School. He was closest to his younger sister Ruth, as
Roy – his nearest brother in age – was eight years older than
him, quite a significant gap for a child. The big city was something of a shock to the artistically minded boy after his carefree
life in the country, surrounded by open fields and plenty of
animals and wildlife. The noise of city life, the huge multi-
storey buildings (skyscrapers were just then beginning to go

up) and the fast-moving automobiles were completely counter to the slower-paced life he'd known. However, the city could be equally exciting, too. He and Roy toured its streets delivering newspapers in all weathers after their father won a contract to deliver the morning *Times* and evening and Sunday *Star* newspapers to 700 local subscribers. That unpaid job (their father kept the income, arguing the brothers' board and lodging was their reward) and school would keep Walt Disney very busy for the next six years.

Walt's school grades improved little in Kansas City, although he read widely – Walter Scott, Charles Dickens and the adventure stories of Robert Louis Stevenson were his favourites (he'd later make movies from several Stevenson stories), alongside the fairy tales he'd grown up with. His drawing skills developed, especially his caricatures of local neighbourhood figures. His brother Roy also finally fled their father's tyranny in 1912, leaving Walt to carry the remaining burden of the newspaper round alone and as the only remaining target of his father's regular wrath. However, Walt had a new school friend, Walter Pfeiffer, and new interests in vaudeville theatre and movies to keep him occupied and away from the fractious family home.

The Pfeiffer family were theatre fans and Walt found their musical, laughter-filled house to be more hospitable than his own rather more austere home life. His visits to the movies and to see vaudeville shows in the company of Walter Pfeiffer had to be undertaken on the sly, as Elias Disney considered such things frivolous. Together the boys imitated the comics they saw, often through the city streets when Pfeiffer accompanied Walt on his newspaper rounds. They began developing their own routines, performing at school and eventually playing in amateur nights at their local theatre. Unfortunately, Walt had the bad luck to be performing on the same night his parents made a rare visit to the theatre, where they were rather startled to see their own son cavorting on stage.

Walt enjoyed entertaining, although he was not a confident

performer. He preferred his cartooning, but he also loved watching Charlie Chaplin shorts at the local movie house. He took additional art classes at the Kansas City Art Institute and took his sister Ruth on trips to Electric Park, a huge amusement park near their home that would influence the eventual design of Disneyland.

Walt Disney graduated from school on 8 June 1917 and stayed behind for the summer in Kansas City to help pass on the newspaper route to new owners when his father took his mother to Chicago in pursuit of a new business opportunity. Elias Disney invested $16,000 ($20 of which belonged to Walt) in the O-Zell jelly factory and became the head of plant construction – he'd been investing in the company since 1912. Now aged fifteen, Walt took a summer job on the railroad selling sodas and snacks on the trains, a role known as a 'news butcher'. He'd claimed he was sixteen in order to secure the position, and his faithful older brother Roy vouched for him.

By that fall, Walt was reluctantly again living with his parents in Chicago, attending McKinley High School during the day and taking night classes three times a week at the Chicago Art Institute. He practised his cartooning for the school newspaper, the *Voice*, often choosing to illustrate topics associated with the First World War, then entering its closing stages. He did odd jobs in his father's jelly factory, or as a security guard, or collecting and delivering mail for the post office. In the summer of 1918, Walt tried to join his older brothers who'd already enlisted in the military, but was turned away as he was still underage.

After failing to get into the Army, his school friend Russell Maas suggested he and Walt try to get into the voluntary American Ambulance Corps, part of the Red Cross. This time, Walt upped his age to seventeen so he would bypass the age restrictions, altering his birth date on the paperwork to '1900'. Walt spent time in the motor pool in Chicago, learning how to drive and repair vehicles, but then had to take some time out in order to recover from a bout of the 1918 influenza epidemic (Walt was lucky; Chicagoans – in common with many world-wide – were dying in their hundreds). Armistice was declared on 11 November, bringing the war to an end, but a week later, on November 18, Walt Disney shipped out to France to spend a year as an ambulance driver. The war was over, but there was plenty of adventure and incident to keep a young man occupied in post-war Paris. It was there that he took up smoking with a vengeance, a habit that was to give him serious health problems later in life.

The city was devastated and there was much to be done. Walt's role as a driver involved shipping supplies across the war-torn urban environment, as well as occasionally driving military officers back and forth to important meetings. He turned seventeen that December, but it was a subdued birthday in a bleak and cold city. He kept up his cartooning, further refining his skills, and sent drawings to publications in the States, but all were rejected. He made money selling caricatures to soldiers who mailed them home and by taking part in card games, mailing any proceeds to his family. Over the following months, life for Parisians began to return to something resembling normality and there was eventually no further requirement for the Red Cross ambulances. In September 1919 the American units left France, and the American Ambulance Corps was soon disbanded. During his year in France Walt Disney had gained a new maturity and he knew upon his return to the United States it would be time for him to find a proper profession.

Whatever he would do for a living, Walt was adamant he wouldn't work alongside his father in the Chicago O-Zell factory. To his father's disdain, Walt announced he wanted to be an actor or an artist, despite warnings that he'd never make an adequate living either way. One thing he knew for sure: his future wasn't in Chicago. Walt moved back to Kansas City once more, taking up residence with his older brother Roy, with whom he was able to share war stories. Hopes of becoming a cartoonist for a Kansas City newspaper, however, were quickly dashed as no one was hiring.

He heard of a vacancy at a commercial art agency, quickly applied, and soon found himself working as an apprentice at the Pesmen-Rubin Commercial Art Studio, which serviced the Gray Advertising Company. For $50 per month, he designed print ads for farm supply companies, local farm produce retailers and – his favourite job – the Newman Theatre weekly programme booklet. It was at Pesmen-Rubin that Walt Disney met a young Dutch artist who would help him on the road to fulfil his artistic ambitions.

Ub Iwerks (his proper full Dutch name was Ubbe Eert Iwwerks) was the same age as Walt and had been at Pesmen-Rubin for just a month. The pair bonded over their work on newspaper advertisements, catalogue illustrations and Christmas-themed promotions. Iwerks would later repeatedly relate an anecdote in which he claimed that Walt would spend his lunch hours practising his own signature – it was even suggested in some quarters that Walt's distinctive graphic signature used as the Disney company logo had been 'created' for him by Iwerks. Once the crush of holiday deadlines passed, however, they were both let go after just six weeks. Walt fell back on a previous temporary job at the post office and began delivering mail, his artistic ambitions set back again.

Walt and Ub decided to go into business for themselves as commercial artists, establishing the Iwerks-Disney Commercial Artists company (they'd tried the names the other way around, Disney-Iwerks, but Walt thought it sounded too much like an opticians) using some of Walt's money from his gambling winnings in France. Disney was the salesman and illustrator, responsible for getting the pair work, while the quieter Ub illustrated and did the lettering on ads. Their first month's work netted them $135, more than they'd been getting at Pesmen-Rubin. Their clients included the *Leather Workers Journal*, an oil well sales firm and the National Restaurant Association. However, that was also their last month's income as in January

1920 the pair saw an ad for a cartoonist at the Kansas Slide Company. They both agreed Walt should apply. He got the job, at $40 per week, and Ub soldiered on with Iwerks-Disney alone. He was no salesman, though, and the business stalled. By March 1920, Ub had joined Walt at the now renamed Kansas City Film Ad Company where they produced illustrations for minute-long advertising films that played in cinemas.

Animation was as old as cinema itself. From seventeenth-century magic lanterns through Victorian gadgets such as the Zoetrope and Praxinoscope that projected limited moving images, artists had tried to represent the world on screens through moving drawings. Traditional hand-drawn animation developed in the early years of the twentieth century, with J. Stuart Blackton – in *The Enchanted Drawing* (1900), *Humorous Phases of Funny Faces* (1906) and *The Haunted Hotel* (1907) – and Émile Cohl – with *Fantasmagorie*, *Le Cauchemar de Fantoche* and *Un Drame Chez les Fantoches* (all 1908) – producing moving images from their artwork. Early frame-by-frame animated films included distinctive works by newspaper cartoonist Winsor McCay, such as *Little Nemo* (1911), *Gertie the Dinosaur* (1914) and *The Sinking of the Lusitania* (1918), many originally presented as part of his touring vaudeville routines.

Cel animation – in which each individual drawing was photographed from a clear animation cel (short for celluloid, the plastic material used for this and as the basis for film itself), rather than involving cut-out paper figures – quickly became the industry standard method of production. Soon animators began to create film series built around specific characters, the most popular of which was Pat Sullivan/Otto Mesmer's Felix the Cat, who debuted in 1919. That same year, Max Fleischer launched Koko the Clown in his 'Out of the Inkwell' series and in 1921 Paul Terry debuted his Terrytoon *Aesop's Fables*. Such short animated films quickly became an established part of any cinema theatre's programme and remained so into the early 1920s.

Animation was something new for Walt Disney. Although

the work produced at the Kansas City Film Ad Company was basic, Walt could see the potential. The short ads were made quickly using cut-out paper figures that were crudely animated one frame at a time. Intrigued by the possibilities, Walt set out to learn all he could about how cartoons were made. To discover more about the practicalities of producing animated short films, Walt had to teach himself the basics. He was aware that the shorts he saw at the cinema coming out of New York were far more realistic and smoothly animated than the cruder material he was working on. He borrowed books from the local library – including human and animal motion studies by Eadweard Muybridge and Edwin George Lutz's *Animated Cartoons: How They Are Made, Their Origin and Development* (1920) – to see how he could make his own work look more like the Koko the Clown and Mutt & Jeff cartoons unspooling at local cinemas. Having discovered cel animation, Walt introduced the idea to his boss at the Kansas City Film Ad Company, A. V. Cauger, who was impressed, but unwilling to change his techniques. The tyro animator rewrote the ad copy he was supplied, adding jokes and coming up with catchier sales lines than the company's best copywriters. Walt also acted in some of the company's live-action ads, playing salesmen and customers, anything the script required.

Walt Disney was earning and learning, borrowing an animation camera from work to practise his new craft long into the night. Early in 1921, practical experiments with the borrowed camera taught him a lot. Such experimentation allowed him to develop the best lighting and animation techniques to make his cartoon-style illustrations look good on screen. He made his own cartoon about a hot button local issue: the poor repair of Kansas City streets. Cartoon-style drivers were depicted getting into all sorts of scrapes thanks to potholes in the roads. Walt took the finished 300-foot cartoon to the Newman Theatre Company, a local business that owned three cinemas in the area (he'd worked on their programme book while engaged at Pesmen-Rubin).

Manager Milton Feld was impressed by Walt's work. He said he could use a new one every week and asked the young animator how much he charged. Never the best businessman, Walt guessed that thirty cents per foot of film would cover his costs, only realizing afterwards that he'd not allowed for any profit. He continued working during the day making animated ads, but at night he'd toil in a makeshift animation studio in his brother Roy's garage. Feld suggested special topics for films, whether political satire or seasonal such as Christmas, and Walt was only too happy to oblige. He called the cartoons Laugh-O-Grams.

During 1921, Walt Disney produced around a dozen Laugh-O-Gram shorts for Milton Feld – they're all lost now, apart from the first. Theatre owner Frank Newman appended his own name to the films, exhibiting them as 'Newman's Laugh-O-Grams'. Walt's demonstration effort depicts the hand of the artist drawing characters that then come to life on screen. He'd lifted this idea from Max Fleischer who used it in his 'Out of the Inkwell' cartoons, but Disney couldn't figure out how to animate his own hand, which he couldn't even fit under the camera mounting, so he used a photographic cut-out, as had been the method of animation at the Kansas City Film Ad Company.

The only surviving example of a Newman's Laugh-O-Gram opens with the young Walt Disney working at his animator's desk. Topical humour mixed with adverts was the order of the day, with the short reel made up of illustrations and cartoons commenting on politics, crime, ladies' fashions, transport in Kansas City and – under the headline 'spring clean up' – police corruption. The success of the shorts made a minor local celebrity of Walt Disney, but he had ambitions beyond this rather basic work.

Walt suggested to his boss at the Kansas City Film Ad Company that they should make short films for distribution to cinemas nationally. This idea was also rejected, so Walt decided to set up on his own once more as the 'Kaycee Studio' (Kaycee derived from KC, the initials of Kansas City – the company was never formally incorporated). He moved his animation set-up out of Roy's garage and into a small shop-front and advertised for additional staff. There was no pay on offer, just a promise of a share of future profits, but Walt was offering to teach those he took on the basics of the new cinematic art of animation. Walt Disney had big ambitions: he wanted to produce fully animated shorts to rival those coming out of the well-known animation studios in New York, such as the work of the Fleischers, the Terrytoons and John R. Bray's colour cartoon *The Debut of Thomas Cat* (1920, only the second ever cartoon made in colour). Among those helping Disney get started were Iwerks and twenty-year-old Fred Harman, another fellow employee at the Kansas City Film Ad Company.

Following some experimental works (the Winsor McCay-inspired *The Little Artist* and *The Old Mill*), the first fully completed film, produced during these evenings, was *Little Red Riding Hood* (1922). Looked at today, the six-minute film (credited on screen as having been 'cartooned by Walt Disney') is rather crude. The Fleischer influence is all-pervasive, from the look of a laughing bearded old man seen in a picture frame on a wall to the animation of a trigger-happy cat, who would evolve into a character called Julius the Cat, that quickly loses all nine of its lives – a gag Walt would use repeatedly. That influence is hardly surprising, as the Fleischer films were the best models available for Disney to imitate.

The action is simple and repetitive; the imagination on display is not on a par with the increasingly freewheeling surrealism of the Fleischer brothers' more inventive work. It was, however, early days, and as a calling card that allowed Walt Disney to begin learning his craft, this modernized – with automobiles and aeroplanes – retelling of Little Red Riding Hood served its purpose. Missing for many years, and listed in 1980 by the American Film Institute as one of the ten 'most wanted' films

for archival preservation, *Little Red Riding Hood* was rediscovered in 1998 in a London film library and has since been
restored as a key work in the development of Walt Disney as an
animator and showman.

Inspired by his self-taught accomplishment with *Little Red
Riding Hood*, Walt Disney resolved to set up properly in business for himself. He finally left his position at the Kansas City
Film Ad Company after two years, giving up his increased
salary of $60 per week. On 23 May 1922 he launched Laugh-
O-Gram Films, funded through $15,000 he'd raised from local
investors who each invested between $250 to $500, as well as
funding from friends and relatives. One significant investor
was a local doctor named John V. Cowles, a prominent Kansas
City figure and a friend of the Disney family through Walt's
uncle Robert. Well-connected financially and politically,
Cowles wrote Walt a cheque for $2,500.

The new company incorporated the remaining assets of
Iwerks-Disney Commercial Artists, with Ub Iwerks joining
Disney as one of the first employees. Others joining the new
outfit included Hugh Harman (brother of Frank), Rudolph
'Rudy' Ising (who'd worked on *Little Red Riding Hood*
with Walt), Otto Walliman, cameraman William 'Red' Lyon
(another old Kansas City Film Ad Company colleague), Lorey
Tague (the only one of the young team who was married)
and Carmen 'Max' Maxwell. There was a business manager,
Adolph Kloepper, who also doubled up as an animation inker
and painter; a short-lived salesman Leslie Mace (previously a
local sales rep for Paramount Pictures); and a secretary. Walt's
old school pal Walter Pfeiffer also joined as a 'scenario direct-
or', which he admitted was basically a joke writer. This group
of enthusiastic young men were dedicated to learning the art
and craft of animation on the job.

Aged just twenty (and at that time, legally speaking, still
a minor), Walt leased a five-room, second-floor suite in the
McConahy Building on the corner of 31st Street and Forest

Avenue in Kansas City. Installed in the workspace was all manner of outré bespoke equipment, including a trio of inker-and-tracer tables, three animation booths, lighting equipment and animation stands – far from the usual office equipment used by the surrounding businesses. Disney had set out on his new enterprise with just one projector, one movie camera and one still camera, but it was to be the beginning of an empire.

The *Motion Picture News* announced the arrival of Laugh-O-Gram Films in June 1922. 'They will produce Laugh-O-Gram cartoon comedies,' the trade paper said, 'cartooned by Walter E. Disney.' No doubt based on exaggerated information supplied by Walt himself, the magazine claimed he'd been making films for the Newman Theatre chain for 'several years' and had already completed six animated films, none of which was strictly true. By July, Walt had placed an advert in the *Motion Picture News* promising his company was already in production on a series of twelve animated shorts.

A distribution deal was struck in September 1922 for the output of Laugh-O-Gram Films with William R. Kelly and Pictorial Clubs of Tennessee, a largely non-theatrical outfit distributing films to schools and churches. A cheque for $100 and a promise of $11,000 more for six cartoons sealed the deal, with payment of the remainder falling due upon delivery of the final cartoon by the deadline of 1 January 1924, almost a year and a half away. Nonetheless, Walt Disney was finally in the animation business.

Sticking with much-loved childhood fairy tales, the company embarked on a further five animated shorts, beginning with *The Four Musicians of Bremen*, which was a significant step up in quality from *Little Red Riding Hood*. The four musicians of the tale are depicted as animals: a donkey, a dog, a rooster and a cat, another forerunner of Julius the Cat – and the loss of the cat's nine lives gag reappears. Although unnamed at this point, Julius featured in the remaining Laugh-O-Gram releases from 1922, all modelled after traditional fairy tales:

Jack and the Beanstalk, *Goldie Locks [sic] and the Three Bears*, *Puss in Boots* (which spoofed silent movie star and heart-throb Rudolph Valentino), *Cinderella* and *Jack the Giant Killer* (the four then-surviving shorts were made available as extras on the 2010 Blu-ray release of Disney's 1991 film *Beauty and the Beast*, while the missing three were rediscovered in 2010).

Walt Disney was 'hands on' during these early endeavours, operating the camera, helping to animate and cleaning used animation cels in order to reuse them. Although nominally the chief executive of his own company, he saw himself simply as one of the workers, learning the business of cinema animation alongside his co-workers. The friendly crew of Laugh-O-Gram Films had a steep learning curve, as none of them were yet adept at animation, learning on the job and through studying their more accomplished rivals.

To make additional money for the organization, Walt affiliated his company as the Kansas City outpost for newsreels from Selznick, Pathé and Universal. The fee was usually $1 per foot of film, with most newsreel reports needing at least 100 feet. When an assignment to cover a local news event came in from New York, work on any in-progress animation stopped: the company's sole camera was separated from the animation unit and used on the street to capture whatever was needed for the newsreels. The team also produced 'Lafflets', very short animated snippets on subjects such as golf, pottery and pirates (none have survived). Everyone was heavily involved and emotionally invested at Laugh-O-Gram Films, so none were too concerned if occasionally their salaries would come up short, with Walt regularly blaming the company's problematic cash flow.

As 1922 drew to a close, it was clear something was seriously wrong. The finished films were being supplied to Pictorial Clubs for distribution but none of the promised $11,000 balance had yet found its way back to Kansas City. As no payment had been due until many months following the signing of the contract, time had been allowed to elapse without much concern on Walt's part (he was developing a habit of being rather laid-back in matters of business). However, in the meantime Pictorial Clubs had quietly gone out of business, leaving Laugh-O-Gram Films with a payment of just $100 for the six completed seven-minute cartoon shorts.

With no salaries, employees began to leave the floundering company, including Ub Iwerks who returned to work at the somewhat more reliable Kansas City Film Ad Company. Walt managed to raise an additional $2,500 from Dr Cowles – still one of his main backers despite the problems – to keep the business afloat. However, Walt had to move out of his rented rooms as he could no longer pay the rent, first bunking with Iwerks and then sleeping in the offices of Laugh-O-Grams Films (with a weekly bath at Union Station, costing a dime a time). Hoping to raise additional funds, Walt advertised an unusual service: he offered to film children as a keepsake for young families (this was before widespread availability of home-movie systems).

With no work on the horizon and money quickly running out, Walt was temporarily saved in December 1922 when a local dentist paid $500 for a short film to promote his business (it seems likely this deal came about through the behind-the-scenes intervention of Cowles yet again). The result was *Tommy Tucker's Tooth* (1922), a mostly live-action – some animated diagrams featured – short filmed in Thomas B. McCrumb's Kansas City dental practice. The ten-minute movie, starring local school kid John Records, was essentially a tutorial on teeth brushing and a warning of what can happen if children ignore their dental health. It was released on 10 December 1922.

This work seemed to revive Walt's dormant ambition, which had taken a knock over the Pictorial Clubs fiasco. He hit upon the idea of reversing the aspect of the Fleischers's work he'd most admired – instead of showing the animator at work creating cartoon characters, what if he put a live-action person into an animated world?

Disney resolved to create a short based upon children's classic Lewis Carroll's *Alice's Adventures in Wonderland* (1865), but he needed an appealing young girl to play Alice. Six-year-old Virginia Davis (who'd previously appeared in an advert produced by the Kansas City Film Ad Company) was hired to play the role, and was filmed against a plain background. Her antics were then combined with those of animated characters and backgrounds to produce *Alice's Wonderland* (1923). She was offered no fee, such were the restricted finances of Walt's company, but her family agreed to be paid 5 per cent of all fees received by Walt when he sold the films.

Walt reached out to the distributors of the 'Out of the Inkwell' series, promoting his new concept as 'live child actors who carry on their action on cartoon scenes with cartoon characters', in the hope they'd take on *Alice's Wonderland* for distribution. While he waited for a response, time was running out for Laugh-O-Gram Films: Walt's financial resources were dwindling despite financial help from his brother Roy, *Alice's Wonderland* was only half done and the rent on the McConahy Building suite of offices was overdue. Despite moving to smaller premises above the Isis Theater just along the street, and struggling to continue in production on the Alice short, time and money simply ran out for Walt Disney.

Most of the staff had left Laugh-O-Gram Films, including his childhood friend Walter Pfeiffer, so Walt struggled on more or less alone to complete the animation on *Alice's Wonderland*. He refused to accept defeat, such was his belief that animated cartoons had a great future. He made a last-ditch attempt to produce sing-a-long films called 'Song-O-Reels' with Carl Stalling, then the organist at the Isis Theater (and later the composer at the Disney studio and for Warner Bros.'s Looney Tunes and Merrie Melodies cartoons).

Through all the ups and downs with Laugh-O-Gram Films, the twenty-one-year-old Walt Disney had learned a huge amount about creating animated cartoons. Eventually, though, even he finally had to face defeat. Running out of funds, the company was declared bankrupt, and although Walt himself was offered another job locally by an animation company, he resolved to leave behind the sense of failure that surrounded him in Kansas City. If he wanted to be a success in the film business, there was only one place for Walt Disney to go now: Hollywood.

2

ALICE, OSWALD AND MICKEY

[Mice] were always cute characters, and they hadn't been
overdone in the picture field . . . I decided it would be a
mouse. I had him 'Mortimer' first, and my wife shook her
head, then I tried 'Mickey' and she nodded the other way,
and that was it.

Walt Disney, *Voices from the Hollywood Past*, 1959
(Walt Disney Archives)

With little more than the clothes on his back, $40 in his pocket, and a suitcase half-packed with animation equipment and an unfinished cartoon, Walt Disney arrived in Hollywood in July 1923 full of hope and optimism. He'd left a mess behind him in Kansas City (it would take many years for the legal and financial fallout from Laugh-O-Grams Films to be sorted out), but he felt he'd learned much that would help forge his way to success in Hollywood, home of the American movie business. His experiences in Kansas City had taught Walt 'what it meant to shift for myself, to take advantage of opportunity, and the thing that every American kid must learn – to take the hard knocks with the good breaks'.

It may have seemed odd for Disney to opt for Hollywood, rather than New York where all the most successful animation houses were then based. There were several good reasons for Walt going West rather than East in 1923. His uncle Robert, who'd always encouraged him, had already made the move to Hollywood, and his reliable older brother Roy was also there, recuperating from a bout of tuberculosis, so he had family connections. Additionally, Disney was – as ever – thinking big. At the back of his mind was the thought of moving beyond animated movies to becoming a producer or director of live-action films. For that to happen, he had to be in Hollywood, especially in the early 1920s when popular filmmaking was just entering its first golden age.

When it came to making movies, Hollywood was nothing if not a town of opportunity. The earliest days of American films had played out in New York between the late 1890s and the early 1900s. The first studios were built there, and the earliest popular films made there. However, as a result of patent wars and inter-company rivalries, several key figures ventured westwards. In 1910, the Biograph Company sent director D. W. Griffith to the West Coast to shoot the movie melodrama *In Old California* (1910), starring Lillian Gish and Mary Pickford. At the time Hollywood was little more than a small village, about ten miles from Los Angeles. Griffith liked the light in the West, as well as the open spaces (much of the area was little more than orange and lemon groves), and decided to stay and make more movies. By 1913 Griffith had been joined by several other filmmakers and companies fleeing from the fees imposed upon them in New York by Thomas Edison enforcing his movie-equipment patents.

Over the next few years, the movie industry set down permanent roots with most studios located in the Hollywood area, causing the town to grow hugely and its name to become synonymous with cinema. Audiences were growing, too, with forty million people (one-third of the American population) going to the cinema every week in the 1920s. Walt Disney arrived in town in July 1923, just as the now world-famous Hollywood sign – then reading 'Hollywoodland', the name of a real estate development it was advertising; 'land' was removed in 1949 – was being erected. It was a place where he'd feel right at home . . .

Walt initially moved in with his uncle Robert, whose home was not far from the gigantic crumbling set of Babylon, built by Griffith for *Intolerance* (1916), then abandoned. It was a metaphor for the opportunities and dangers awaiting all who tried to make their names and fortunes in the picture business, but it didn't put Walt off. He rapidly got to know the geography of the movie studios, and still had his old business cards proclaiming him the Kansas City representative of Universal and Selznick (stretching his minor newsreel experience somewhat). It was enough to get him through the doors of some of the studios, where he was able to watch filmmakers in action. He got access to Universal, Vitagraph Studios and the Paramount lot. He saw the buzz of studio life, first hand. This was what he wanted to do.

Fearing he was too late to make an impact with cartoons, Disney tried to secure work at the studios, preferably as a director. His lack of demonstrable experience, if not confidence, meant that he failed to progress and quickly found himself out of money and options once more. He'd been in Hollywood for two months, and now had to borrow money from his brother Roy in order to pay his rent to his uncle. Although he briefly considered becoming a movie extra, Disney eventually concluded that if he wanted to make his way in the movie world, he'd better stick to what he knew: making cartoons.

By September he'd recreated his original Kansas City makeshift animation studio in Uncle Robert's garage using the few bits of equipment he'd brought with him and whatever he could find lying around to build a camera stand. Although he managed to interest Alexander Pantages, of Pantages Theatres, in recreating something like the Laugh-O-Gram Films,

Disney pinned his hopes on the Alice comedies. After all, he had a nearly finished version of *Alice's Wonderland* to show to potential distributors. He then managed to interest New York-based cartoon distributor Margaret Winkler in handling the Alice series, with the proviso that he'd improve on the quality of the first try-out short.

Margaret Winkler had begun in the movie business as a secretary to New York-based Harry Warner, one of the founders of Warner Bros. studios. By 1917, she was handling distribution of Warner's cartoons in New York and New Jersey, and then took on the 'Out of the Inkwell' series from the Fleischer brothers. She established her own company, Winkler Pictures, and by 1922 had added the Felix the Cat cartoons from Pat Sullivan Productions to her roster of movies, distributed on a 'states' rights basis, which meant that sales were done individually state-by-state.

By 1923, when Walt Disney approached her, Winkler was open to new avenues as she had lost the Fleischer account when they set up their own distribution system, and she was having trouble with the difficult Sullivan. Margaret Winkler needed Walt Disney almost as much as the neophyte animator needed her. She was prepared to offer him $1,500 per seven-minute cartoon, with payment upon delivery of each negative. There was only one condition: Alice must be played by the same little girl as before to maintain continuity between the shorts. The only problem was that Walt no longer had access to his Kansas City Alice, Virginia Davies.

This was, however, Walt's big chance to establish himself in Hollywood, but he knew he needed the help of his brother Roy to get things started. Visiting his brother's tuberculosis sickbed that October, Walt explained that he could complete each cartoon for around $750, meaning they'd make a 100 per cent profit on each one. That was enough for Roy to accept the deal, putting up $200 of his own money and persuading their rather reluctant uncle Robert (who feared that Walt was gaining a reputation following his adventures in Kansas City as someone who didn't pay his debts – he still owed older brother Ray $60, that being his investment in Laugh-O-Gram Films) to put in a further $500, albeit at a stringent 8 per cent interest. Walt secured a loan of $275 from Carl Stalling, still the organist at the Isis Theater back in Kansas City.

The deal with Winkler was sealed on 16 October 1923, with Walt and Roy jointly signing a contract that would pay them $1,500 for each of six Alice comedies and $1,800 each for six further films, with an option for two more series to follow. Disney obtained office space behind a real-estate office for the sum of $10 per month, and bought a second-hand movie camera for $200. Roy quickly learned how to operate the camera, perhaps because he wanted to protect his $200 investment and keep an eye on Walt. The next task was to secure the further services of the young Virginia Davies. Her parents, perhaps star struck by Hollywood or because they had few ties in Kansas City, agreed to move the family out to California so their daughter could appear in Disney's new movies. The fee paid would be $100 per film, with a built-in escalator of an additional $25 every two months up to a total of $200 for the first twelve shorts. Together, the Disney brothers were in the animation business.

The second Alice comedy, *Alice's Day at Sea* (released in March 1924), in which a shipwrecked Alice battles an octopus, was completed (Walt did the animation and Roy shot the live action) and supplied to Winkler Pictures by Christmas 1923. The first payment allowed the brothers to relocate to new premises on the corner of Hollywood Boulevard and Rodney Drive, again for $10 per month, where their live-action shooting took place. There they embarked upon the next film – after Winkler had rejected an Africa-themed instalment as below par – *Alice's Spooky Adventure* (April 1924), for which Disney employed local kids alongside Virginia Davies for a fee of fifty cents each. Alice now had a German shepherd dog, which was actually Walt's Uncle Robert's dog Peggy, and the film was hailed by Winkler as the best Walt had produced.

By February 1924, Disney had employed his first animator,

Rollin Hamilton, and moved premises yet again to an office on Kingswell Avenue (near Robert's house), which had a garage that became Walt's office, at the cost of $35 per month. A sign above the door announced this was the location of 'Disney Bros. Studios'.

The first few of the Alice comedies, released between March 1924 and the end of that year, show an artist learning his skills on the job. There was no doubt that Walt Disney could draw, if not exceptionally well, and he could animate cartoon characters and minimal backgrounds, even if he still owed a large debt to the Fleischer style. His biggest deficiencies – as pointed out to him by Margaret Winkler – were in plot and comedy. These early films featured plenty of incident, but none of it was particularly funny, even by the undemanding standards of the mid-1920s. He was essentially trying to compete with Hal Roach's incredibly popular 'Our Gang' series of comedies, which featured a troupe of cheeky young performers. Winkler encouraged Disney to improve his stories and to include more comedy. She was encouraged by the interest in the series from exhibitors nationwide, but was smart enough to know that the product must improve if that interest was to be maintained in the longer term.

By May 1924, the first six instalments as called for in the first contract had been completed, adding *Alice's Wild West Show* (May 1924), *Alice's Fishy Story* (June 1924) and *Alice and the Dog Catcher* (July 1924) to the growing series. Disney knew he needed help, so he turned to the one man he felt he could rely on, Ub Iwerks. Walt persuaded Iwerks to give up his $50 per week job with the Kansas City Film Ad Company and move to Hollywood in June 1924 on a salary of $40 per week, despite the fact that Iwerks was still owed $1,000 in unpaid salary from the collapsed Laugh-O-Gram Films (he eventually received $450 from the bankruptcy settlement). With Iwerks handling the animation alongside Hamilton, Walt decided he could take a step back and do more work on improving the stories and the comedy for the next batch of Alice films.

Just as Walt retreated from animation, so his distributor also quit the business. In 1924, Margaret Winkler had married Charles Mintz, who worked for her in film distribution, and handed the company over to him so she could focus on raising a family. Walt found Mintz harder to deal with, and the distributor began sending only 50 per cent payments for each film, even though the animation quality had markedly improved under Iwerks, as had the frequency of production. The second series of Alice shorts started with *Alice the Peacemaker* (August 1924) and continued with *Alice Gets in Dutch* and *Alice Hunting in Africa* (both November 1924), although Mintz was still unhappy with the lack of comedy. Things improved with the final three films of the year, *Alice and the Three Bears* (December 1924), *Alice the Piper* (December 1924) and *Alice Cans the Cannibals* (January 1925). Of the final film, Walt told Mintz: 'We have endeavoured to have nothing but gags, and the whole story is one gag after another.'

The series began to get good notices in the press, with London's *Kinematograph Weekly* noting 'the artists' work and the living player are capitally united' in *Alice and the Three Bears*, while the *Moving Picture World* marked the release of *Alice Cans the Cannibals* with the encouraging comment that 'each of these Walt Disney cartoons . . . appears to be more imaginative and clever than the preceding, and this one is a corker'.

This was enough for Charles Mintz at Winkler Pictures to re-contract the Disney Bros. Studios for a further eighteen Alice shorts at $1,800 each in December 1924. The new deal also gave the Disneys a share of the rental profits from the theatres where the films played, potentially putting the company on a more secure financial footing. Walt quickly hired two further colleagues from the Laugh-O-Gram days, Hugh Harman and Rudy Ising, to come to Hollywood and join the company as animators, bringing the total number of employees to nine. Another new hire at the Disney Bros. Studio was Lillian Bounds, an inker and painter two years older than

Walt who lived near the studio premises and was paid $15 each week. Soon Walt and Lillian would see much more of each other: they'd be married in the summer of 1925 and would stay together until his death in 1966. Walt also changed his appearance, growing the moustache that would become something of a trademark later in life in an attempt to make him appear older than his twenty-three years, so giving him more authority with his staff and in negotiations with executives in Hollywood.

In July 1925 the Disney brothers made a down payment of $400 on a lot at 2719 Hyperion Avenue near Griffith Park in the Silver Lake District, which would become the location of the new Disney studio until 1939. During 1925 the company would produce two Alice comedies every month, although Mintz began to complain that this was too frequent for his distribution arrangements. The contract was renegotiated, with each film bringing Disney a reduced fee of $1,500, plus a 50 per cent share of any rental profits above $3,000, allowing production to continue on the series through 1925. Looking to the future, Walt also negotiated an equal share of any ancillary right beyond films, such as toys, games or books. As ever he was thinking of bigger things. By January 1926 the new expanded studio property had been completed at Hyperion Avenue and the company had a new name: the Walt Disney Studios.

Mintz continued to suggest improvements for the Alice comedies, including the development of the Felix the Cat lookalike character called Julius. While unhappy at so directly imitating another animator's work, Walt did as he was asked and Julius the Cat began to take a larger role.

At the same time, the face of Alice herself changed. With the cut in the budget, Virginia Davies's mother withdrew her daughter from the role of Alice, hoping she could find success elsewhere in Hollywood (she didn't). Her last regular appearance was in *Alice Gets Stung* (February 1925). Her first replacement was Dawn O'Day, who appeared in one Alice comedy, *Alice's Egg Plant* (released in May 1925). A more modern-looking Alice was found in the form of four-year-old Margie Gaye, who sported a pageboy hairstyle more reflective of 1920s fashions and was hired at a day rate of $25. She made her debut in *Alice Solves the Puzzle* (February 1925) and held the role until 1927, appearing in thirty-one of the Alice shorts. Professional child actress Lois Hardwick took over the role for the final series of Alice comedies from *Alice's Circus Daze* (April 1927) through to the final instalment, *Alice in the Big League* (released in August 1927).

Between 1923 and 1927 Walt Disney had created a total of fifty-six Alice comedies, many of which remain lost, with a good selection of those that survived available on various Disney DVD releases. Since Disney didn't control the Alice series, many were later re-released in the era of sound movies with added soundtracks to cash in on the animator's growing fame, and it is mostly these later versions of the films that have survived.

Towards the end of 1926, Walt Disney knew that the Alice comedies were running out of steam. There was only so much 'funny business' he could devise for the little girl to get involved in, and he'd done just about everything. At the same time, Charles Mintz had been approached by Carl Laemmle of Universal requesting a cartoon series featuring an animated rabbit. Although not entirely happy with the business arrangements on the Alice series, Disney agreed to develop sketches of a possible rabbit character for Mintz to replace the Alice series. In turn, Mintz sent the work on to Universal, who approved the concepts. Mintz came up with the character name of Oswald the Lucky Rabbit, and commissioned Walt Disney Studios to begin production on the new series.

Rushed into production in April 1927, the first Oswald the Lucky Rabbit cartoon, *Poor Papa*, was rejected by Universal due to its poor production quality (the film was not released until 1928 and is now lost). Among the criticisms from Universal were 'poor animation', 'repetition of action', 'lack of character' for Oswald and no 'thread of story'. Much work would have to be done, both on the character of Oswald and on the quality of the animated films Disney was producing, before the series could proceed any further.

The Oswald the Lucky Rabbit series would be Disney's first all-animated professional film series, with no live-action sequences as in the Alice shorts. As Julius the Cat had taken on greater prominence as those films went on, and through study-ing the output of his New York competitors, Walt had come to realize that having a strong character was central to making a success in animation. He brought that awareness to his second attempt with Oswald, creating a younger-seeming, more hip character than before in the hope that he would connect with audiences in cinemas countrywide. It would take a few more films to get Oswald ironed out, but the pace of change and development was rapid, with as much attention paid to his character as to the gags. Rough animation was filmed and viewed to ensure it worked before Walt would give the okay for the full process to proceed (a process he would rely on heavily in future). This cost time and money, but very quickly Oswald the Lucky Rabbit developed into a distinctive character not influenced by the likes of Felix, Koko or any other successful cartoon headliner of the mid-1920s.

The first Oswald cartoon to be released was *Trolley Troubles* on 5 September 1927, in which Oswald ran into comic difficul-ties as a conductor on a 'Toonerville' trolley car. Oswald was a 'lucky rabbit' because he could detach his own foot and rub it for good fortune, but that wasn't the only limb that was remov-able. Throughout the cartoons Oswald would be seen to use his arms and legs, often separated from himself, as tools to achieve whatever endeavour he was engaged in. This deconstructive ele-ment of a new animated character that was not a cat quickly caught on with audiences, making Oswald the Lucky Rabbit one of the most popular cartoon series of that year.

The new shorts met with positive reviews from the growing film press. Oswald the Lucky Rabbit was described as 'a riot' by *Film Daily*, while *Moving Picture World* described the series as 'a new note in cartoons . . . bright, speedy, and genuinely amusing'. For *Motion Picture News* the new Disney shorts were 'chock full of humour'. Oswald was a break-out character who began to be featured on tie-in merchandise, from chocolate candy bars to button badges and stencil sets allowing fans to draw their own Oswalds. Due to the contract arrangements with Mintz, Disney received no income from these products, but he reluctantly viewed it all as good publicity for the series.

The new character proved a success for Walt Disney Studios, with 1927 being a great year for the ambitious company. Producing a new Oswald cartoon every two weeks resulted in a steady cash flow, allowing the Disney brothers to purchase two lots adjacent to their Hyperion Avenue property for $7,000 each, which would enable them to expand their studio premises. However, there was trouble on the horizon. Mintz had first sent his brother-in-law George Winkler (Margaret's brother) to Hollywood to supervise Walt's productions during the later Alice comedies. According to Ub Iwerks, Winkler was making his presence felt beyond simply checking the films and collecting the reels and the lobby posters Iwerks created for each Oswald short. Iwerks told Walt that he'd seen Winkler deep in conversation with some of the other animators and he thought something was going on. Walt dismissed his friend's suspicions and set out on a trip to New York with Lillian in February 1928 expecting the renewal of the contract for the Oswald films to be a mere formality. The meeting to negotiate the contract took place in Mintz's office on 42nd Street, with Walt hoping for a raise in his per picture fee from $2,250 to $2,500. Instead, Mintz suggested knocking the price down to just $1,800 per picture, putting Walt back to the level of income he was getting for the Alice films. When Walt argued this would make producing the films at their current level of quality impossible, Mintz countered by telling the would-be studio mogul to agree to his terms or he'd hijack Disney's best animators. According to Mintz, he already had the key people signed up to work for him. Stunned, Walt asked for time to think it over.

Back at his hotel he called Roy on the West Coast and asked him to look into the situation. The news was bad: Roy reported that virtually all the Disney animators, with the exception of Ub Iwerks, had agreed to work for Mintz, including Harman, Ising and recent hire Friz Freleng. Walt knew he was backed into a corner: he didn't own Oswald, Universal did. There was nothing to stop them switching production of the cartoons to another animation house, and although it was poor practice, there was nothing in law to stop Mintz from poaching Disney's staff to set up his own animation team. Walt put out feelers to other bigger distributors, including Fox and Metro-Goldwyn-Mayer (MGM), to see if they'd like to take on Oswald with his studio attached, but to no avail. It soon sunk in that Walt had spent his time, money and creative effort on developing a valuable movie property that he had no ownership stake in. 'Never again will I work for somebody else,' he vowed to Lillian before conceding defeat in early March. The couple returned to Hollywood, leaving ownership of Oswald the Lucky Rabbit behind in New York. It would take a further seventy-eight years, but in 2006 the Walt Disney Company re-obtained the rights to Oswald (in exchange for ABC sports commentator Al Michaels) from NBC Universal, as Universal had become. Oswald was happily welcomed back into the Disney family of animated characters and continues to be used to this day.

Out of the ashes of the Oswald debacle would come another character that sealed the fortunes of Walt Disney once and for all: a mouse called Mickey. The exact origins of this world-famous icon have been lost to legend, myth and the remembrances or fantasies of those involved. Walt Disney claimed he'd either dreamed up the new character on the return train trip to Hollywood in March 1928 while doodling on a sketch pad, or he'd based him upon a mouse he used to see around the Laugh-O-Gram offices back in Kansas City. Both might have some basis in fact, but the often overlooked input of Walt's one faithful supporter Ub Iwerks would prove to be pivotal to the development of Mickey Mouse, who visually had clearly evolved from Oswald. Iwerks claimed the character had emerged from a brainstorming session between him, Roy and Walt in search of a new cartoon personality after they'd lost Oswald to Mintz.

There were outstanding obligations facing Walt upon his return to the studio. His turncoat animators wouldn't be leaving until June 1928 and he had a commitment to complete three remaining Oswald shorts on the current contract. While the departing animators were put to work finishing off the contracted job for Mintz, Walt and Iwerks secreted themselves away in a separate part of the studio to begin work on the launch cartoon for their new Mickey Mouse series, entitled *Plane Crazy*. They told everyone it was about the then recent success of Charles Lindbergh's non-stop solo flight to France in 1927. No one mentioned the new mouse character featured in the film.

While Mickey would become the most famous, he was far from the first animated mouse. Paul Terry's animated 'Aesop's Fables' had often featured mice in the stories, while Walt himself had included mice in his films, often as the required antagonists for Julius the Cat in several Alice comedies including *Alice Solves the Puzzle* (February 1925), *Alice's Tin Pony* (August 1925), *Alice Rattled by Rats* (November 1925) and *Alice the Whaler* (July 1927). The posters for some of the Oswald comedies (many by Iwerks), including *The Ocean Hop* (1927), *Great Guns* (1927) and *Sky Scrappers* (1928), featured a distinctive long-eared mouse who would cause trouble for the rabbit, which may have provided some inspiration for Mickey. According to Lillian Disney, though, the real reason for choosing a mouse was 'because we thought it would make a cute character to animate'. It was also Lillian who persuaded Walt to change the name of the mouse from his suggestion of Mortimer to the more casually friendly-sounding Mickey.

The arrival of sound was changing filmmaking in the late 1920s. The premiere of *The Jazz Singer* in New York on 6 October 1927 brought synchronized sound – if primitively – to film for the first time. The first full 'talking picture', *Lights of New York*, was released in July 1928. By the end of 1929, almost 5,000 cinemas across the country would be equipped for sound. Disney knew his new cartoon series would need to feature music, sound effects and even dialogue if it was to succeed in the new market sound film had created. In the early days, though, several different methods for presenting sound on film were competing. Particularly popular was Warner Bros.'s Vitaphone system, where the soundtrack accompanied the film from a recorded disc, but Walt was convinced that the future lay in sound recorded on to the film itself. He was to be proved right in this. One thing did concern him: would cinema audiences take to talking animated animals and other cartoon characters? Disney would find out by making Mickey Mouse the first cartoon character to talk.

By the autumn of 1928 things were rather different at Walt Disney Studios than a few months before. Most of the animators had left to take up the offer from Charles Mintz to work directly for him, leaving Walt and Roy with Ub Iwerks, Les Clark, Wilfred Jackson (who'd be a key figure in Walt's later endeavours) and Johnny Cannon as animators, three women inker-and-painters and a janitor. Despite this, they quickly completed the work on a trio of Mickey Mouse cartoons: *Plane Crazy*, *Gallopin' Gaucho* and *Steamboat Willie* (a riff on the 1928 Buster Keaton movie *Steamboat Bill Jr*).

Mickey Mouse had been seen for the first time publicly at a test screening of *Plane Crazy* in a Sunset Boulevard cinema on 15 May 1928. The short was liked, despite being rather crude in animation and character terms, but it failed to secure a distributor for the new series. Encouraged, but determined to improve, Walt set Iwerks to work on the second film, *Gallopin' Gaucho*, a spoof of the Douglas Fairbanks movie, *The Gaucho* (1927). The films were then screened for MGM in the hope they'd take on their distribution, but they also declined. At this time, all the major Hollywood filmmaking studios still maintained their head offices in New York, so Walt realized that's where he'd have to sell his movies. He hired a local film agent to open doors for him, but eventually made the trip there himself that September and October, both to add a soundtrack to *Steamboat Willie* – the most accomplished of the three cartoons completed to date – and to tout his wares around the major distributors in person.

Adding a specially created soundtrack was not a simple process in the early days of sound film, and it took a lot of time, money and patience on Walt's behalf to achieve his aims. In order to save money, Walt himself ended up providing the voice for his new creation (at first just whistles, but from the ninth instalment, *The Karnival Kid*, 1929, dialogue) and would continue to do so until 1946 on the theatrical films, and again between 1955 and 1959 for *The Mickey Mouse Club* television series on ABC.

Although he personally presented his work to each of the major studios that October, none of them agreed to take on Mickey Mouse. Walt was convinced he had a winner, and he was perplexed as to why no one wanted to back him. It had been an expensive business getting *Steamboat Willie* and the other two films into shape, but he was sure it would all pay off. He'd written to Roy: 'This [deal] may mean the making of a big organization out of our little dump. Why should we let a few dollars jeopardize our chances? I really think our big chance is here!' Walt finally won backing from forty-four-year-old experienced movie publicist Harry Reichenbach, who ran the Colony Theater on Broadway for Universal. He explained that movie executives never knew whether anything was good or not until the public told them. He offered to exhibit *Steamboat Willie* at the Colony for two weeks at a fee of $500 per week. Although doubtful of this strategy, Walt knew his cash-strapped organization needed the $1,000 on offer, so quickly agreed to the deal.

Steamboat Willie premiered on 18 November 1928 and became a breakout sensation (the short was added to the National Film Registry of important movies in 1998). On a bill that included the talking movie *Gang War* (1928) and a live stage show by Ben Bernie and his orchestra, it was *Steamboat Willie* that became a talking point with audiences. This was the first cartoon with genuine synchronized sound, and *Variety* decided it should be 'recommended unreservedly'. Walt took to standing at the back of the theatre each night, taking in the audience reaction to his seven-minute cartoon. He particularly welcomed the write-up of *Steamboat Willie* in the *New York Times* describing it as 'an ingenious piece of work with a good deal of fun. It growls, whines, squeaks, and makes various other sounds that add to its mirthful quality.'

Distributors were now very interested in Walt Disney's Mickey Mouse cartoons as *Steamboat Willie* had proven popular with audiences, but they wanted to buy them on the old terms; either for a weekly payment or for outright ownership. Either way, just as with Alice and Oswald, Disney would not own his character through these deals. Desperate for all his work to pay off and anxious to secure the future for his floundering animation studio, Walt was keen to make a deal, but given his recent experiences it had to be on his own terms. He alone had to own Mickey Mouse.

With none of the big studios and distributors offering him the terms he wanted, Walt entered into a deal with movie maverick Pat Powers. Powers had been involved in the early days of film in New York and had taken part in the patent battles and dubious business practices that marked the early days of movie making, renting films through 'film exchanges' to the nickelodeons. He'd once co-owned Universal, before he was ousted following a battle with Carl Laemmle. Now he was pushing his film sound system called Cinephone – a sound-on-film system – and was prepared to take on Walt's Mickey Mouse cartoons for distribution through his company Celebrity Pictures on a 10 per cent/90 per cent split of the profits in Walt's favour, as long as the Disney company committed to using his sound equipment for a period of ten years (a deal that would potentially cost Disney $26,000 each year). With no other offers on the table, Walt agreed – only to be greeted by a furious Roy on his return to Hollywood. The other Disney brother – who was handling the business and finance of their company – didn't like the contract terms, but Walt explained he had little other choice.

Sound effects and new scores by Walt's Kansas City friend Carl Stalling were added to *Plane Crazy*, *Gallopin' Gaucho* and the newly completed *The Barn Dance* to prepare the first quartet of Mickey Mouse cartoons for national distribution. Another four animators had been recruited to the studio, readying the organization for the new workload that 1929 would bring in producing a continual stream of Mickey Mouse cartoons.

Walt was worried about becoming over reliant on a single character again, just as he had been with Alice and Oswald. The novelty of sound on the Mickey Mouse cartoons was no longer exclusive to Disney, as all the other animation houses, including Walter Lantz (who had been hired by Mintz to produce the Oswald shorts), the Fleischers and Terry, were now also using synchronized sound. It was important to the future of the Disney studio, Walt felt, for it to diversify beyond just Mickey Mouse, however successful he looked likely to be. Creatively, too, Walt welcomed the challenge of creating something new and hated repeating himself. The result would be the macabre yet amusing 1929 short, *The Skeleton Dance*, that launched Disney's second series of animated shorts.

The film was the creation of Ub Iwerks based upon the idea of a 'graveyard frolic' suggested by composer Carl Stalling. Inspired by the material, Iwerks threw himself into the project wholeheartedly, refusing to give up the animation to anyone else and completing all the 'in-between' images usually delegated to junior animators (this added to the growing tensions between Iwerks and Disney that would eventually drive them apart). Impressed by the finished movie, Walt declared that 'the music sounds like a little symphony' so inspiring the name for the overall series: 'Disney's Silly Symphonies'. This umbrella title would allow Walt and his animators a strand in which they could experiment with new characters, one-off stories or new animation techniques while continuing to produce the separate hit Mickey Mouse cartoons that ensured their regular income.

The Skeleton Dance, however, proved a tough film to sell at first. Walt sent it to Pat Powers in New York, who quickly replied saying he couldn't sell it: audiences 'don't want this. More mice!' As Walt had feared, all the distributors and, seemingly, cinema audiences wanted from Disney were more Mickey Mouse cartoons. Trying to repeat the trick he'd pulled off with *Steamboat Willie*, Walt arranged to screen *The Skeleton Dance* in a Los Angeles theatre. While Walt felt the audience had enjoyed the funny, spooky short, the manager told him he couldn't recommend it to his cinema chain as it was 'too gruesome'.

Never one to give up easily, Walt persevered, managing to get a booking for his newest short at the new Carthay Circle Theatre on San Vicente Boulevard in Los Angeles (where the later Disney production *Snow White and the Seven Dwarfs*, the first American feature-length animated film, would premiere in 1937). As had happened at the Colony with *Steamboat Willie*, the response of the audience and critics was hugely positive, resulting in the film winning a booking at the prestigious Roxy Theatre on Broadway in New York. The Silly Symphonies had found their place; in 1994 *The Skeleton Dance* was voted by animation professionals as no. 18 on the list of '50 Greatest Cartoons of All Time'.

Meanwhile, 1929 saw Mickey Mouse and his gal pal, Minnie, become a bona fide cultural phenomenon. While Mickey Mouse Clubs grew all over the country (there would be one million members by 1931), Walt continued to spend time and money improving his animation techniques so that each individual film was now costing in the region of $5,000, seriously affecting the company's profitability. Late running payments from Pat Powers's Celebrity Pictures weren't helping, resulting in the Disney brothers and their lawyer confronting the film executive with their grievances in early 1930.

As had happened before with Charles Mintz, Powers pulled a surprise rabbit out of the hat when he announced he'd signed Disney's disgruntled head animator Ub Iwerks to a $300 per week contract to make animated cartoons directly for him. Walt was astonished, as Iwerks now held 20 per cent of the Disney company in shares. They'd developed in the animation business together from their Kansas City adventures through to their triumph with Mickey Mouse, a character who had now made the Disney name known worldwide. In quitting the Disney organization, Iwerks blamed 'creative differences' between him and Walt, but the real issue was the lack of recognition of his role in the creation of Mickey Mouse. Just as Walt felt he got nothing out of Oswald the Lucky Rabbit's success, so Iwerks felt he was gaining nothing from Mickey Mouse (of course, if he'd hung in there a while longer his one-fifth share of the Disney company would have proved to be a hugely valuable asset over time). Iwerks cashed out his shares for just under $3,000 and left the Disney company.

By January 1930 the Walt Disney Studios had completed twelve Mickey Mouse cartoons and six Silly Symphonies, with a further three Mickey Mouse cartoons for the second series already done. The costs had been so high that the company had made little money on each cartoon. Despite this, and despite the loss of Iwerks, Walt walked away from his deal with Pat Powers, much to Roy's relief. Unlike before with Alice and Oswald, the creator of Mickey Mouse was now welcome in the offices of the big studios and high-powered New York distributors. Walt Disney himself was now a player in Hollywood. Four days of hard negotiations with MGM to take on Mickey Mouse resulted in deadlock, allowing Harry Cohn's maverick Columbia Pictures to step in to sign up the similarly maverick mouse on the recommendation of his house director, Frank Capra. Cohn offered an increased $7,000 advance per cartoon. As part of the deal, Walt had to pay off Powers to relinquish the continuing contract, which he managed with the financial backing of Columbia. The deal was done by early February 1930.

Each animated Disney short was handmade, and it proved to be an expensive business. Even with the new deal with Columbia, the finances of Walt Disney Studios proved continually precarious, especially when Walt insisted on hiring more animators to help improve the quality of the films that were going out under his name. For Walt, quality was to be the mark of superior Disney product, his unique selling point that differentiated his efforts from those of other studios. Some of the new faces were experienced hands who'd worked on rival series like Felix the Cat, Krazy Kat and Mutt & Jeff, while others were newcomers just out of art school, eager to learn the Disney way of animation.

The stress of running the expanding studio got to Walt, affecting his health through 1930 and into 1931. Although a doctor prescribed a complete rest and some time away from the strains of the company, Walt refused to slow down the pace of his work: he couldn't, as he had contracts to honour and he knew audiences were always waiting hungrily for the next Mickey Mouse cartoon. Despite this, Roy persuaded Walt he could look after the firm while he and Lillian took a much needed recreational trip to Washington, DC. After sightseeing there, they travelled on to Key West and then to Cuba, where they stayed in Havana, and then back to the West Coast via the Panama Canal. Walt enjoyed the relaxing cruise and came back to work energized and ready for the next phase of development for the growing Disney studio.

3

DISNEY'S FOLLY

*All the world's great fairy tales are essentially morality tales,
opposing good and bad, virtue and villainy . . . Without such
a clash of good and evil and the prevalence of goodness, fairy
tales like Snow White, Cinderella, Pinocchio, [and] Sleeping
Beauty long since would have died because they would have
no meaning.*

Walt Disney, interviewed by David Griffiths, 1959
(Walt Disney Archives)

By 1930, Mickey Mouse had supplanted Felix the Cat (whose
creator Pat Sullivan had failed to adjust to the sound revolution) as the most popular cartoon character in America, if not
the world. The Mickey Mouse Clubs were going from strength
to strength across the US, with an estimated 800 chapters made
up of up to a million members, all Mickey Mouse mad American
kids. There was a syndicated Mickey Mouse comic strip running in newspapers, initially written by Walt Disney (Floyd
Gottfredson would illustrate the strip continuously from 1930
to 1975). There was even a Mickey Mouse figure in London's

Madame Tussauds waxworks hall of fame – clear recognition of his widespread impact and stature. Mickey's new-found celebrity would be the focus of the 1933 cartoon instalment *Mickey's Gala Premier*, which sees a host of animated then-contemporary Hollywood stars, including Edward G. Robinson, Buster Keaton and the Marx Brothers, among many others, attend the opening of a new Mickey Mouse short.

Many have attempted to explain the seemingly instant appeal of Mickey Mouse. For some it was the way he was drawn – as Mickey evolved, he came to be made up of a series of circles and curves, pleasing shapes to the human eye (and, not coincidentally, easier for Disney's animators to draw rapidly). Mickey became less mouse-like and more human-like, almost child-like, as he evolved. Walt, celebrating Mickey's twenty-fifth anniversary, said: 'Mickey is so simple and uncomplicated, so easy to understand, that you can't help liking him.' The mouse may have been 'simple', but his appeal was not so easy to understand.

For some, Mickey was a Depression-era figure, a 'little guy' comic like Chaplin or Harold Lloyd, who refused to give up no matter the obstacles, a go-getter symbolic of the age – one supporter of this theory was *New York Times* film reviewer Frank Nugent, a regular Disney booster. One commentator went so far as to position Mickey as the counterpoint to what looked to be an 'age of dictators and tyrants'. In 1934 a Harvard professor claimed that Mickey Mouse hypnotized the audience, sending them back to childhood in spans of seven minutes – the length of a cartoon short – at a time. For most Americans, Mickey was just that: a symbol of American achievement and character. United Artists, in taking over distribution of the Disney studio films, simply stated that in Mickey Mouse, 'Disney has created a character whose type has never been equalled in motion picture history'. He was a movie star, plain and simple, and for a while was equal to any made of flesh and blood.

The rapid appearance of bootleg Mickey merchandise prompted Walt Disney quickly to set up his own official licensing deals to get Mickey products into the hands of young fans. From early items, such as Mickey and Minnie hand-kerchiefs, to stuffed Mickey dolls (initially individually handmade), Disney was one of the first studios to tap into the power of tie-in merchandising. Walt was often dissatisfied by the quality of some of the early merchandise produced, believ-ing it reflected poorly on him personally and on his company's films. Kay Kamen, a Kansas City ad man, was soon appointed to handle Disney's licensing (a post he held until his early death in 1949 in a plane crash), imposing strict quality controls as part of any deals made.

Oddly, the term 'Mickey Mouse' would come to denote something of low quality or cheap manufacture, rather than of the high standard that Walt insisted upon – the phrase was used in Australia and elsewhere to mean 'cheap and unreliable', and may have originated with poorly made knock-off Mickey Mouse watches not manufactured under licence. The numbers were huge, with Mickey Mouse merchandise achieving a value of $35 million by 1934. A $3.75 Mickey Mouse watch saved manufacturer Ingersoll from bankruptcy, with Macy's store selling 11,000 watches in a single day upon their launch. Walt would claim that his company was rapidly making more money from the merchandise than it did through producing cartoons.

The Mickey Mouse films developed from the early musical numbers – basically an excuse for Mickey to dance around, giving rise to a handful of slapstick gags – to more character-driven tales. Supporting characters developed, with Minnie becoming Mickey's regular girlfriend, and Peg-Leg Pete his frequent antagonist. There were other regulars, from Horace Horsecollar and Clarabelle Cow to a new dog that appeared to be Minnie's pet. First seen in *The Chain Gang* (1930) as one of a pair of anonymous dogs, he reappeared called 'Rover' in *The Picnic* (1930). By 1931, the character became Mickey's pet and was called Pluto.

Other characters introduced through the Mickey Mouse shorts would go on to have lives of their own as major Disney animated characters. These included Donald Duck, who first appeared in the Silly Symphony, *The Wise Little Hen*, in 1934, noted for the raspy voice provided by former milkman and birdsong impressionist Clarence Nash, and the dog-like Goofy, first seen in 1932's *Mickey's Revue*. These characters were evidence of Walt's new emphasis on 'personality animation': each character had to be more than just a participant in a series of gags. Following the example of Mickey, they had to have distinctive characteristics of their own that would be maintained from film to film.

As Mickey lost some of his edge, became less mischievous and more benevolently childlike, so Donald Duck stepped into that vacated character space. He was unashamedly self-centred, cheeky and careless of others' feelings or well-being. That made him the perfect foil for the ever more innocent Mickey. Donald was dressed in a blue sailor suit because, according to Walt, 'being a duck, he likes water. Sailors and water go together.' According to Disney animator Ward Kimball, pairing the mouse and the duck as antagonists for the first time in *Orphan's Benefit* (1934) was a breakthrough, as it saw a bad-tempered Donald react angrily to an audience that disparaged his poetry recitations. The first colour Mickey Mouse cartoon, *The Band Concert* (1935), repeated the trick, but put the spotlight firmly on the cantankerous Donald. 'It is a bad, wicked duck,' wrote the *New York Journal* of Donald in *The Band Concert*, 'a malicious and mischievous duck, a duck corresponding to all the maddening attractiveness of bad little boys and girls – a superb character'. Walt Disney had discovered his second breakout cartoon star, and Donald Duck had his own series from 1935.

Mickey, Donald and Goofy were often at their best when seen together as a trio in such classic Disney animated shorts as *Mickey's Service Station* (1935, first uniting the trio), *Clock Cleaners* (1937) and *Lonesome Ghosts* (1937), in which they rivalled such live-action comedy teams as Laurel and Hardy or the Three Stooges.

* * *

The Silly Symphonies – initially distributed through Columbia, then United Artists – had not been quite as successful as Mickey and company, as they were running against Ub Iwerk's Flip the Frog (subject of the first colour sound cartoon) and Max Fleischer's incredibly popular cartoon flapper Betty Boop. The musically based fanciful shorts also suffered from the loss of composer Carl Stalling, who suggested the idea of musical-based cartoons in the first place. Some were based around seasons, such as *Springtime* (1929), *Summer* (1930) and *Autumn* (1930), or wildlife, such as *Frolicking Fish* (1930) and *Monkey Melodies* (1930). The series was drifting without a strong direction.

Things picked up with the switch to colour. *Flowers and Trees* (1932) was abandoned halfway through in black and white and retooled for full colour in the three-strip Technicolor process – Disney negotiated an exclusive deal to use it for two years. The short – which featured a variety of plants, flowers and trees performing musical numbers – won the first Academy Award (later known as the Oscar) for Best Animated Short Subject; the series would win a total of seven Oscars, a feat in animation only matched by MGM's later Tom and Jerry cartoons. *Flowers and Trees* first screened at Grauman's Chinese Theatre on Hollywood Boulevard accompanying MGM's prestigious *Strange Interlude* (1932). Colour brought a new lease of life to the Silly Symphonies, and they branched out in a new direction tackling a series of fairy-tale subjects, including *The Ugly Duckling* (1931), *The Three Little Pigs* (1933, another Oscar winner, followed by three sequels as it was so popular in its appeal to Depression-era audiences) and *The Tortoise and the Hare* (1935, also an Oscar winner).

The Three Little Pigs broke ground in several ways. It was the first time that Walt felt his team had properly mastered his sought after goal of 'personality animation'. Animator Fred Moore gave the pigs more than distinct personalities: he managed to bring them alive in a way few other animated characters

had been to that point, setting a new style for Disney animation in the process. Walt said there 'was a certain recognition
from the industry and the public that these things could be
more than just a mouse hopping around . . . [We] put real feeling and charm in our characterizations.'

The film connected with audiences, and it played in
extended runs nationwide with many newspapers writing it up
as the latest sensation from Disney. The song 'Who's Afraid
of the Big Bad Wolf?' quickly caught on, becoming a defiant
Depression anthem. Although Walt denied it, some critics read
a political message into the popular film, seeing the wolf as representing the terrible economic conditions of the Depression
and the three pigs (two lazy and laid back, the third hardwork-
ing and forward-looking) as depicting possible responses to
the national turmoil. The nation's censor, Will Hays, president
of the Motion Picture Producers and Distributors of America,
would claim the nation 'literally laughed the "big bad wolf" of
depression out of the public mind through the protagonists of
The Three Little Pigs'.

In preparing for the feature film *Snow White and the Seven
Dwarfs*, which he hoped to direct personally, Walt Disney took
upon himself the task of directing a Silly Symphony, *The Golden
Touch* (1935) – the first time in five years he'd done so. A riff on
the story of King Midas, Disney was unhappy with the results,
fearing it moved too slowly and the character animation was too
stiff. Walt had hoped to set an example for his animators, but *The
Golden Touch* only resulted in putting him off from directing a
cartoon ever again. He realized he was far better as a director
of men and their talents than he was of individual pictures – he
would be content as the ringmaster of his animated circus. The
Silly Symphony series would end with a remake of *The Ugly
Duckling* in 1939, the series' final Oscar winner. Although nine
Mickey Mouse cartoons (in colour from 1935) were also Oscar-
nominated, none would win until 1949. Instead, Walt Disney
himself was presented with a special Oscar in November 1932
at the fifth annual Academy Awards, recognizing his creation

of Mickey Mouse who had become an international icon and the corporate logo for the Walt Disney studio.

Between them, the Mickey Mouse cartoons and the Silly Symphonies demonstrated the dichotomy of Walt Disney's approach to animation, as both art and a business. Hamilton Luske, an animator who started at the studio in 1931, was aware that Walt himself began to see animation as more than 'the cartooning of broad caricatures, gags and comic situations'. Instead it could be 'a means of bringing life and motion to fine illustration. The Silly Symphony shorts were the proving ground.' If they were the art, animator Ward Kimball knew what the business end of the organization was: 'If you were a top animator at Disney, you would work on the Silly Symphonies because they were the artistic cartoons. Mickey Mouse was the pot boiler.'

The early to mid-1930s were a period of expansion and growth for the Disney studio. New animators were regularly hired as the volume of production increased, including David Hand from the Fleischer studio. The ideas for films now came from a growing number of 'story men', gag writers and script writers. As the personnel grew (there were 200 employees by 1933), so the animation and storytelling quality of the cartoons improved and became ever more sophisticated.

Although he used free association in a group setting to develop ideas and comedy business, Walt Disney controlled all aspects of production. He introduced streamlined animation methods and introduced the innovation of having his animators sketch out their filmmaking intention in the form of 'storyboards', named after the cork notice boards upon which sketches of individual scenes were pinned and could be rearranged as the story was revised. Changes and alterations could be made at this stage before a foot of film was even shot. Roughly drawn 'pencil tests' were sometimes shot, simply to demonstrate how a new idea might look on film – an idea revived from Walt's Kansas City days. Everything was subject to Walt's approval, which often involved long hours in an air-less screening room that became known as 'sweatbox sessions'. As far as Walt was concerned, everything came secondary to keeping up the quality of the films his studio was producing. He would often tour the studio late in the evening, examining the work left on animators' desks. Several of his animators became trusted directors and were handed all responsibility for particular cartoons, including Wilfred Jackson (who'd been with Disney since 1928) and Ben Sharpsteen.

Walt arranged for his animators to attend night classes in art at the Chouinard Art Institute, believing they could benefit (as he had) from basic tuition in life study, human dynamics and the implications of physics for cartoon animation. As a result, the animators' use of 3D space and acknowledgement of the force of gravity began to improve the cartoons. Within a short time, the classes were being run by Chouinard staff on Disney premises, led by lecturer Don Graham and known as the Disney Art Classes. Running things less like a commercial enterprise and more like an art collective, Walt spent $100,000 per year on training his staff in the Disney way of animation, much to his business-minded brother Roy's annoyance. Attendance reputedly shot up when the classes featured nude female models as life-drawing subjects.

Recruitment was ongoing, with a Disney ad requiring candidates to display 'an ability to draw well, creatively, plus a certain amount of imagination that would be helpful in the study of dramatics, which animators must acquire'. The recruitment process was exhaustive and exacting, with mere handfuls of the thousands who applied actually winning jobs at the studio. Walt often said that the lack of jobs elsewhere during the Depression enabled him to recruit the top people, but he was also offering above-normal salaries for his key people. By now he had a central core of trusted animators upon whom he relied (they'd come to be known as Disney's 'nine old men', after the members of the US Supreme Court, even though they were mostly in their thirties at the time). They comprised Les

Clark (who joined in 1927 and handled many Mickey Mouse cartoons), Milt Kahl (who joined in 1934 for *Snow White*), Frank Thomas (another 1934 recruit), Marc Davis (who started on *Snow White* in 1935), Wolfgang Reitherman (who joined in 1933 and directed all the Disney animated films after Walt's death until his own retirement), Eric Larson (a 1933 recruit who often trained younger animators), John Lounsbery (a key character animator who joined in 1935), Ward Kimball (a 1934 recruit whose signature character would be Jiminy Cricket in *Pinocchio*) and Ollie Johnston (another 1935 arrival for *Snow White*). This group would develop and expand the fundamentals of the Disney style in animation and would rightly each be inducted as 'Disney Legends' by the studio (a programme established in 1987 by the company to recognize those who made significant contributions).

As the Disney cartoons became more sophisticated and moved to colour, they also became more expensive to produce. Unable to persuade Columbia to pay more for the Disney shorts, the company switched distributor to United Artists, a studio founded by actors Charlie Chaplin (Walt's comedy hero), Mary Pickford and Douglas Fairbanks, and director D. W. Griffith in 1919. The wit and invention on display in the Disney Mickey Mouse and Silly Symphony cartoons was unrivalled, but it was proving to be expensive. Popular though it was (grossing around $250,000 during its extended first run), *The Three Little Pigs* had cost $22,000 to make, way above the $7,000 Columbia had been paying. Cinemas were screening fewer shorts, too, as double bills became popular on economic terms if not always for their quality. It was ever more important to Walt Disney that his studio earned a decent income as he had big plans that would prove expensive: he would produce America's first full-length, full-colour animated feature film, quickly regarded by some as 'Disney's folly'.

Snow White and the Seven Dwarfs was not Walt Disney's first choice of subject for his first full-length animated feature

film. Walt considered Frank L. Baum's *The Wizard of Oz*, and
would come back to the idea repeatedly after *Snow White*.
However, he quickly returned to the subject that had brought
him into the world of animated films in the first place: *Alice
in Wonderland*. He lost interest, however, when a 'talkie' live-
action film version was released in 1931, starring Ruth Gilbert.
A few years later, Walt was planning another Alice movie, this
time featuring Mary Pickford as a live-action Alice lost in a
cartoon wonderland (as in his old Alice comedies), but again
abandoned his plans when he heard Paramount were planning
a star-studded version featuring Cary Grant, Gary Cooper
and W. C. Fields, among other big Hollywood names. Disney's
plan to film *Rip Van Winkle* with Western star Will Rogers was
also thwarted by Paramount who owned the rights and refused
permission. Walt's search for a suitable subject for his first animated feature then turned to the Victor Herbert operetta *Babes
in Toyland*, a planned co-production with Merian C. Cooper
(*King Kong*). In that case, RKO held the rights, and they were
planning to use the story as a vehicle for comic duo Laurel and
Hardy – it was released in 1934.

Finally, Walt turned to Snow White, a character he'd planned
to feature in a Silly Symphony, despite the fact that she'd featured in a 1933 Max Fleischer cartoon (played by Betty Boop).
He happily recalled seeing a silent version of *Snow White* (1916)
in January 1917 in Kansas City, one of his earliest and certainly
most vivid memories of attending the cinema. 'My impression
of the picture has stayed with me through the years,' Walt later
wrote to a friend, 'and I know it played a big part in selecting
Snow White for my first feature production.' Promoting the
planned film to the status of a 'Feature Symphony', Walt reckoned the fairy tale of Snow White and the Seven Dwarfs had
enough story potential to fill a feature film's ninety-minute
running time. 'It was well-known,' he said of the fairy tale,
'and I knew I could do something with seven "screwy" dwarfs.'
He saw in the subject matter the basic element of any entertaining film: a good story. Walt's enthusiasm for the idea of an

animated feature film wasn't shared across Hollywood. Surely, received wisdom went, no one would want to sit through a ninety-minute cartoon?

Disney's secret weapon was to be the team of talented animators and storytellers he'd recruited in recent years and who had tested their mettle on the Mickey Mouse and Silly Symphony shorts. One evening early in 1934, Walt Disney sent his core animators out for dinner on his dime, asking them to return to a late meeting on the studio soundstage afterwards. Through to midnight, Walt then explained his plans for a feature-length cartoon to the animators, including his by now customary acting out of key characters and key moments in the proposed film. He had already worked out a detailed plot, noting where songs or musical numbers could feature. His enthusiasm for the concept was infectious, and while the majority of the studio's animators continued toiling on Mickey Mouse and Silly Symphony cartoons, he assembled a core team who would work exclusively on developing *Snow White and the Seven Dwarfs*, a process Walt confidently predicted would take between a year and eighteen months and would cost only $250,000, ten times as much as a Mickey Mouse or Silly Symphony short.

Based on the Brothers Grimm original of 1812, Walt produced a written synopsis of his story in August 1934 that was then expanded upon by various contributors. This story differed in significant places from the final film, with Snow White en route to the dwarfs' house travelling through 'sleepy valley' and its huge poppy fields (echoes of his interest in *The Wizard of Oz*), as well as the 'morass of monsters' and the 'valley of dragons', and even weirder places like 'upside-down' and 'backward lane'. The document pointed out that while all the dwarfs would be of a similar type, each of them needed to have distinct, individual personalities reflected in their names and characters.

In an office next to his, Walt installed a team of writers to develop the story, as well as artists charged with designing the main characters, under the guidance of two animators, the Swiss-born Albert Hurter and 'story man' Joe Grant. Thousands of drawings were produced long before a frame of film was ever exposed. These images gave Walt something to react to in his decisions about what the characters would be like. Originally, the dwarfs were a little too earthy (reflecting his own farmyard humour), so Walt directed that they should be more cartoony. Early on, Snow White was a round-faced blonde princess, who became sharper featured and darker haired, modelled after actress Janet Gaynor. Walt described the Prince as a younger Douglas Fairbanks, Jr type. Considerable development time was devoted to the Queen, as she proved an elusive figure, until Walt defined her as 'a mixture of Lady Macbeth and the Big Bad Wolf. Her beauty is sinister, mature, plenty of curves. She becomes ugly and menacing when scheming and mixing her poisons. [She] transforms into an old witch-like hag.'

In October 1934 a trio of lengthy story meetings were held to further define the characters, especially those of the dwarfs that were central to Walt's interest in making the film. Among the staff involved were 'story men' Richard Creedon, Larry Morey, Ted Sears and Pinto Colvig. Around fifty possible names for the seven dwarfs were listed, including Jumpy, Dizzey [sic], Wheezy, Baldy, Gabby and Burby. From this long list, the final seven were selected, starting with Doc for the self-important leader of the group. Grumpy, Happy, Sleepy and Bashful were quickly finalized, although Jumpy and another unnamed seventh were still included, before Sneezy and Dopey were settled on, the latter very late in the process. Their characteristics were modelled after silent film clowns, with Dopey described as a mix of Harry Langdon and Disney's own Pluto.

As was Disney's practice at the time for the shorts, the original outline of *Snow White and the Seven Dwarfs* was gag-laden and far more humour-driven than the final film would be. The main focus for gags were the dwarfs, but Snow White, the handsome Prince and even the evil Queen were all subject to moments of slapstick and character humour, almost as though Walt were not sure his material could dramatically stand alone without endless gags. Working from this group outline, Walt then developed the project himself for most of the remainder of 1934, gradually working out a 'straighter', more serious and confident version of the romantic fairy tale in which the humour would largely be confined to the antics of the dwarfs. 'You couldn't possibly realize all the things we had to learn, and unlearn, in doing *Snow White*,' Walt told a reporter. 'We started out gaily, in the fast tempo that is the special technique of short subjects. But that wouldn't do; we soon realized there was danger of wearing out an audience. There was too much going on.'

Deciding the human characters would be depicted with greater realism, Disney set about using the Silly Symphonies as a training ground for his artists in techniques they would need for *Snow White*. Human figure animation had been tried in *The Pied Piper*, a Silly Symphony released in September 1933, but Walt had been disappointed with the results. *The Goddess of Spring*, a November 1934 Silly Symphony based upon the Greek legend of Persephone and directed by Wilfred Jackson, provided the setting for Disney artists to again practise rendering a more realistic depiction of the human figure. However, Walt was once more very disappointed, and even began to doubt the wisdom of a fully animated feature-length film. The project was on hiatus for most of 1935 while the company focused on producing such notable Mickey Mouse cartoons as *Mickey's Garden* (July 1935, the first colour appearance of Pluto), *Mickey's Fire Brigade* (August 1935) and *On Ice* (September 1935, the first colour appearance of Minnie Mouse who still appeared to be Mickey in drag), alongside the ongoing Silly Symphonies series.

There were some encouraging successes. In *Playful Pluto* (1934), director Burt Gillett was able to depict the dumb dog as something more like a genuine thinking and feeling character. As he became embroiled in a tangle with some sticky flypaper,

Pluto's frustrations, happiness and anticipation of events all combined to suggest a character with an inner life. In these mid-1930s Disney cartoons, there weren't just a series of gags – things happened to or befell recognizable, almost human, personalities. Similarly, *The Flying Mouse* (1934, directed by Dave Hand) saw a mouse granted his wish for wings imbued with some genuine emotion.

A summer trip to Europe in 1935 with Lillian, as well as Roy and his wife, gave Walt time to reflect on his animated feature project and regain his confidence. It included a tour of Paris, where Walt had spent the year immediately after the First World War, and Rome, where the Hollywood pioneer was greeted by Mussolini – 'He was most pleasant and cordial,' said Roy of the Italian dictator.

By November 1935 Walt was once again enthusiastically driving *Snow White and the Seven Dwarfs* forward, at the expense of his attention to the Mickey Mouse and Silly Symphony shorts (which had been left to the reliable supervision of Ben Sharpsteen), issuing a memo that outlined the core personnel's key responsibilities on the film. Dave Hand would be the supervising director responsible for coordinating the work of the other animators on the film. Five experienced Disney shorts directors were given key responsibility for certain sequences: Perce Pearce, Larry Morey (who would co-write the film's songs with Disney musical director Frank Churchill), Wilfred Jackson, Ben Sharpsteen and William 'Bill' Cottrell.

A variety of art directors worked on the designs for the characters and environments. Concept artists Ferdinand Hovarth (from Hungary) and Gustaf Tenggren (from Sweden) brought a suitably darker European fairy-tale sensibility to the look of the film's locations and backgrounds. They borrowed ideas for atmosphere and style from the illustrations of Arthur Rackham and John Bauer. Joe Grant focused specifically on developing the look for the wicked Queen when in her Witch guise, while Grim Natwick, who'd previously animated the curvy Betty

Boop for the Fleischer brothers, was given responsibility for designing Snow White herself.

There was constant feedback between the writers, who were further refining the story with Walt and working out detailed gag sequences for the dwarfs, and the artists, who were also refining the characters' looks and the locations. As always, Walt Disney presided over every aspect, but he continued to operate the collegiate approach he'd always had in the creation of the studio's animated films: everyone would have their input considered and anyone could contribute to any aspect of the project, but everyone had to recognize that only one name would be overtly attached to the finished film: Walt Disney.

The inevitable side effect of all this effort would be a variety of sequences that were developed but that would not be included in the movie, often for reasons of pacing. One such deleted sequence saw the Queen hold the Prince prisoner in her dungeon, where she used magic to make the skeletons of her previous prisoners dance for her amusement (a call back to one of Disney's earliest animated movies, *The Skeleton Dance*, and an idea later recycled in *Sleeping Beauty*, 1959). A fantasy sequence was planned to accompany Snow White's song 'Some Day My Prince Will Come', in which she visualizes herself dancing among the clouds with her dream Prince. Even scenes featuring the dwarfs were abandoned, including one in which they build an elaborate bed for Snow White with the help of dozens of woodland animals, and another in which they noisily eat soup before Snow White teaches them better manners (both sequences were worked upon by animator Ward Kimball, who considered leaving the studio when they were cut, until he was made a supervising animator on *Pinocchio*, 1940).

As ever, Walt Disney's drive for quality above all else meant he was willing to sacrifice months of creative effort if he came up with something he felt better fitted the developing tone of the film, even if his actions upset many of those involved in the seemingly never-ending project.

*   *   *

After almost three years of development work, actual animation began in earnest in February 1936. Fred Moore, who'd handled the animation of the title characters in *The Three Little Pigs*, was put in charge of animating the dwarfs, along with Bill Tytla, Fred Spencer and Frank Thomas. A group of newer, younger animators were given charge of the various woodland creatures. Wolfgang Reitherman handled the Magic Mirror sequences, Art Babbitt dealt with the Queen's scenes and Norm Ferguson took over for those scenes in which she transformed into the Witch (a look that owed something to actress Helen Gahagan in *She*, 1935). The rather limited character of the strait-laced Prince then fell to Grim Natwick, while Hamilton Luske finally landed the plum job of animating the star of the film, Snow White.

There were outstanding technical issues to be solved before shooting could be completed. Disney determined that the standard size of animated drawings used on the shorts was not large enough for the detail and scope he wanted for this film, especially given the 'painterly' nature of much of the background artwork, so he insisted the company use drawings one-and-a-half times larger than usual. It was a costly innovation that meant the development of new camera equipment, as well as new larger sized animation boards for all the animators, inkers and painters to work on.

Walt wanted his first animated feature film to contain depth, not only in the characters, story and in the world his team were creating, but also visually on the screen. He wanted to see authentic layers, where objects and people on screen would appear to be in the foreground, middle ground or background naturally. To achieve this, Disney's head of the camera department, William Garity, devised what became known as the 'multiplane' camera, a 12-foot tall contraption built in the Disney studio's machine shop. The huge multiplane set-up – which needed at least four people to operate it – allowed a motion-picture camera to shoot down through up to seven (appropriately enough) layers of art on animation cels and glass, offering several planes in any scene separate from each other, so giving an illusion of depth. This parallax process was successfully tested on the atmospheric Silly Symphony *The Old Mill* in 1937, which won the Oscar that year for Best Animated Short Film.

Learning from the mistakes made in animating the figure of Persephone in *The Goddess of Spring*, Walt devised a different approach to creating Snow White. He enlisted a young dancer and actress, Marge Belcher, to act out the part of Snow White (complete with costume) in live action, as reference for the animators. Similarly, actor Lewis Hightower stood in as the Prince and three small people were recruited so that the animators could accurately depict the dwarfs in motion. Tracing animation over live-action footage is known as 'rotoscoping', a process pioneered by Max Fleischer in his 'Out of the Inkwell' series, but many Disney animators disapproved of the practice. They preferred to use the live-action footage for reference, but create their own caricatures of human figures for their animation. However, some sequences featuring Snow White and the Prince were fully rotoscoped over animators' objections, probably in the interests of speeding up the production process.

The next challenge for Walt was giving voice to his film's characters. The dwarfs were relatively easy, especially as Disney animator Pinto Colvig himself voiced Sleepy and Grumpy (he'd also voiced Goofy and the Big Bad Wolf for various shorts). Radio and vaudeville performers played the others, including Otis Harlan as Happy, Scotty Mattraw as Bashful and Roy Atwell as Doc. The biggest name was movie comedian Billy Gilbert, cast as Sneezy. As it was largely a singing role, Harry Stockwell gave voice to the Prince, while Moroni Olsen voiced the Magic Mirror. Disney studio employee Stuart Buchanan took on the part of the Huntsman, and movie veteran Lucille La Verne played the Queen and the Witch.

Walt was determined that the musical interludes in *Snow White* should be more than just entertainment between the action sequences. He wanted the music to push forward the story, illuminate character or illustrate a major event. 'We should set a new pattern,' said Walt. '[We need] a new way to use music, [to] weave it into the story so somebody doesn't just burst into song.' This would later become a standard approach to movie musicals, but in the mid-1930s it was far from fashionable. Three of the film's eight songs – 'Heigh-Ho', 'Whistle While You Work' and 'Some Day My Prince Will Come' – were popular hits.

The biggest problem came in the quest for the perfect Snow White. Over a hundred people were auditioned, including a young Deanna Durbin, singing various songs from the movie including 'Whistle While You Work', but none fitted Walt's idea of the character. Disney's casting director sought the advice of Los Angeles singing coach Guido Caselotti, whose then nineteen-year-old daughter Adriana asked if she could try out for the role. As soon as Walt heard her distinctive singing voice, he knew he'd found his Snow White. She was quickly signed up, spent forty-eight days recording the role, and was paid a total of $970.

Walt had originally estimated the cost of *Snow White and the Seven Dwarfs* to be around $250,000, or about ten times the cost of a Silly Symphony short in 1934. The amount of time, effort and expense spent on development pushed the estimate to $500,000, much to the consternation of Roy Disney who had harboured doubts about the ambitious project from the very beginning. The seemingly endless development and the lack of a clear endpoint caused many arguments between Walt and Roy, with Walt pushing his 'quality above all' mantra, and Roy becoming ever more anxious about the studio's financial risk. When some early footage was screened to Disney employees and feedback sought in the form of notes deposited anonymously in a box, one note that read 'Stick to shorts' was widely believed to have been written by Roy.

Finally, the Bank of America refused to advance the studio any further financing unless they saw something of the epic work in progress. This spurred Walt into reluctantly producing a rough cut of everything that had been shot so far, padded out with pencil animation tests and storyboards for yet un-filmed or incomplete sequences. That September in 1937, the work-in-progress showreel, which also featured an incomplete soundtrack (Walt would improvise and fill in where material was missing), was screened for the company's bankers and executives from RKO (Disney's new distributor), whose col-lective quiet response convinced Walt they would get no more funding. When walking Joseph Rosenberg – who handled the Disney account at the Bank of America – out to his car, Walt was relieved when the banker finally said: 'That thing is going to make you a hatful of money.'

While this was a relief to Disney, the rest of the world con-tinued to crow about the non-appearance of *Snow White and the Seven Dwarfs* some three years after it had been officially announced. Worried by the negative comments, Walt dis-cussed the matter with his distributors. They responded with a variation of Oscar Wilde's famous quote: 'There is only one thing in life worse than being talked about, and that is not being talked about.' Despite the delays, anticipation was build-ing for the film among the public. *Esquire*'s film critic tested whether it was possible to watch cartoons for ninety minutes by viewing ten Disney shorts one after another and writing a feature about it. *Life* magazine speculated that the discussion of the long-delayed movie had reached 'such proportions that Mr Disney may well worry lest the public expect too much!'

For the final six months of production on *Snow White*, Disney had the studio operating twenty-four hours a day, seven days a week, with animators working in shifts to complete sequences, sometimes sleeping by their drawing boards rather than going home. Final animation wasn't completed until early November, with the last cels painted at the end of that month and the photography on *Snow White* concluded on the first day of December, a mere six days before the first scheduled public preview in Pomona, an hour east of Los Angeles. There was a sense of a righteous crusade in the studio's work, as if everyone

involved in making *Snow White* were collectively dedicated
to proving the naysayers wrong. Even towards the end, ever
the perfectionist, Walt still wasn't happy. 'I've seen so much
of *Snow White* that I am conscious only of the places where it
could be improved,' he said. 'We've learned such a lot since we
started this thing. I wish I could yank it back and do it all over
again!' Animator Frank Thomas said of Walt's focus on *Snow
White* that he 'lived every sprocket hole of this film'.

Finally, the movie was done towards the end of 1937, at a
total cost of $1,488,423 – almost six times the originally esti-
mated budget. Near the end of production, Walt found himself
in conflict with his distributor United Artists, who demanded
that television rights to the Disney cartoons be included in
their deal. Walt explained, rather disingenuously: 'I don't know
what television is, and I'm not going to sign away anything I
don't know about.' The relationship with United Artists came
to an end, so *Snow White and the Seven Dwarfs* would be distributed by RKO, who'd also handle the shorts from now on.

The premiere of *Snow White and the Seven Dwarfs* took place
at the Carthay Circle Theatre (where *The Skeleton Dance*, the
first of the Silly Symphonies, had played eight years earlier) on
21 December 1937. Big Hollywood names, among them Marlene
Dietrich, Charles Laughton and Judy Garland, attended. The
eighty-three-minute film, made up of around two million individual drawings, concluded to a rapturous response, winning a
standing ovation from the crowd. To the surprise of the many
cynics who'd denigrated the project during its protracted
development, 'Disney's folly' turned out to be a masterpiece.

The press agreed upon the film's wide release in February
1938, with the *New York Herald Tribune* writing of the film:
'It is one of those rare works of inspired artistry that weave
an irresistible spell around the beholder . . . *Snow White and
the Seven Dwarfs* is more than a completely satisfying entertainment, more than a perfect moving picture, in the full
sense of that term. It offers a memorable and deeply enriching

experience.' For *Time* magazine (which featured Walt on the cover), *Snow White* was 'an authentic masterpiece', a declaration with which the *New York Times* agreed. 'It is a classic, as important cinematically as *The Birth of a Nation* or the birth of Mickey Mouse,' wrote its film critic, Frank Nugent, concluding by noting, 'If you miss it, you'll be missing the 10 best pictures of 1938.' The *New Republic* saw the film as an achievement that transcended mere film, calling it 'among the genuine artistic achievements of this country'. Hollywood's trade paper, *Variety*, wrote: 'so perfect is the illusion, so tender the romance and fantasy, so are certain portions where the acting of the characters strikes a depth comparable to the sincerity of human players, that the film approaches real greatness'. No more would anyone doubt whether audiences were ready to sit through an animated film at feature length.

Walt Disney's cinematic hero Charlie Chaplin was present at the Los Angeles premiere and noted the movie 'even surpassed our high expectations. In Dopey, Disney has created one of the greatest comedians of all time.' Starting from January 1938, the film unspooled in spectacularly successful exclusive runs at Radio City Music Hall in New York and at a cinema in Miami, before going on to a wider release through RKO from 4 February.

The film quickly became a major box office hit, rapidly earning $3.5 million (four times its cost of production) in the US and Canada. By May 1939, the total international gross takings of the movie had reached $6.5 million, making it the most successful sound film to that point, replacing Al Jolson's *The Singing Fool* (1928) – it would later itself be surpassed by *Gone with the Wind* (1939). By the time the movie closed, it had earned just under $8 million worldwide. The average cinema ticket price in 1938 was twenty-three cents, or a dime (ten cents) for children, who probably made up the majority of the audience.

Snow White and the Seven Dwarfs would be re-released to US cinemas in 1944 to help raise revenue for the Disney studio during the war years, beginning a tradition of re-releases of their major animated films every seven to ten years to capture each new generation. The lifetime theatrical takings of *Snow White and the Seven Dwarfs* would reach an impressive $416 million (that doesn't include television screenings, videotape and DVD releases, all of which have further added to the film's ever-growing revenue). Adjusted for inflation, the film still makes it into the top ten of all-time box office champions.

The film played in forty-nine countries and was dubbed into ten different languages. There were over 2,000 *Snow White* tie-in products and merchandise items, all of which brought additional income to the studio for many years. In May 1938, Walt's merchandise man Kay Kamen reported that $2 million worth of *Snow White* toys had been sold, while Walt himself was pre-empting modern animation art collectors by selling individual animation cels from the movie to the Courvoisier Art Gallery in San Francisco. And then there were the awards . . .

The 11th Annual Academy Awards took place in February 1939 and saw Walt Disney win his second special honorary Oscar for 'creating *Snow White and the Seven Dwarfs*, recognized as a significant screen innovation which has charmed millions and pioneered a great new entertainment field for the motion picture cartoon'. In honour of the film, the Oscar consisted of one main statuette with seven mini-Oscars on a stepped base. The award was presented to Walt by a then ten-year-old Shirley Temple. At the same ceremony the Silly Symphony *Ferdinand the Bull* (1938, about a bull who hated bullfighting) also won an Oscar for Best Short Subject (Cartoons).

Snow White even reached the Soviet Union, with Russian filmmaker Sergei Eisenstein singing Walt Disney's praises: 'Although as yet there are all too few examples of the true cinematography of sound-and-sight consonance (only a few scenes, for instance in Disney's wonderful *Snow White* or individual scenes from *Alexander Nevsky*, such as the "Attack of the Knights"), advanced cinema directors are engrossed in the problem of spectacle synthesis, experimenting in this field and accumulating a certain amount of experience.' The film was even a smash hit in Hitler's Germany.

Films that built upon the success of *Snow White* include MGM's perennial *The Wizard of Oz* (1939), which incorporated Walt's approach of having songs advance the narrative, and Max Fleischer's animated feature film *Gulliver's Travels* (1939). By 1943, the lasting impact of 'Disney's folly' was assured when it was parodied (in the period's politically incorrect way) as the Warner Bros. Merrie Melody short *Coal Black and de Sebben Dwarfs*, directed by Bob Clampett (whose aunt had made the first licensed handmade Mickey Mouse dolls for Walt Disney back in the late 1920s).

Seven years after the film's initial release, director Michael Powell would write about it in the British magazine *Film Review*, citing Walt Disney as:

> one of the three persons necessary to the evolution of film making – Griffith, the master showman; Chaplin, the lonely genius; Disney, the experimenter and planner; the director of the future will partake of all of them; without them he could not exist, whether he ever heard of them or not . . . At one stride, with this feature-length cartoon in colour, for making which he had been ridiculed, Disney became one of the world's greatest film producers. Few of them realized it; few of them realize it now, seven years later, such is the momentum of film production. Yet, in *Snow White*, Disney abolished naturalism, established stylistic settings and backgrounds (echoed recently in Laurence Olivier's *Henry V*), controlled his design of colour and sound (a feat not yet in the power of any other producer) and held audiences enraptured all over the world.

Over the weekend of 4–5 June 1938, the Disney company held a now notorious staff party, essentially a delayed wrap party, for *Snow White and the Seven Dwarfs*, attended by up to 1,400 employees, family and friends. Officially called 'Walt's Field Day' (achievement in competitive sports events during the day was rewarded with trophies), the event came to be known among those who were there as the 'Snow White orgy'. Intended as a reward for all the hard work involved in making the movie and as a celebration of its unprecedented success, the festivities soon got out of hand, largely thanks to a free open bar (the company would pick up the tab, including for the overnight room rentals). This was to be no traditional company picnic.

Held at the Norconian Club, a desert resort on Lake Norco, close to Palm Springs, things started out sedately enough but, according to Ward Kimball's recollections, rapidly deteriorated into a drunken bacchanal that carried on non-stop for two whole days and nights. Stories told after the event included Walt and Roy and their wives arriving some time after the party had begun to truly swing and soon leaving again when they saw how things were going. One story told of Fred Moore (chief animator of the dwarfs) falling from a third-floor window while drunkenly relieving himself, only to land in a tree. Someone else was said to have ridden a horse drunkenly along a second-storey hallway.

With the Disney staff having suffered through three years of stress and overwork, animator Bill Justice admitted that 'something just snapped. An animator picked up an ink and paint girl and dumped her into the pool fully clothed . . . followed by others jumping in and all hell broke loose pretty quickly. Swimsuits flew out the windows. There were naked swim parties, people got drunk and were often surprised what room they were in and who they were sleeping next to when they awoke the next morning.' Whatever else may have gone on has been lost to history, but suffice it to say that Walt Disney never sanctioned such a studio party ever again.

Things had changed a lot at Walt Disney Studios through the 1930s. Walt himself had risen from the setbacks of the Alice comedies and the betrayals he felt over Oswald the Lucky Rabbit and by Ub Iwerks from the early days of Disney. He'd built the world's best animation studio from a very small beginning, developing Mickey Mouse and Donald Duck, characters loved the world over, and had expressed his artistic sensibilities through the Silly Symphonies. With America's first full-length animated feature film, Walt Disney had launched a new type of movie and had innovated in the field of motion pictures. He was at the height of his powers and his studio was top of the heap in Hollywood. The trouble with reaching the top is that often the only way to go next is down.

4

THE GOLDEN AGE OF ANIMATION

Our most important aim is to develop definite personalities in our cartoon characters. We don't want them to be just shadows, for merely as moving figures they provoke no emotional response from the public. We invest them with life . . . a caricature of life.

Walt Disney, interview, *New York Times*, March 1938

During the production of *Snow White and the Seven Dwarfs*, Walt Disney had become a family man. Following Lillian's earlier miscarriages, they'd tried again for children, this time successfully. Diane Marie Disney had been born on 18 December 1933, almost two weeks after Walt's thirty-second birthday. Walt expanded the family by adopting Sharon Mae Disney on 31 December 1936, as both he and Lillian were worried about her attempting another pregnancy. During much of his life, Walt went to great lengths to keep the fact of Sharon's adoption out of the media, only because he didn't believe it mattered one way or another and he didn't want his second daughter to become a curiosity to the press. By the time *Snow White* was on wide release in early 1938, both Disney girls were of an age that they could begin to enjoy viewing their father's work.

Prior to and throughout the lengthy production of *Snow White and the Seven Dwarfs* the Hyperion Disney studio had grown like Topsy. In a series of opportunistic expansions, adjoining lots had been developed and buildings put up in a rather uncoordinated fashion. During 1937 and 1938 a feature animation building had been added, three film vaults constructed and a new inking-and-painting building erected, among other haphazard structures. The result was a cluster of buildings with animators and administrators, writers and management spread across a site rather like an unplanned college campus. While Walt and his animators enjoyed that atmosphere, he knew that if the studio was to focus on animated feature film production in future following the astonishing success of *Snow White*, they would need to expand again, and there was simply no room for that on the existing Hyperion site.

The only option was to start again with a new, purpose-built studio complex. A fifty-one-acre site was secured on Buena Vista Street in Burbank with a deposit of $10,000 (against a final purchase price of $100,000) put down at the end of August 1938. Walt personally supervised every aspect of the new studio, even though the actual planning was carried out by a team of professional architects and designers. It had to meet a mix of requirements as a suitable place for the production of movies, but also an environment that would encourage the creativity and quality of output that Walt always looked for from his employees.

At three storeys high and with four wings, the new Animation Building dominated the site. Natural light was deemed paramount, and the building was designed to allow as much light in as possible to facilitate the animators, with adjustable slatted blinds helping eliminate glare. The building housed Walt's offices, the story department, production man-agers, supervising animators, in-betweeners (who filled in the images between the animators' key poses) and 'checkers' (who passed the drawings before they went off to the ink-and-paint department). There was a reference library used by both the story people and the animators, and in the basement was the 'morgue' where old animation drawings were stored (and would be accessed decades later by students at CalArts). Surrounding buildings of the campus-like studio grounds included the ink-and-paint department, and others for editing and cameras, a sound stage for recording music and voice tracks, and a grand projection theatre. Unlike at the old studio, everywhere in the new complex was air-conditioned (although that didn't stop the animation review sessions with Walt still being called 'sweatboxes'). Walt even involved himself in designing new chairs and tables for the studio's hard-working animators – it was all good experience he would later put to use in creating Disneyland and Disney World.

The new studio was in operation by the end of 1939 and remains the headquarters of the much expanded Disney operation to this day. With the new studio came an overhaul of the organization of the company. The production process of *Snow White* had been rather haphazard and disorganized, largely because the company was discovering exactly how to produce a feature-length animated film for the first time. For the future, things would be much more structured, and the Disney company lost some of its previous collegiate feel in the process, giving rise to later staff problems. The new studio structure cemented Walt's position as top dog, with his Executive Producer role defined as authorizing and controlling everything the company was involved in.

In the wake of Mickey Mouse and *Snow White*, Walt Disney found he had to cope with becoming famous, a side-effect of his success. 'I never have time to ponder over the fact that I may have become what they call a "celebrity",' he once wrote to a friend, 'and if I am one, it has never helped me to make a better picture.' The only benefit he could recall was scoring a better seat at an American football game when he was recognized, but that also came with being 'pounced on' after the game for autographs. 'No,' Walt concluded, 'being a celebrity doesn't mean so much.' In later years, though, he'd find a way to positively embrace and use his celebrity, especially on television.

Disney biographer Neal Gabler, however, thought he saw something else in Disney's occasional comparison between the animator and God in their control over creation. Gabler reckoned that among his employees, at least during the production of *Snow White*, Walt Disney himself was perceived as God-like. There was an atmosphere at play during the production of that movie: not only were all the staff united in pulling in the same direction to achieve Walt's goal, but there was also a need among them to somehow please their mentor, to have their work reach his high standards of quality. In this Gabler saw something cultish. 'The effect was that the Disney studio did not operate like any other studio in Hollywood,' he wrote in *Walt Disney: The Triumph of the American Imagination*. 'In fact, it didn't operate like a commercial institution at all. By the mid-1930s the Disney studio operated like a cult, with a messianic figure inspiring a group of devoted, sometimes frenzied acolytes.' In Disney's aspiration to animate the perfect human, at first in cartoons and later through animatronic robots, he was trespassing on the territory of the divine creator. Regardless of whether Gabler was overreaching with this comparison, the atmosphere in and around the Disney studio would change dramatically, and not for the better, as the new decade of the 1940s dawned.

In the wake of the success of *Snow White*, the demands of Disney's distributors were nothing if not predictable. Then as now, whatever has most recently succeeded will be repeated. So, following the distributors' call for 'more mice' after Mickey and 'more pigs' after *The Three Little Pigs*, came the call for 'more dwarfs' after *Snow White*. Other studios obliged, with

Max Fleischer making *Gulliver's Travels* (1939) for Paramount and Walter Lantz embarking upon *Aladdin and His Wonderful Lamp* for Universal (a project never to be completed). Walt Disney refused to repeat himself, even though he could see as well as anyone that there was much more comic mileage in his 'screwy' dwarfs.

However, the story of Snow White had been told, and it was time for the Disney studio to expand into other areas, although many of the new stories would also be based upon fairy tales or folk tales. Walt outlined six subjects he wanted to develop as movies: Pinocchio, Bambi (which had been in development even before *Snow White*), *Alice in Wonderland* (Disney's long-time favourite), Cinderella, Kenneth Grahame's *The Wind in the Willows* and J. M. Barrie's *Peter Pan*. Walt also had an interest in doing a film based on A. A. Milne's Winnie-the-Pooh stories. Some would be completed in the next few years, while others would have to wait a lot longer before they saw the silvery light of cinema projection.

Rather than follow *Snow White and the Seven Dwarfs* with something easier, Walt Disney hit upon the picaresque adventures of Pinocchio, as told by nineteenth-century writer Carlo Collodi. The 1880 book *The Adventures of Pinocchio* had been brought to Walt's attention by animator Norman Ferguson in September 1937, while everyone at the studio was rushing to finish *Snow White*. Intended to be the third animated feature film that Disney would tackle, it was brought forward due to the ongoing development problems with *Bambi* (the animators were finding it difficult to realize realistic-looking forest animals). According to Ferguson, Walt was 'busting his guts with enthusiasm' for *Pinocchio*, seeing in the title character another childlike figure akin to Mickey Mouse and the dwarfs in *Snow White*.

Adapting the story was a fraught process. Although *Snow White*'s basic tale could be built up and elaborated upon in any number of ways, the *Pinocchio* story had a fixed conclusion, and the character as originally written was rather harsh, although the tale was full of comic incidents that could potentially make great material for the screen. The Disney artists' first attempts at rendering Pinocchio were deemed too grotesque by Walt, who had them soften his characteristics. At the same time, he had the writers revise his character in order to make him more appealing as the hero of an adventure aimed at a family audience, rather than the wilful and often disobedient puppet boy of the Collodi stories. Although animation had been started by Frank Thomas and Ollie Johnston in January 1938, Walt called a halt to the project after just six months, unhappy with the way it was going. He knew he'd be expected to top *Snow White*, and what he was seeing so far on *Pinocchio* was far from that.

The key problem was making Pinocchio sympathetic. To get around this, the writers and animators had devised a conceit where Pinocchio would debate with himself the rights and wrongs of each situation in which he found himself. This proved difficult to maintain and hard to pull off without it appearing mannered and wearying. Walt felt his team were on the right lines, though, and hit upon one sequence in the book in which Pinocchio (now redesigned to be more appealing by Fred Moore and revised again by Milt Kahl, who gave him Mickey Mouse-style gloves) encounters a talking cricket. When Pinocchio doesn't like the cricket's advice, he squashes him with a hammer. Walt, however, decided that if they made the cricket function as an external conscience for Pinocchio it would solve many of the adaptation's problems. Recalling a 1934 Silly Symphony, *The Grasshopper and the Ants*, which had featured a smartly dressed, violin-playing grasshopper, Walt could see the basis for a great character in the cricket. They gave him a name and personality, resulting in Jiminy Cricket. The original version was described by Walt as 'a pompous little fellow . . . a kind of a windbag', but he was changed with the casting of Cliff Edwards as the voice. The character was revised as younger and livelier to fit with Edwards and his performance of two songs in the film, 'Give a Little Whistle' and

'When You Wish upon a Star' (which would become a Disney signature tune). The character was the perfect companion for the naive Pinocchio, able to help him to learn lessons and figure out the right and wrong way to go about things, while being entertaining in his own right.

Supervising animators on the film were Disney veterans Ben Sharpsteen and Hamilton Luske. The animation of Jiminy Cricket fell to Wolfgang Reitherman, Don Towsley and Ward Kimball (who was prevented from quitting Disney after the travails of *Snow White* thanks to becoming lead animator for Jiminy Cricket). Kimball redesigned Jiminy to be less cricket-like and more human, resulting in a far more appealing character. Mistaken for an honest fellow by Pinocchio, the fox conman J. Worthington Foulfellow was animated by the originator of the whole project, Norman Ferguson, with John Lounsbery, and was voiced by Walter Catlett. Stromboli the puppet-master was animated by Bill Tytla and voiced (in Italian gibberish) by Charles Judels. Evelyn Venable voiced the Blue Fairy, which was modelled after Marge Belcher, the live-action inspiration for Snow White. Woodcarver Geppetto, Pinocchio's 'father', was animated by Art Babbitt and brought to vocal life by Christian Rub, an Austrian character actor on whom the look of the character was based. The voice of Pinocchio would be key to the film, believed Walt. He rejected the usual approach of having an adult voice a child character, deciding instead upon child actor Dickie Jones (*Mr Smith Goes to Washington*, 1939).

Animation was resumed in September 1938, with Joe Grant heading up the character-modelling department, which decided upon the look for each individual character, modelling them as three-dimensional clay figures that aided the animators in their work. Several other key props, such as Geppetto's clocks, and vehicles, like Stromboli's gypsy wagon, were also initially visualized in this way. A marionette of Pinocchio was created for the animators to study. As on *Snow White*, Albert Hurter and Gustaff Tenggren provided backgrounds, while animators took daytrips out to Catalina Island to observe the marine gardens from a glass-bottomed boat and collect seashells for their work.

If *Snow White and the Seven Dwarfs* had made breakthroughs in character animation, proving in the process that audiences could be made to sympathize with and even be moved to tears by mere 'cartoon' characters, then *Pinocchio* innovated further in the field of effects animation. Natural effects – such as rain, snow, lightning and wind – were much focused upon, with the animators creating scenes as big as violent storms and as small as flickering candles with equal attention to detail and craft. Underwater scenes were given a rippling effect by shooting through specially created groundglass panels. The effects for 'fairy dust' and the Blue Fairy's wand were handled by Oskar Fischinger, who would be instrumental to *Fantasia* (1940).

Walt was especially keen to develop use of the multiplane camera further in *Pinocchio*; it had been sparingly used in *Snow White* as it was developed late in the production of that movie. The camera was especially effective in *Pinocchio* in the sequence depicting the awakening of the village as the shot begins in the rooftops, moving down through the twisting streets, to a final scene packed with people. That single shot was said to have cost in the region of $48,000, almost twice as much as an entire average Mickey Mouse or Silly Symphony short.

There were technical improvements in the animation for *Pinocchio*, but the storytelling remained fractured. As with *Snow White*, several sequences planned for *Pinocchio* ended up being abandoned or dropped from the finished film. Among them was a much longer series of adventures on Pleasure Island, and a sequence that saw Geppetto tell Pinocchio about his 'grandfather', an old pine tree. Woodland storm and forest-fire sequences were worked up but dropped, only to be revived for use in *Bambi*. By the time it was completed, *Pinocchio* far exceeded the cost of *Snow White*, coming in at $2.6 million.

Opening on 7 February 1940 (about eighteen months after its originally planned release date), *Pinocchio* was a critical hit but a financial failure, at least, at first. The song 'When You Wish Upon a Star', with music by Leigh Harline and lyrics by Ned Washington, became a huge hit, winning an Oscar for Best Music, Original Song, with the film also winning for Best Music, Original Score. Ever a supporter of Disney, Frank Nugent in the *New York Times* ironically said *Pinocchio* was 'superior to *Snow White* in every respect but one: the score', while the *New Republic* claimed it brought 'the cartoon to a level of perfection that the word "cartoon" will not cover'.

By late 1940, *Pinocchio* had only taken around $1 million at the US box office, well under its cost of production and the huge amounts taken by *Snow White*, simply due to the fact that fewer people went to see the film. Perhaps the novelty of an animated feature film had worn off since *Snow White*, or the growing war in Europe was on people's minds more than frivolous entertainment. Estimates of the film's first run worldwide box office range between $1.4 and $1.9 million, a major disappointment to Walt Disney and to RKO (who recorded a formal loss of $94,000 for the movie). The problem was compounded by the loss of many European and Asian markets due to the outbreak of war – an issue that would dog the next few Disney releases as up to 45 per cent of the studio's income was estimated to come from overseas releasing. Reissues of *Pinocchio* after the end of the Second World War were more successful, starting in 1944 in the US. By 1973 the film had grossed about $13 million (including the 1940 release and four further reissues), while later theatrical reissues would bring *Pinocchio*'s lifetime box office to a total of just over $84 million. In 1994 it was added to the National Film Registry of culturally important movies. The American Film Institute's 2008 list of the top ten animated films puts *Snow White* in first place and *Pinocchio* in second. In 2011, *Time* magazine put Pinocchio at the top of its 25 Best All-Time Animated Films. Not bad for a 'failure' of a film.

*   *   *

Meanwhile, progress was slowly being made on *Bambi*. An in-betweener on *Pinocchio*, Chinese-born Tyrus Wong submitted drawings for *Bambi* that took Walt's fancy and would become the defining style for the movie. With *Bambi* still essentially stuck in development hell (it had first been considered before *Snow White* and was the subject of a series of story conferences in August 1937), Walt Disney had a new obsession that would come to be known within the studio as 'The Concert Feature', but would be released as *Fantasia* in 1940.

Walt's interest was first captured by the tale of *The Sorcerer's Apprentice*, a 1797 poem by Goethe adapted as a fantasy scherzo by Paul Dukas in 1896–7. Walt envisioned the music matched with a Silly Symphony-style film starring Mickey Mouse, whose appeal was slightly on the wane with audiences compared with the ever-more popular Donald Duck and Goofy (who also had their own film series from 1937 and 1939 respectively). The story of an ambitious youngster's attempts to become a great magician while experimenting with his master's tools was ideal material – Walt could easily see Mickey failing to cope with the magic broomstick and the marching buckets of water and the chaos that followed when the enchantment runs out of the apprentice's control.

There was debate within the studio, though, as to whether the material would work with Mickey. One faction suggested using Dopey, from *Snow White*, as he was a character that could be developed further and could work well with the material. Walt, though, was adamant that he would not revive any of the dwarfs. 'I feel that to separate Dopey from the other dwarfs, to take him away from his surroundings, to place him in a strange world to fend for himself, would be wrong,' he said. Developing better business instincts than before, Walt knew that Mickey needed a boost to restore his popularity, so in May 1937 he set about acquiring the rights to use the Dukas symphonic poem.

Following a long dinner at Chasen's restaurant in West Hollywood, when the men met by happenstance, Walt invited acclaimed conductor Leopold Stokowski to conduct the music for *The Sorcerer's Apprentice*, which was recorded in January 1938. Stokowski, conductor of the Philadelphia Orchestra since 1912, had become something of a Hollywood personality following appearances in several movies, including *The Big Broadcast of 1937*. In a letter Disney said he was 'all steamed up over the idea of Stokowski working with us . . . The union of Stokowski and his music, together with the best of our medium, would be the means of a success and should lead to a new style of motion picture presentation.'

The animation of *The Sorcerer's Apprentice* was put in the hands of Les Clark and Fred Moore, with Moore making revisions to Mickey's appearance, giving him eyes with pupils for the first time (they went from all black to white with black pupils). The resulting ten-minute film had cost $125,000, making it too expensive and too long to function as a stand-alone Silly Symphony. When others at the studio suggested the only thing to be done was to cut *The Sorcerer's Apprentice* down to the usual cartoon length of seven or so minutes, Walt – ever the innovator – went in the opposite direction. He decided that they could take the work of other composers and give them the same animated treatment, thus making an entire concert film. As with *Snow White* – the first American animated feature – Walt Disney sensed there was new ground to be broken in the field of animated cartoons driven by music, beyond the Silly Symphonies.

In September 1938 a five-person team, consisting of Walt Disney, Joe Grant (head of the character-modelling department), animator Dick Huemer, composer and musical commentator Deems Taylor (who provided intermission commentaries during radio broadcasts of the New York Philharmonic, and who would narrate the resulting film) and Stokowski, gathered to begin exploring other musical compositions that might be suitable in the creation of several new shorts that could be joined with *The Sorcerer's Apprentice* to make 'The Concert Feature' film.

Between them they devised a shortlist of music to include.

It had to be dramatic and lend itself to animated sequences if the overall movie was going to work. Two straightforward choices were the contrasting *Night on Bald Mountain* by Mussorgsky and Schubert's *Ave Maria*, while Stravinsky's *The Rite of Spring* was chosen to accompany a planned animation sequence of the evolution of life on earth through to the extinction of the dinosaurs. Tchaikovsky's *The Nutcracker Suite* was deemed a suitable accompaniment to images of the natural world, including magical fantasy fairies, while Bach's *Toccata and Fugue in D Minor* would open the film accompanying images of the orchestra and a sequence of abstract graphics. 'Dance of the Hours' by Ponchielli (from the opera *La Gioconda*) would accompany a series of comic ballet dances (modelled upon live-action dance footage of Marge Belcher) by ungainly animals including hippos, elephants and alligators. Beethoven's Sixth Symphony ('The Pastoral'), replaced Gabriel Pierné's *Cydalise et le Chèvre Pied* to accompany figures from Greek mythology including fauns, the god of wine Bacchus and Zeus, father of the gods. The Hollywood Hays Office that enforced the movie Production Code insisted that the female centaurs in this sequence should sport bras (they don't in the finished film, they just don't have any nipples). Walt wanted all his collaborators to imaginatively interpret the music through the ever-expanding art of animation.

Although he felt his knowledge of music was merely 'instinctual', Disney was excited by the project. He didn't suggest much of the music used, but he was pivotal in choosing what among the others' suggestions might work best when married up to animated images. A variety of works by composers such as Stravinsky, Paganini and Rachmaninoff were sampled by the group but ultimately rejected. According to those working on the film, Disney appeared to thoroughly enjoy his involvement in the development work on what would ultimately be titled *Fantasia*, much more than he had on *Pinocchio*. That film, he seemed to feel, was under pressure to repeat the success of *Snow White*, whereas 'The Concert Feature' was a brand new, exciting creation unto itself unlike anything else produced in American motion pictures, just as *Snow White* had once been. It appealed to Walt's constant desire to innovate, to pursue the new and exciting, that was always more interesting to him than merely repeating what he had done before – whereas Roy would always prefer more of the same, safe material than anything dramatically unproven, as that tended to be expensive.

Given that the success of this film would depend upon the music as much as the animation, the sound reproduction would be of central importance. Stokowski worked with Disney's William Garity, head of the sound and camera department, to develop a new form of four-track recording (dubbed Fantasound) that saw elements of the soundtrack recorded separately, meaning they could then be selected and emphasized to match what was being shown on screen. The system required the installation of a trio of speakers behind the cinema screen and sixty-five others placed strategically around each auditorium.

While internal artists like Albert Hurter handled the mythological creatures for 'The Pastoral' symphony, Walt brought in Danish artist Kay Nielsen from outside the Disney fold to provide illustrations for the *Night on Bald Mountain* sequence that would close the film. Nielsen didn't find working for Disney to be rewarding, though, and the association was short-lived, as was that of Oskar Fischinger, who worked with Disney's Cy Town on the opening Bach sequence only to quit 'in disgust and despair' before the sequence was completed.

Where some thought that *Snow White* was going to be 'arty' in comparison to the then-standard cartoon short, there could be no doubting that *Fantasia* was always intended to be a highbrow product using what had widely been perceived to be a largely lowbrow medium, the animated cartoon. The project attracted a large number of accomplished visitors to the studios, such as author Thomas Mann, choreographer George Balanchine and architect Frank Lloyd Wright, who criticized the work-in-progress as simply 'too damned artistic'. Dr

Edwin P. Hubble of California's Mount Wilson Observatory and biologist Sir Julian Huxley lent their expertise to the evolutionary scope of *The Rites of Spring* sequence.

Walt had the idea of perhaps re-releasing *Fantasia* at different intervals with new music and animated sequences added and others dropped, making it an infinitely changeable film (this would eventually happen with 1999's *Fantasia 2000* revised version of the movie). In this way he could incorporate some of the ideas he'd had to drop, including animating the 'Ride of the Valkyrie' from *The Ring of the Nibelung*, or Rimsky-Korsakov's *Flight of the Bumble Bee* (which Walt felt could make for a great animated short). As it was, the finished work had cost a total of $2.3 million, including $400,000 on recording the music alone.

The title of *Fantasia* was only decided upon as the film neared completion. 'In a profession that has been an unending voyage of discovery in realms of colour, sound, and motion,' Walt said, '*Fantasia* represents our most exciting adventure.' Presentationally, Walt Disney hoped *Fantasia* could break new ground. He conjured up several unfulfilled concepts, such as making the film in 3D, pumping fragrances into the auditorium to accompany certain sections of the movie, or widescreen or multi-screen presentations. None of this was to happen, but the release of *Fantasia* would be handled carefully as a 'roadshow' presentation, making the film more of an event than simply another run-of-the-mill cinema release.

RKO, still Disney's distributor despite the financial disappointment of *Pinocchio*, didn't know how to handle such a unique movie and agreed to allow Walt to distribute this one himself. Walt gave responsibility for the release of *Fantasia* to salesman Irving Ludwig, who outfitted major theatres in big cities with the 'Fantasound' audio reproduction system (at a cost of $30,000 per cinema) especially for exclusive engagements of *Fantasia*. Opening on 13 November 1940 at New York's Broadway Theater (formerly the Colony, where Mickey Mouse had debuted in *Steamboat Willie*), *Fantasia* was liked

by critics, if not by general cinema-goers who didn't respond
to it in the way Walt would have hoped. 'Motion picture history was made last night,' wrote the *New York Times* critic
Bosley Crowther after viewing *Fantasia*. He noted that the
new Disney movie 'dumps conventional formulas overboard
and reveals the scope of film for imaginative excursions . . .
Fantasia is simply terrific.' *Time* magazine felt the film was
'stranger and more wonderful than any of Hollywood's', while
Variety dubbed *Fantasia* 'a successful experiment to lift the
relationship from the plane of the popular, mass entertainment to the higher strata of appeal to lovers of classical music'.
Generally, classical music critics took against the film as it
was not deemed to be reverential enough to the music, which
it had demeaned by running it over mere 'cartoons'. Music
critic Virgil Thomson took issue with the 'musical taste' of
Stokowski, and Olin Downes of the *New York Times* wrote
that 'it is clear that in many cases Mr Disney's noble and highly
provocative experiment separated certain lovers of the respective arts [cinema and music] than united them'.

The biggest controversy surrounding the film, however, was
political. With the rise of the Nazis in Europe and the outbreak
of war, many saw *Fantasia* – especially in its choice of music –
as reactionary in a time of international crisis. Writing in the
left-wing *Daily Worker*, Harry Raymond noted that in the
movie, 'the forces of evil are not shown as the exploiters and war
makers, but as a mythical devil on a mountain top against whom
human powers are helpless'. Even more stringent in her attack
was columnist Dorothy Thompson, who dubbed *Fantasia* nothing less than an 'assault . . . a brutalization of sensibility in this
remarkable nightmare . . . [It is a] caricature of the decline of the
West.' Walt welcomed the additional publicity the unforeseen
political controversy brought to *Fantasia*, claiming he himself
was apolitical. The fuss, he noted, 'couldn't have been sweeter.
The public responded by lining up at the box office with the
result that our advance sale has been simply terrific.'

The film ran in Los Angeles and San Francisco, as well as

Boston, Cleveland, Chicago and Detroit, but the only sustained engagement was in New York where it ran for a full year. 'Roadshow' prices were higher than general admission, and many parents got the idea that *Fantasia* was not a suitable movie for children – for some the earlier *Snow White* had its frightening moments too. Some children who did attend were frightened by the dark and foreboding *Night on Bald Mountain* sequence that closed the picture (screen Dracula Bela Lugosi had provided live-action footage as demon Chernobog for the animators to work from). Finally, Walt very reluctantly agreed to RKO releasing a cut-down version of the two-hour film across the country. RKO's editors trimmed the movie to eighty-one minutes without Walt's input and released it second on a double bill with a Western.

Despite that, *Fantasia* failed at the box office. By April 1941, the roadshow presentations had taken $1.3 million, but much of that was taken up by the additional cost of installing the bespoke Fantasound system in theatres. RKO's release brought in an additional $325,000, but many European markets were closed to the film due to the war. A reissue in 1942 helped, but still did not bring *Fantasia* into profit. It wouldn't be until 1969, after several reissues and following Walt's death, that *Fantasia* would finally enter profit, when its re-release coincided with the rise of hippy youth culture and psychedelia, which brought the film a new (stoned) audience that Walt could never have anticipated.

Consolation came to Walt at the Academy Awards in 1942 when the film won two honorary Oscars. One went to Walt Disney, William E. Garity, John N. A. Hawkins and the RCA Manufacturing Company for 'their outstanding contribution to the advancement of the use of sound in motion pictures'. The second Oscar was for Leopold Stokowski and his collaborators for 'their unique achievement in the creation of a new form of visualized music . . . [and for] widening the scope of the motion picture as entertainment and as an art form'. *Fantasia* also made the list of the Top Ten Pictures of 1940 by the National Board of Review and in 1990 was listed for preservation in the United States National Film Registry by the Library of Congress as being 'culturally, historically, or aesthetically significant'. Once more with the benefit of time and changing tastes, Walt Disney beat his critics and had the last laugh.

Bambi, based on the novel *Bambi, A Life in the Woods* by Austrian writer Felix Salten, had been on Walt's mind for a while, but he had failed to progress it. He feared his artists were not yet capable of the necessarily realistic animal animation that would be required to adequately tell the story of the deer fawn Bambi's coming of age in the wild after the death of his mother. The film rights had been with MGM since 1933 for a planned live-action version, but Walt Disney acquired them in 1937 for an animated film. Originally intended to be the studio's first fully animated feature film, the project was repeatedly stalled by Walt as he waited for his animators to gain further experience in representing animals realistically. It was also necessary to lighten the material, as the original novel had been aimed at adults rather than children. *Bambi* was finally put into full production in 1939, overlapping with the ongoing work on *Pinocchio* and *Fantasia*.

The study of animal movements – under painter Rico Lebrun – had become an important part of the Disney Art School experience, and the animators tasked with working on *Bambi* went on trips to the local Los Angeles Zoo to watch and sketch animals in motion, as well as to source live-action footage that could be studied later. A small mini-zoo was established within the studio grounds, including rabbits, ducks, owls and skunks that the animators could spend time studying. Maurice Day shot footage in the Maine woods, allowing artists to study not only the animals but the environment in which they lived, including the changing light quality at different times of day. His material would be heavily used in the film's backgrounds. A pair of real fawns, as well as rabbits, mice and skunks were filmed in their natural habitats, providing a jumping-off point for the Disney animation teams headed by Disney's younger animators Milt Kahl, Eric Larson, Frank Thomas and Ollie Johnston.

Despite this attention to realism, changes still had to be made to make a deer the central character of an animated movie. A realistically proportioned and recreated deer's head, with widely separated eyes, would not have worked as an animated character with personality. Although based upon the real animals, the animators found they had to make the characters more 'cartoony' while still sticking close to the 'realistic' mantra that had come from Walt. Marc Davis redesigned Bambi to give him more of a human aspect. It was important that Bambi had an attractive personality, a feat that proved easier to achieve with the movie's sidekick characters.

At the same time as the animation approach was being developed, the writers were struggling with the story. Larry Morey decided the way in was to give Bambi a pair of companions, Thumper the rabbit (narrowed down from the original idea to feature six rabbits, in a call back to the seven dwarfs) and Flower the skunk. These two would provide the humour that was otherwise lacking in a tale that in the original book often invoked the harshness of nature, red in tooth and claw. As it was, generation after generation would be traumatized by the death of Bambi's mother, shot by a hunter (an event that happens off screen, although many viewers would claim to remember seeing it as children). The hope was that younger viewers would connect with the younger, clumsy, questioning Bambi and be prepared to follow the journey of the character through to adulthood. The film would stand or fall on the quality of the animation, as the story lacked the opportunities for slapstick or gags that Disney usually employed: there were no dwarfs in this forest. It would be July 1940 before a storyline was even agreed upon.

What the film did have were several stunning dramatic sequences that allowed the Disney animators to push themselves, including the forest fire that causes the animals of the

woods to flee (depicted in rather abstract, but effective, silhou-
ette), and the battle of the stags, a stylized scene that pitted
two of the forest's alpha-male animals against each other in
mortal combat. Problems would come about with the patterns
on Bambi's skin: the need to replicate the spotting from drawing to drawing slowed down production immensely – it was to
be a problem the studio would face again in the 1960s with *One
Hundred and One Dalmatians*.

Both *Pinocchio* and *Fantasia* had been major disappointments
to Walt Disney personally, despite their undoubted technical
and artistic achievements, and their immediate failure at the
box office was causing problems for his company more widely.
Since the advent of war in Europe the Disney company's foreign earnings – which, as mentioned, accounted for up to 45
per cent of their overall income in any given year – had been
severely curtailed. Spending on *Pinocchio* and *Fantasia* had
hugely exceeded their estimated budgets, and the films under-
performed at the North American box office, while *Bambi* had
spent years stuck in development.

The studio now employed almost 1,000 people (meaning a
hefty payroll had to be met every month) at its new Burbank
headquarters, which, at four times the size of the old studio
on Hyperion, had seen the cost of building strain company
finances. The huge profits made through *Snow White and the
Seven Dwarfs* were long gone, and loans and other bank support meant the Disney company was now once again in debt,
to the tune of $4.5 million. Roy Disney's solution was a reluc-
tant 1940 public stock issue, which quickly raised $3.5 million
while leaving the Disney brothers in control of their company.
The money enabled the completion of *Fantasia*, but by the
end of 1940, the 1939 surplus of $1.25 million had once again
become a deficit of $120,000.

Drastic action was required, beginning with cuts in personnel to reduce the cost of wages. Production would be scaled
down by 20 per cent, reducing the number of shorts made and

bringing the Silly Symphonies to an end. While work continued in production on *Bambi* and in development on two new pictures – *Peter Pan* and *The Wind in the Willows* – Walt recognized he had to get new product into cinemas quickly in order to keep the company financially sound. He also had something to prove to Hollywood – after the protracted production processes of his recent movies, he had to show he could produce a film on time and on budget. It was all right taking years to make a movie if it made *Snow White*-level profits, not so much if it failed at the box office in the way *Pinocchio* and *Fantasia* had. The result was two new, rapidly made movies, one mostly live action (a first for Disney) – *The Reluctant Dragon* – and the other animated – *Dumbo*.

The Reluctant Dragon (1941) was something of a cheat. Budgeted at $600,000, the live-action picture, a vehicle for humorist Robert Benchley, was essentially a behind-the-scenes guided tour of the Walt Disney Studios. Since *Snow White*, Walt had been inundated with questions about how his cartoons were made: *The Reluctant Dragon* was his answer, as well as hopefully being part of the answer to his studio's financial troubles. Benchley tours the studio, briefly meets Walt and attends a screening of the company's latest picture, *The Reluctant Dragon*. The opening twenty minutes of the seventy-four-minute movie were in black and white, as was a cartoon featuring *Dumbo*'s Casey Junior, with the fifty or so minutes of live action and animation in Technicolor. The three colour cartoons were *Baby Weems* (another cheat, as it was simply still storyboards), *How to Ride a Horse* (featuring Goofy and later released on its own in 1950), and the twenty-minute *The Reluctant Dragon*, based on a tale by Kenneth Grahame. Central to the film were its teases of the forthcoming Disney movies, *Bambi* and *Dumbo*.

Released in 1941, the film failed in its stated aim of making money, meeting a mixed critical reception and only grossing $400,000 so posting a loss of $200,000 in production costs. *The Reluctant Dragon* is perhaps of more interest in retrospect for the glimpse behind the curtain it offers. While actors were engaged in the main parts, several Disney animators appear in the movie, including Ward Kimball, Fred Moore and Wolfgang Reitherman, as well as Walt's original animation partner Ub Iwerks, who had recently returned to Disney to work on developing new cameras. Iwerks's own studio had collapsed, and he'd spent time working for Warner Bros. and Columbia. Ben Sharpsteen had originally brought Iwerks back to Disney as an animation checker, but following a rapprochement over lunch Walt offered Iwerks the more suitable role of developing new techniques for Disney.

Dumbo, a short animated feature, fared rather better than *The Reluctant Dragon*. It was originally planned as a thirty-minute film, based on a recently published children's story – written by Helen Aberson and illustrated by Harold Pearl – about a big-eared baby elephant who discovers he can fly. Walt bumped *Dumbo* up to 'feature' length (barely, at just sixty-four minutes, a complaint aired by distributors RKO who wanted another ten minutes) in the hope that it would make more at the box office. The straightforward story was ideal for a project that could be made rapidly, in a simpler animated form. Supervising director Ben Sharpsteen endeavoured to work quickly, so the backgrounds and characters were less detailed than those in the first three Disney animated features.

Bill Tytla animated the baby elephant Dumbo, the star of the film, and made him a cuter 'cartoony' figure than the usual Disney characters, resulting in a more 'picture book' look to the film. *Dumbo* took just a year to make and was completed for just under $1 million. The film would become an enduring family favourite and featured a classic sequence in the 'Pink Elephants on Parade' section, when both Dumbo and Timothy Q. Mouse accidentally drink alcohol-spiked water and are assailed by a series of comic hallucinations. Cliff Edwards voiced the leader of the crows, and the film produced a hit song in 'When I See an Elephant Fly'.

Released on 23 October 1941, Dumbo went on to become

one of the most successful Disney animated films of the 1940s at the box office. It grossed $1.6 million in the US and Canada, immediately making a profit and adding to its take with each subsequent re-release over future decades. *Variety* called the film 'a pleasant little story [with] plenty of pathos mixed with the large doses of humour, a number of appealing new animal characters, lots of good music, and the usual Disney skilfulness in technique'. *Dumbo* won an Oscar for Best Original Music Score, and was awarded Best Animation Design at the 1947 Cannes Film Festival when the film was seen for the first time in post-war Europe.

While *Dumbo* was in production, unrest was growing at the Disney studio. Ever since the move to the Burbank location and the necessary reorganization of the company, the studio had lost much of its collegiate nature from the early days. There was increased stratification of staff and a more formal atmosphere. An influx of new staff and the financial growing pains of the company all added to the strained atmosphere in and around the new Burbank studio. There was a much more factory-production-line feel to Disney's animation now, exacerbated by the studio's recent financial failures. Where *The Reluctant Dragon* depicted a happy, busy animation team hard at work, the reality during 1941 was very different. Animators felt isolated from each other in their production 'silos' and the creative energy that had driven their work on *Snow White* had dissipated. The studio's figurehead, Walt Disney himself, seemed to be ever more distant from the staff doing the actual work of animating his features.

Disney had always paid higher than average wages, aiming to attract the best artists to the studio. There were other studio benefits, including paid holidays, sick pay and company loans at favourable interest rates. However, the atmosphere at the studio had turned sour following the first suggestions of cost-saving staff layoffs, with experienced animators fearing they were to be replaced by cheaper new recruits, including the large number of women who had come into the workforce. An unnecessarily complicated bonus system had also served to alienate staff from management and each other, with the belief that a favoured few were being privileged over the rest spreading rapidly. At the time of the share issue, around 20 per cent of the company's shares had been given to the workforce. As the share price was slipping, many of the discontented chose to quickly cash in their shares, much to Walt's disgust and concern. Alarmed by the share-price fall, Walt decided to personally buy back the shares of employees who wanted to sell.

Following the Depression, the rise of labour unions in Hollywood – such as the Screen Actors Guild (founded in 1933) – was beginning to have an effect on the way the studios did business. The Fleischer studio had suffered an animators' strike in 1937, leading to the formation of the Screen Cartoonists Guild in 1938. Left-wing leader of the Guild, Herbert Sorrell, set about unionizing the other animation studios, including Walter Lantz Productions, Terrytoons and Warner Bros.'s Looney Tunes/Merrie Melodies staff, whose animators had gone on strike following an attempted lockout by management. Next on Sorrell's hit list was the Disney studio.

One of the first to sign up was Disney animator Art Babbitt, who rapidly became the leader of the union branch at the studio. Babbitt had been with the studio since 1932, animating the Witch in *Snow White*, and sequences in *Fantasia* and *Dumbo*. He also married the real-life model for *Snow White*, Marge Belcher, a development that had served to annoy the prudish and proprietorial Walt Disney. Walt saw Babbitt's union activities as rallying discontented staff against management, rather than as a cooperative effort to protect workers' rights and salaries. Sorrell approached Disney in the hopes of getting the studio to sign up to an agreement with the Screen Cartoonists Guild to protect the animators' salaries. Walt refused, preferring instead to put the matter to a staff vote to be organized by the National Labor Relations Board. Sorrell was wary, having lost a recent ballot in similar circumstances by a single vote, and threatened strike action, claiming he had already signed up the majority of the Disney animators.

Aiming to bring the matter to an end, Walt addressed the Disney employees in February 1941 at a mass meeting. He presented a scripted address, stretching to twenty-six typed pages, that outlined the history of the studio, explained the risks and hardships endured by the Disney brothers and early employees in making theatrical animation a success, and the company's struggles with critics and bankers in the effort to make the world's first animated feature film with *Snow White*. Describing animation as 'one of the greatest mediums of fantasy and entertainment yet developed', Walt went on to address what he saw as the employees' grievances, including matters of efficiency and organization that had been introduced since the studio's relocation to Burbank. He defended the recruitment and promotion of women in animation due to their 'right to expect the same chances for advancement as men'. He described what he saw as the bright future for animation and the studio, if only they could all weather the current storms and bring the spiralling costs of the studio's animated features under control.

Walt's pleas did little to curb the unrest. Things came to a head when Goofy animator Art Babbitt was finally fired, having been described as a 'troublemaker' and 'Bolshevik' by Walt. Sorrell saw his chance, and claiming that Babbitt had been sacked because of his legitimate union activities, he called an animators' strike at the Disney studio. The strike began the following day, 29 May 1941, with almost 300 employees walking out, bringing work on *Dumbo* to a near halt (the finished film would feature caricatures of some of the strike leaders as clowns who attempt to 'hit the big boss for a raise').

Those actively participating had a variety of motives. Some were acting to build union power, others wanted their legitimate concerns about the way things were run at Disney to be addressed, while others felt they had a personal score to settle with Walt. Although 60 per cent of Disney's employees crossed the picket line outside the studio, others took industrial action not because they were particularly militant, but because they sympathized with their colleagues and wanted to show solidarity, including *Dumbo* animator Bill Tytla. The striking animators held placards with slogans such as 'The Reluctant Disney' and (in reference to the company's signature character, Mickey Mouse) 'Are We Mice or Men?' Given the strikers were talented artists, many of the placards were heavily illustrated with colourful artwork, including one of Pinocchio next to the slogan 'There are No Strings on Me!'

Walt hoped the strike would blow over in a matter of days, but the atmosphere on the picket line quickly soured, resulting in a near physical confrontation between him and Babbitt. Driving into the studio, Walt was harangued by Babbitt through a loudspeaker, provoking him to leave his car and attempt to remonstrate with the striking animator. Only studio guards (Walt had hired fifty private police as security during the strike) restraining their boss averted a more serious incident. Walt took to photographing the strikers, claiming not to recognize many of the people turning up daily to picket his studio. He passed the images on to the Federal Bureau of Investigation (FBI) and investigators for the House Un-American Activities Committee (established in 1938), and said they told him: 'The fellows in those photos have been at every strike Sorrell has called!' With tempers fraying on both sides, there were threats of violence, just as *The Reluctant Dragon* was released to theatres in June 1941, depicting the Disney studios as a place of industrious harmony.

While the summer of 1941 saw various discussions and negotiations, the strike continued and was expanded with Sorrell also bringing out workers at Technicolor (so reducing the supply of film to Disney) and using the press to attempt to paint a picture of the Disney studio as a 'sweatshop' that exploited its workers, with Walt as the 'J. Worthington Foulfellow' (the venal fox character in *Pinocchio*) at its apex. Walt saw the actions of the striking workers as yet another betrayal, following those by Mintz over Oswald the Lucky Rabbit, and by the now rehabilitated Iwerks when he defected to work with Pat Powers. 'The spirit that played such an important part in the building of the cartoon medium has been destroyed,' he lamented.

When the opportunity came (through Nelson Rockefeller) for Walt Disney to make a tour of Latin America as a United States goodwill ambassador (an act intended to limit Nazi influence in South America and in furtherance of America's 'good neighbour' policy), he leapt at the chance to escape from his troubled studio. Walt wasn't sure how to be a 'goodwill ambassador', but he saw the trip as a chance to gather material for new animated shorts, funded by the US government with a budget of $70,000 for the first, and $50,000 for a further four (funding the near broke Disney company welcomed).

Non-striking animators Norm Ferguson and Frank Thomas, writers Ted Sears, Bill Cottrell and Webb Smith, and a handful of other studio personnel (totalling seventeen, including a few wives) accompanied Disney on the trip. From mid-August the troupe (who called themselves 'El Grupo') toured South America, including Rio de Janeiro and Buenos Aires, attended the Brazilian premiere of *Fantasia*, and returned over two weeks later via New York City in time for the premiere of *Dumbo*. The result of the trip would be *Saludos Amigos* (1942) and *The Three Caballeros* (1944), the first in a series of pro-American wartime propaganda films.

Walt returned to the studio to discover the animators' strike had been settled in his absence after five weeks, with the help of a federal negotiator and with Sorrell claiming victory. 'The method used to settle it,' recalled Walt of the divisive strike fifteen years later, 'was simplicity itself. The negotiators gave Sorrell practically everything he wanted.' Every department at the studio was unionized, as much as anything to prevent further trouble, according to Walt. Art Babbitt was reinstated at the studio, and an agreement was made to ensure that future layoffs would be split equally between strikers and non-strikers to avoid any victimization (although the practical results were to be unsatisfactory for all). Much bad blood remained and many of the returning strikers never felt comfortable working at Disney again. Within two years, many had left (reducing studio staffing to just under 700), including Babbitt.

Although he was often painted as the villain of the piece in subsequent years, Walt saw the weeding-out process as the strikers quit the studio as positive. 'It eventually cleaned house a lot more thoroughly than I could have done,' he said. 'An elimination process took place I couldn't have forced if I wanted to.' Along the way, some of the studio's most talented people would depart, including *Dumbo* animators Bill Tytla, Walt Kelly and Virgil Partch. Ex-Disney animators would contribute to the development of animation at United Productions of America (UPA), MGM and Warner Bros.

The initial freewheeling creative spirit of the Disney studio that made the company feel like a family and that had resulted in *Snow White and the Seven Dwarfs* was replaced by an efficiency-dictated style of management, with production driven by the newly installed time clocks. One outcome of the Disney animators' strike of 1941 was to push the usually rather liberal Walt Disney to become more conservative and anticommunist, tendencies that would rise further to the surface in later years.

Any good news for Disney about the ending of the animators' strike and the successful release of *Dumbo* was soon eclipsed by the Japanese attack on Pearl Harbor on 7 December 1941 – the event that brought America fully into the Second World War.

5

WALT IN WARTIME

Tomorrow will be better for as long as America keeps alive the ideals of freedom and a better life. All men will want to be free and share our way of life. I thank God and America for the right to live and raise my family under the flag of tolerance, democracy and freedom.

Walt Disney, 'Our American Culture', radio address broadcast during an intermission of the Metropolitan Opera, 1 March 1941

It had been long anticipated, but America's entry into the Second World War at the end of 1941 still shocked many. The effect on the Walt Disney Studios was immediate, with the US Army commandeering one of the studio sound stages for vehicle repair on the very day of the assault on Pearl Harbor – at least according to Disney legend (*Variety* reported that the troops moved in a week after the attack on the US).

The Army planned to use part of the Disney studio complex as a staging post for 500 soldiers to protect the nearby Lockheed aircraft plant, seen as a potential target of enemy bombing raids. Vehicles, spare parts and three million rounds of ammuition were stored at the studio, taking up part of the employees' parking area. The Army would remain on the site for the next eight months, until fears of a Japanese attack on the US mainland had receded. Studio employees – even Walt and Roy – were fingerprinted and issued with US government identity cards to facilitate their access to the studio.

Some of their work now included fulfilling a US government commission for a series of short training films to be supplied to the Navy Bureau of Aeronautics. Others were commissioned by the Department of Agriculture, the Treasury Department and the Army Air Force. Work on several slowly developing animation projects – including *Alice in Wonderland*, *Peter Pan* and *The Wind in the Willows* – was put on hiatus for the duration of the conflict. The information, training and educational films were a new challenge for Walt Disney, and he leapt upon it, even though the studio would have fewer personnel (due to the draft) and be charged with producing many more cartoons, ever more rapidly.

To begin with, the Disney studio was involved in the production of shorts for the National Film Board of Canada (Canada was already involved in the war effort as a 'dominion' of the British Empire), using the famous Disney characters to promote the sale of Canadian war bonds. Four films resulted, including *The Thrifty Pig* (1941), which employed the characters from *The Three Little Pigs* but made the Big Bad Wolf a caricatured Nazi, and *7 Wise Dwarfs* (1941), featuring the dwarfs from *Snow White* and repurposing some of that film's animation, with new material showing the dwarfs visiting the post office to purchase war bonds. The 'Heigh-Ho' song was rewritten to include patriotic lyrics. Two other shorts for Canada – *All Together* (1941) and *Donald's Decision* (1941) – made the same points.

Walt Disney was also dealing with the aftermath of a pair of family tragedies during this period. Back in 1938, Walt and Roy had brought their parents Flora and Elias from Portland to Los

Angeles, establishing them in a North Hollywood bungalow. They celebrated their golden wedding anniversary that year, but their happiness was to be short-lived. On 26 November 1938 a defective furnace in their new home asphyxiated Flora, leaving the brothers devastated and blaming themselves as they'd bought that house specifically for their parents. Walt would avoid talking about his mother's death for the rest of his days. His father, Elias, did odd carpentry jobs around the Disney studio before the war, but he died three years later at the age of eighty-two in 1941, while Walt was off on his South American tour.

Within a year of American involvement in the war, the production of war propaganda and training films would be the main focus of the Walt Disney Studios, with government contracts worth $2.6 million. A punishing schedule of production was instigated, as the material was needed rapidly, and the quality of the usual Disney animation was diluted using stills, cut-outs, models and other tricks to get the films done on schedule. All the same, Walt used the opportunity to develop some new animation techniques and to experiment.

As well as the rather dry training films, Disney continued in production on its usual shorts, with most given over to wartime topics. Mickey Mouse, whose outgoing geniality and optimism seemed out of step with the times, was largely side-lined in favour of Donald Duck and others. Goofy featured in films such as *Victory Vehicles* (1943), in which he demonstrated the options available for wartime travel; Pluto popped up in *The Army Mascot* (1942), *Private Pluto* (1943) and *Dog Watch* (1945); while Donald made the most wartime appearances, including *Donald Gets Drafted* (1942, in which he willingly signs up to fight rather than 'Get Drafted'), *The Vanishing Private* (1942, in which he experiments with invisible paint), *Fall Out-Fall In* (1943) and *Commando Duck* (1944, which sees Donald sent on an assignment behind enemy lines to take out a Japanese airfield).

Although propaganda for the home-front audience, these films still allowed for the usual Disney humour to prevail in dark times. These early war shorts continued the boisterous fun familiar from the pre-war films, making them more palatable to audiences uncertain about where involvement in the war might take America. One of the earliest produced was the Donald Duck short *The New Spirit* (released in January 1942) for the US Treasury, which depicted Donald as a tax avoider persuaded to mend his ways when he is shown what his taxes are spent on and how important the money is to the war effort. The rapid production process was fraught, and then Walt had trouble getting the government to pay for the finished film they had commissioned, with Congress even accusing Disney of being an 'unpatriotic war profiteer'. The House of Representatives debated the war appropriations bill that February, with Congressman John Taber of New York declaring that he supported 'Billions for defence . . . but not one buck for Donald Duck!' Although the short had cost $83,000 to produce, the government eventually paid only $43,000 towards it.

Despite this setback, Walt was fully committed to producing films in support of the war effort, and he followed *The New Spirit* with a sequel, *The Spirit of '43*, the following year. By mid-1942, around 93 per cent of all studio production was related to the war effort. Other war work included *Food Will Win the War* (1942, for the Department of Agriculture) and the Minnie Mouse-starring *Out of the Frying Pan and into the Firing Line* (1942, which advocated that housewives should save cooking oils). More entertaining were *Mickey's Birthday Party* (1942, a colour remake of 1931's *The Birthday Party*), *Orphan's Benefit* (1941, another colour remake of a 1934 short), *Symphony Hour* (1942, with Mickey as an orchestral conductor) and the Oscar-winning *Lend a Paw* (1941, in which Pluto adopts a rescued kitten in a colour remake of 1933's *Mickey's Pal Pluto*).

The series of shorts featuring Goofy solo was now under the charge of Jack Kinney and had been modelled after Robert

Benchley's well-known 'How To' film series. Goofy would feature as an incompetent exponent of whatever sport or pastime he engaged in, including *The Art of Skiing* (1941), *The Art of Self-Defense* (1941), *How to Play Baseball* (1942, in which every character was Goofy), *How to Swim* (1942), *How to Fish* (1942) and *How to Play Golf* (1944). Pinto Colvig, the animator who'd been voicing Goofy previously, had a personality conflict with Walt and had left the studio (he'd return in 1944 and resume voicing Goofy), so the later wartime 'How To' films featured little dialogue and a narrator. Some of Colvig's old recordings were reused, although occasionally an actor was brought in to imitate his sound.

Donald Duck prospered under the direction of Jack King, with his anti-establishment blustering suiting an agitated wartime audience. He continued with his Army antics in the likes of *Sky Trooper* (1942, in which Donald's flying ambitions see him crashing into his own HQ) and *The Old Army Game* (1943, in which Donald matches wits with Peg-Leg Pete). Donald's image was to be found painted (sometimes crudely) on to the nose cone of many an American plane flying into action throughout the war, and he was a prominent wartime mascot. In fact, one part of Disney's war work consisted of the creation of over 1,200 combat insignia for US military and naval units by studio artists featuring a host of Disney characters, without charging a fee. Donald Duck's non-military adventures continued in the likes of *Chef Donald* (1941, in which he cooks along with a radio show), *Donald's Gold Mine* (1942, in which an uncooperative donkey thwarts his attempts to get rich quick) and *Donald's Crime* (1945, an effective, Oscar-nominated film noir parody).

Finally, after four and a half years in production, the feature animation *Bambi* was released on 13 August 1942. Whether it was due to the wartime atmosphere, or simply a sign that critics were tiring of Disney's approach to animation, *Bambi* was the first Disney film to be met with largely negative reviews upon first release. The loss of the fantasy elements that had made *Snow White* and *Pinocchio* so attractive hurt *Bambi* in cinemas, especially when playing to adult audiences in the evening. Hunters claimed the movie was 'an insult' to American sportsmen, and the *New York Times* (normally a Disney booster) complained that 'in the search for perfection, Mr Disney has come perilously close to tossing away his whole world of cartoon fantasy'. The *New York Post* had queried whether young audiences would appreciate such a 'serious and elemental' movie. The realism of the movie, for which Walt had spent so many years striving, compared badly with the fantasy of *Snow White* and *Pinocchio*, while it lacked much of the humour so evident in the delightful *Dumbo*.

Costing over $1.7 million to make, Bambi took around $3 million in 1942, making a small profit for the studio. The film was to make the bulk of its $102 million total earnings upon regular theatrical re-releases, with a 1947 post-war re-release adding $2.2 million; a 1957 re-release bringing in $6 million; another $9 million added in 1966; a further $20 million in 1975; and finally $23 million and $39 million being added in 1982 and 1988. In 2008 *Bambi* was listed third in the American Film Institute's top ten animated movies (behind *Snow White* at no. 1 and *Pinocchio* at no. 2), although the film's 'primal shock' of the death of Bambi's mother also saw the film listed in *Time* magazine's Top 25 Horror Movies of All Time!

The lack of European markets and the tendency of cinemas to play the movie as a matinee and not as a main evening screening hit *Bambi*'s box-office potential. Audiences seemingly preferred the escapist fare of *The Road to Morocco*, *Talk of the Town* and *Holiday Inn* to Walt's wildlife cartoon. As with the previous Disney animated features, though, the film would go on to later be regarded as a classic.

The South American film *Saludos Amigos* was released in the US in February 1943, following an earlier August 1942 South American engagement. A forty-three-minute feature made up of four shorts (including *El Gaucho Goofy*) linked with Walt's personal 16 mm footage of the trip, the film took $1.3 million at the US box office.

As well as their own shorts, Disney was employed in producing animated inserts for Frank Capra's 'Why We Fight' propaganda series, starting in 1942 with *Prelude to War* (which won an Oscar for Best Documentary feature). Capra had been a persuasive voice when Columbia's Harry Cohn committed to distributing Disney's early Mickey Mouse cartoons. Around 25 per cent of each forty- to seventy-five-minute 'Why We Fight' film (mainly consisting of newsreel and stock footage) was made up of black-and-white animated maps and charts produced by the Disney studio. While utilitarian in approach, there was room for the occasional artistic flourish on behalf of the Disney animators. Such instances included an image of Nazi insects devouring the foundations of a castle that represented France, and a gauntlet-clad Nazi fist stamping the island of Crete with a Nazi swastika seal. The studio contributed animated work to two other Frank Capra projects late in the war: *Know Your Enemy: Japan* (1945) and *Here is Germany* (1945).

Chicken Little (1943) was among a number of Disney's wartime films for the home front that included powerful messages for American audiences and that saw Disney animation take a darker turn as the war wore on. Taking the well-known 'The Sky is Falling' fable of Chicken Little, the short was a warning about the consequences of believing misinformation in relation to the war effort. Foxy Loxy is seen to manipulate the chickens (reading passages from Hitler's *Mein Kampf*, although it is labelled on screen as a psychology text) so he can eat them, with their bones laid out as though in a war grave.

In a similar way, *Reason and Emotion* (1943) depicted two cartoon characters piloting a human brain. These two – representing Reason and Emotion – are in conflict and fight for the right to control their human host. In the end, however, it is shown that they must cooperate, as they both have strengths, if they are to pilot their charge responsibly. *Education for Death*

(1943) was more explicit and extreme in its message. In just ten minutes the short follows the growth of a young boy in Nazi Germany, from birth to youth, with him pledged (by his parents) in service to Hitler. Hans becomes ill and is threatened with death by a Nazi officer, as he is of no use to the Fatherland. He recovers, attends a Hitler Youth school and is declared a dunce for his sympathy for a 'weak' rabbit attacked by a 'strong' fox. A book-burning crusade follows, in which stark imagery has the Bible transform into *Mein Kampf* and a crucifix into a Nazi sword. Hans is sent off to war, just one of many stormtroopers sent into a hopeless battle having been 'educated for death'. It's one of Disney's darkest and strongest slices of anti-Nazi propaganda.

Walt Disney was more personally involved in the 1943 animated feature *Victory Through Air Power*, a non-government-inspired project based upon an influential non-fiction 1942 book by Alexander P. de Seversky. With US military leaders downplaying air power in favour of naval offensives, Russian-born de Seversky (himself part of the US Air Corps Reserve) argued for the importance of strategic air power to an Allied victory over the Axis powers. Interested in producing an aviation film (following his experiences flying across South America), Walt latched on to de Seversky's bestselling book, purchased the film rights and signed up the author as a consultant and on-screen presenter of his arguments. Financed by the studio, not the government, the resulting sixty-five-minute movie was a daunting challenge. Walt feared that it might upset his military employers, who were against air power, and he worried that it might not find an audience among an increasingly war-weary, and equally war-film-weary, American population.

Despite these concerns, he was personally committed to the film. He had the movie open with an amusing, comic history of aviation (later released separately as a short), with supervising director Dave Hand (responsible for *Snow White*) coordinating the work of various animators, including Ward Kimball and John Lounsbery. H. C. Potter (director of the zany

Hellzapoppin', 1941) was recruited to handle the live action featuring de Seversky. The remainder made the hard sell for air power as part of America's military arsenal, although one inventive animated sequence saw the symbolic American eagle battle an equally symbolic Japanese octopus, whose tentacled grasp was threatening to encompass the entire world.

Released in July 1943, *Victory Through Air Power* had a seismic impact. Walt sent a print of the film direct to US President Franklin D. Roosevelt. According to animation historian Leonard Maltin, 'It changed FDR's way of thinking – he agreed that de Seversky was right. It was only after Roosevelt saw *Victory Through Air Power* that [America] made the commitment to long-range bombing.' The film grossed $11,000 more than its overall cost of $788,000, so could be counted a success for the bottom line, as far as Roy Disney was concerned. This single film might have been Walt Disney's most effective contribution to the Allied war effort.

Much more amusing was the Oscar-winning *Der Fuehrer's Face* (1943), starring Donald Duck. Donald dreams he's a worker in a 'Nutziland' ammunition factory, where – in the style of Chaplin's *Modern Times* (1936) – he struggles to keep up with the impossible production demands of der Fuehrer, which culminates with a thrown tomato connecting with Hitler's face. The highlight is a surreal sequence that sees the shells Donald is building turn on him. The film, as with almost all of the others produced during the war, contained the usual racist caricatures of Germans and Japanese. However, *Der Fuehrer's Face* achieved its aim in undermining the figures of Hitler, Mussolini and Hirohito by making them figures of fun, rather than fear, and the theme song, recorded by musical humorist Spike Jones, was a wartime hit. The lampoon was quickly recognized as one of the more potent forms of wartime propaganda. The film won the Academy Award for Best Animated Short Film, the only Donald Duck short ever to win (although eight others were nominated). In 1994, *Der Fuehrer's Face* was placed at no. 22 in the 50 Greatest Cartoons of All

Time poll voted on by animation professionals. After the war, the film was kept from re-release due to its depiction of Donald Duck as a Nazi (albeit in a nightmare scenario), and it didn't get a consumer release until Walt Disney Treasures's third wave of DVDs in 2004.

Inspired by *Victory Through Air Power* and still exploring his interest in aviation in a wartime context, Walt Disney found himself deep in development on a project that would never come to fruition. It began simply enough, with his desire to make a film from a Roald Dahl story called 'Gremlin Lore', about malevolent fairy creatures who caused wartime air crashes by tampering with engines. The unpublished story was based on stories Dahl heard while serving in the Middle East, and he wrote it while serving with the British Embassy in Washington. The story came to Walt through friends of Dahl, with negotiations with the British Air Ministry required before he could buy it. Dahl decided he would give all his income from the project to the RAF Benevolent Fund.

Keen to make another film that mixed live action and animation in the style of *The Reluctant Dragon* and *Victory Through Air Power*, Walt saw the possibilities of the mischievous Gremlin characters and felt the story had wartime audience appeal (despite the fact that the Gremlin phenomenon was an almost exclusively British folklore). However, the British Air Ministry decided they must approve all elements of the project, so restricting Walt's freedom to develop the tale. Attempting to prepare the public for the movie, the Disney company placed stories concerning Gremlins in the press and began developing designs for a series of tie-in dolls and figures. The original story was published by the Walt Disney Company under the title *The Gremlins* in 1943, with illustrations, but the supporting movie never appeared. The story told of the peaceful Gremlin folk who lived in a secluded wood that was demolished to build an aircraft factory, resulting in the Gremlins swearing to bring down 'those big tin birds wherever they go'.

WALT IN WARTIME 103

The notion of the Gremlins had caught on in the US thanks to Disney's efforts, and other movie studios were quicker to jump on the bandwagon Disney had started rolling, with MGM and Universal planning Gremlin-themed films. Roy Disney was able to talk them out of it, with only Warner Bros. persevering with their planned project. By August 1943 Walt had downgraded 'The Gremlins' to the status of a short, and by October that year he'd abandoned the notion entirely, fearing that the popularity of Gremlins would be short-lived and interest would have waned by the time Disney had a film out in theatres. Advance work on the project had run up a bill of $30,000 at a time when the company could ill afford to be extravagant in funding projects with no return. The work the studio undertook for the government as part of the war effort had resulted in a loss of $13,000 for the first year of activity.

Many of Disney's best animators had either been drafted or volunteered for war service, so depleting the studio's personnel. Frank Thomas and Wolfgang Reitherman were just two among the many who volunteered for the Army. Walt attempted to argue that the studio was undertaking important war work in order to stave off the loss of more people, but his arguments were rejected and many of the supposedly 'unskilled' inkers and painters were drafted. As a way of bringing in some much-needed funds without requiring new work (as there weren't the people), Walt hit on the idea of re-releasing *Snow White and the Seven Dwarfs* to cinemas during 1944. He hoped the fantasy film would help distract audiences from the privations of war, while at the same time exposing a new generation to the wonders of Disney animation. It had been seven years since the film was first out, and Walt reckoned there was a new generation of potential filmgoers growing up every seven years – it would lead to a seven-year cycle of frequent re-releases for the best Disney product.

The second of the films sourced from Walt's South American sojourn was released in February 1945 (following a debut in Mexico the previous Christmas) as *The Three Caballeros*. A shortage of Technicolor film, due to the war, had added to delays in completing the project earlier. The film focused on Brazil and Mexico, and incorporated specially shot performance footage of Aurora Miranda (sister of Carmen) and other singers and dancers. This film overall had a more polished appearance then the earlier *Saludos Amigos*, with the self-contained segments (comprising animation and live action) linked together by Donald Duck opening a series of birthday gifts from Latin American friends.

The seven segments that make up *The Three Caballeros* comprised *The Cold-Blooded Penguin*, *The Flying Gauchito*, *Baía*, *Las Posadas*, a travelogue of Mexico and a song, 'You Belong to My Heart', concluding with Donald's *Surreal Reverie*, in which the duck finds himself in a sequence not unlike *Dumbo*'s 'Pink Elephants on Parade'. The mix of various animation styles and different approaches to each of the shorts made for a rather jumbled feature, despite the efforts to tie it all together with Donald's antics. The technique of combining live action and animated characters pioneered here would be developed further in later films, especially *Mary Poppins* (1964). Poor reviews didn't seem to damage *The Three Caballeros* at the box office, with the film ultimately taking $3.4 million, well above its production costs, so bringing a welcome influx of cash to the Disney company. As well as the production of the propaganda shorts produced as entertainment and the hundreds of dry instructional films intended for the military, Disney produced health education films for the Coordinator of Inter-American Affairs – including *The Winged Scourge* (1945), which featured the seven dwarfs demonstrating protections against malaria-carrying mosquitoes, and the 1944 animated short *The Amazon Awakens*. As a result, the Disney studio had been kept busy, if not particularly profitable, during the war years. The war work was necessary economically for the studio (as well as being patriotic), but it was not what Walt wanted to do. There were other compensations, as Walt himself noted: 'We had acquired a wonderful education and a determination to diversify our entertainment product.'

Walt's collaborator Frank Capra was rewarded for his 'Why We Fight' series with the Distinguished Service Medal. There were no medals for Walt Disney or any of his animators. Instead, Walt had the satisfaction of having stayed in business, and through supporting the American war effort, the company had reduced the $1 million deficit it was carrying at the outbreak of war to just $300,000 by the war's end in 1945. However, *Bambi*, *Victory Through Air Power* and *Saludos Amigos* had all lost substantial money for the studio. The military films had brought in few funds, and the theatrically released wartime shorts featuring Donald, Goofy and Pluto had all suffered falling grosses as the American populace lost its movie-going habit. A short-lived post-war detour into educational and industrial films proved unfulfilling, and Walt yearned to return to full-length fairy-tale animated features.

Since the Disney animators' strike of 1941, Walt had joined the millions of Americans in business who were virulently anti-communist. He saw – and was encouraged to see by others – the machinations of communists who had supposedly infiltrated Hollywood behind the strike, and had personified them in the form of Disney animator and union organizer Art Babbitt.

Walt hadn't particularly reacted against his father's socialist beliefs, but neither had he really formulated a particular political outlook for himself prior to the strike. He loved small-town traditional values and the life reflected in early-twentieth-century Marceline, so was likely to take against anything that threatened such an idyllic (as he saw it) way of life, even though he'd long ago left that life behind. For Walt, the communist threat was against his business interests, not his personal interests, and on that basis he was going to fight back.

Walt became a vice-president of the conservative Motion Picture Alliance for the Preservation of American Ideals (MPA), established in early 1944 to combat perceived infiltration of

Hollywood by communist elements, especially through the unions like the Screen Actors Guild and the Screen Writers Guild (the MPA was eventually disbanded in 1975). Its aim was to oppose 'the effort of Communists, Fascists, and other totalitarian-minded groups to pervert this powerful medium [film] into an instrument for the dissemination of un-American ideas and beliefs'. Despite the declared catch-all targets, almost everything the MPA did was exclusively anti-communist. Others who signed up included actors Clark Gable, Ronald Reagan, Gary Cooper, John Wayne and Irene Dunne, and directors Victor Fleming, Cecil B. DeMille and Norman Taurog.

Walt's involvement was used to justify a call to Congress to investigate, as tensions between the left and the right in Hollywood rose through the 1940s. Although claiming non-partisanship, there was no doubt that Walt Disney was a right-winger (he donated to the Republican Party and allowed a rally for Republican Presidential nominee Thomas Dewey to be held on studio grounds). His affiliations became crystal clear when he gave testimony to Congress's House Un-American Activities Committee (HUAC) as a so-called 'friendly' witness to communist influence in the movie world. On 24 October 1947 – twenty years on from his creation of Mickey Mouse – Walt Disney suggested there were no longer any communists within the Disney studio and that his staff were now '100 per cent American'. He discussed his work producing wartime propaganda, and gave his version of events behind the 1941 animators' strike, claiming that union organizer Herbert Sorrell had threatened to smear Disney's reputation unless he gave in to his demands to unionize. Walt described the Communist Party as 'an un-American thing', but he stopped short of agreeing that it should be banned.

Oddly, Walt didn't name Art Babbitt, whom he had blamed at the time, but instead brought up the name of animator David Hilberman who had been involved, but was hardly a leader or instigator. 'He had no religion,' said Walt of Hilberman, 'and he had spent considerable time at the Moscow Arts Theatre'. Others at the studio who were left-leaning in their politics, such as Ward Kimball and Maurice Rapf (named at the HUAC hearings as a communist), were happily tolerated by Walt as long as they didn't make trouble. Walt had been one of the first to 'name names' before HUAC in 1947 (his testimony fell on the second day), but he was far from the last. Ten of the 'unfriendly' witnesses, largely screenwriters, were jailed for contempt of Congress and a blacklist operated in Hollywood denying work to around 300 individuals (including many animators) and removing credits from others until the mid-1960s.

Walt Disney's anti-communist activities extended into the 1950s, when he was registered as a 'Special Agent in Charge [SAC] contact' for J. Edgar Hoover's FBI. While some biographers have taken this to mean that Walt was an active FBI agent, there is little evidence for this assertion. It is true that – according to Walt's FBI file – he contacted the Bureau in 1954 offering 'complete access to the facilities of Disneyland for use in connection with official matters and for recreational purposes', although this may have just been another attempt by Walt to push his new park. Being an SAC contact was a largely honorary position, simply indicating to the local SAC that Walt Disney was likely to be a 'friendly' contact in their area. There's no evidence Walt was ever used in this capacity, or that he ever volunteered any information to the FBI about his employees or anyone else. Hoover and Disney exchanged letters of mutual admiration, but that didn't mean Walt was above the FBI's suspicion – his attendance at two 'leftist gatherings' in the 1940s was noted in his file. For his part, while Walt produced a special 'Inside the FBI' segment for *The Mickey Mouse Club* offering career suggestions, he was not afraid to satirize the organization, as in *Moon Pilot* (1962) and *That Darn Cat!* (1965).

By September 1945 the Second World War had come to an end, with the signing of the armistice by the defeated Japanese whose initial attack on Pearl Harbor had brought the US into the conflict. Disney had played one last part in the war: the phrase 'Mickey Mouse' was used by soldiers as an identifying codeword during the planning of the Normandy invasion of June 1944. Walt was optimistic, as he usually was, about the future, about the prospects for his company and about the as yet unexplored possibilities of animation in the new world of peace that was awaiting the country. However, just as there were challenges nationwide in the turbulent post-war period, there would be some painful adjustments for the Disney company in the aftermath of the conflict. It wouldn't be until the mid-1950s that Walt Disney Studios once again became the home of the animated fairy-tale film.

PART TWO: THE DISNEY GENIUS

6

POST-WAR WOES

*Too many people grow up. They forget. They don't
remember what it's like to be 12 years old. They patronize,
they treat children as inferiors. Well, I won't do that. I'll
temper a story, yes. But I won't play down, and I won't
patronize.*

Walt Disney, quoted in *Walt Disney World: Then,
Now, and Forever*, 2008

The post-war years were a time of struggle for the Walt Disney
organization. The challenges of recovery from the conflict
were many, including finding places within the studio for those
men returning from their time in the US Army. Walt Disney's
creative energy had been thrown off course by the war work,
resulting in a loss of focus on what precisely the Disney studio
uniquely had to offer American cinema audiences. In the
immediate post-war years, the studio failed to produce movies
that could rival its pre-war titles for either artistic achievement
or critical acclaim. Like the men coming back from combat,
the studio and its staff were out of touch with changing public

tastes, and unlike other Hollywood studios – the majority of which had prospered during the war producing escapist entertainment – the Disney studio was facing difficult financial times in returning to civilian production.

While production during the war years had focused on rather dull training films and the occasional propaganda cartoon, some work had been done in developing ideas for entertainment subjects that could serve as the basis for Disney's immediate post-war films. Among these projects (which were internally valued at around $4 million in potential, as yet unrealized, revenue) were the fairy tale *Beauty and the Beast*, some Hans Christian Andersen tales including *The Snow Queen*, *Doctor Dolittle*, Don Marquis's *Archy and Mehitabel* (about a cockroach and a cat) and even Beatrix Potter's *The Tale of Peter Rabbit*. More obvious fare included the self-explanatory sequel *Return of Snow White*, a sequel to *Fantasia* (music had been selected, including works by Ravel, Saint-Saëns and Wagner), and original creations by Disney writers, including stories about a camel, an owl and a dog detective. Whatever was made, the Disney studio needed to get new movies into the marketplace rapidly in order to generate much needed income.

One of the more unusual projects undertaken by Walt Disney after the war was *Destino*, a short film made in collaboration with renowned Spanish surrealist artist Salvador Dalí. The painter had made two films with Luis Buñuel, *Un Chien Andalou* (1929) and *L'Age d'Or* (1930), and had worked in Hollywood on the surreal dream sequence in Alfred Hitchcock's *Spellbound* (1945). Disney and Dalí had met in 1945, and in the spirit of his musical inspiration for *Fantasia*, the filmmaker asked the artist to contribute to a film that had been inspired by Walt's South American trip. He wanted to make an animated short inspired by a romantic ballad by Mexican songwriter Armando Domínguez and sung by Dora Luz, who had featured in *The Three Caballeros* (1944).

Disney invited Dalí to come up with a storyline and images for *Destino* (Spanish for 'Destiny'). The artist responded by claiming 'Dalí and Disney will produce the first motion picture of the Never Seen Before'. The collaboration was another example of Walt's continual push to challenge himself by committing to something new and previously never achieved. 'People try to keep me in well-worn grooves,' Disney complained, explaining his need to keep on 'breaking new trails'. Neither party could have known that their work would not be completed for another fifty-eight years, in 2003.

Dalí based himself at the Disney studio, making a series of sketches and paintings for *Destino*. Walt outlined the story as 'a simple story about a young girl in search of her real love', but Dalí was an artist for whom nothing was ever 'simple'. He embarked upon the project by applying much of his unique surrealist imagery to Disney animation, including the landscape of his home in Figueres in Catalonia. 'I have been given absolute freedom,' declared Dalí, '[and] that is paradise for the artist.'

'Ordinarily good story ideas don't come easily,' said Walt, 'but with Dalí, it was exactly the reverse. He constantly bubbled with new ideas.' Storyboard artist John Hench was tasked with organizing Dalí's material into a structure that could be turned into a Disney film. For eight months they worked on the film, with Dalí creating twenty-two complete paintings and 135 story sketches, but they only produced around fifteen seconds of actual animation. It soon became clear to Walt that he and Dalí were operating on different artistic wavelengths and the project was abandoned. The pair talked of working together on something else, such as a version of *Don Quixote*, but nothing came of it.

Destino remained on the shelf at Disney until 1999 when Walt's nephew Roy E. Disney (the last member of the family to work at the studio) revived the project. Dalí and Hench's work was sent to Disney's outpost in Paris, France, where animator and director Dominique Monfery completed the film. Around twenty-five animators worked to figure out Dalí and Hench's intentions (Hench himself was still around to act as a consultant – he died in 2004), using a mix of traditional and computer animation to complete the seven-minute film. It was released in 2003 and was nominated for an Oscar as Best Animated Short.

The ever-present money troubles (a feature of the Disney studio since the relative failures of the post-*Snow White* films to generate comparable profits) contributed towards the abandoning of experimental works like *Destino* and a renewed concentration on what Walt referred to as 'mashed potato and gravy' filmmaking: basic movies that would draw in audiences. Work continued on story development for long-in-gestation animation projects such as *The Wind in the Willows*, *Cinderella*, *Alice in Wonderland* and *Peter Pan*, but it would take a few more years before any of them reached a cinema screen.

Income was down dramatically for 1945; the war work had not been particularly profitable – simply keeping the studio solvent – and the focus on government contracts had thrown the creativity of the Disney staff off course. Once more, Roy Disney was forced into the position of attempting to rein in his more artistically focused brother. He pointed out that works like *Fantasia* and the films resulting from the South American trip had essentially been a series of shorts strung together to form a feature-length film. He wanted Walt to do the same with some of the unfinished or in-development shorts, cutting the studio's output of standalone shorts to just one a month, half the number produced annually before the war.

During the 1930s and into the 1940s, Disney faced some serious competition in the field of animated shorts. The Looney Tunes and Merrie Melodies series from Warner Bros. had proved themselves to be more anarchic, smarter and wittier than anything Disney had recently produced (even the acerbic Donald Duck), and much more suited to the post-war disillusionment of the late 1940s than Mickey Mouse. Their smart-alec characters – like Bugs Bunny, Daffy Duck and Porky Pig – were capturing the imagination of the young and the young-at-heart in the way Mickey Mouse had once done in 1929. Additionally, MGM were on a winning streak with their Tom and Jerry series (from 1940). Disney films had won Oscars for best cartoon every year (except once) between 1934 and 1943. Tom and Jerry (directed by animators William Hanna and Joseph Barbera) would go on to win seven animation Oscars, every year between 1943 and 1946, again in 1948, and in 1952 and 1953. It would be another decade before Disney would reclaim the annual animation Oscar with Ward Kimball's *Toot, Whistle, Plunk and Boom* in 1954.

The first of the post-war anthology music films released was *Make Mine Music* (1946), a popular music version of *Fantasia*. The seventy-six-minute feature comprised ten animated segments, including *Blue Bayou*, that used animation originally intended for a section of *Fantasia* that was to have featured Claude Debussy's *Claire de Lune*. Jazz and swing musician Benny Goodman contributed two sections, *All the Cats Join In* and *After You've Gone*. The most accomplished sequence was *Peter and the Wolf*, an animated short built around Prokofiev's 1936 composition (itself inspired by the work of Walt Disney). The musical range of *Make Mine Music* made for an uneven audience experience, with a host of clashing animation styles, and some barely adequate (such as *Johnny Fedora and Alice Blue Bonnet*). *Blue Bayou*, the Goodman numbers and the *Peter and the Wolf* section stand out from the rest as worthwhile, but overall the film is a mess. The *New York Times* called *Make Mine Music* 'a bit questionable in spots', while the *Herald Tribune* dubbed the film 'a Disney pot-boiler'. The film was symptomatic of the sense of confusion at the Disney studio, and the pressure to produce 'product' for financial reasons.

The next Disney movie would become notorious: *Song of the South* (1946). Based on the 'Uncle Remus' stories of life on the plantation by Joel Chandler Harris, the film was to be a combination of live action (quicker and easier to produce) and animated tales (making up just a third of the film) of the clever Br'er Rabbit and his enemies, Br'er Fox and Br'er Bear. The studio's best animators, among them Milt Kahl, Eric Larson, Marc Davis and John Lounsbery, worked on the film, with Wilfred Jackson as the supervising director. James Baskett starred as Uncle Remus, the African-American former slave who tells an audience of children the stories of Br'er Rabbit. In 1947, the film won an Oscar for Best Song for the catchy 'Zip-a-Dee-Doo-Dah', which Baskett sang surrounded by animated animals. Baskett himself was awarded a special Oscar (actively campaigned for by Walt) for 'his able and heart-warming characterization of Uncle Remus, friend and storyteller to the children of the world' – he died within months of receiving the accolade.

Song of the South is widely seen in retrospect as racist, especially in the figure of Uncle Remus, but even at the time critics were gunning for it. *Time* magazine said it would 'enrage all educated Negroes, and a number of damn yankees', while the National Urban League criticized the movie for its 'stereotype casting of the Negro in the servant role'. Even the tune of 'Zip-a-Dee-Doo-Dah' was problematic, based as it was on an 1830s American folk song 'Turkey in the Straw', popularized by blackface performers and used as the basis for the pre-Civil War racist song 'Zip Coon'. Uncle Remus happily serving in the home of wealthy whites caused the National Association for the Advancement of Colored People (NAACP) to decry the film's depiction of an 'idyllic master-slave relationship which is a distortion of the facts', while some New York screenings were met with picket-line protesters wielding placards that read 'We fought for Uncle Sam, not Uncle Tom!'

Regular film critics were no more easy-going when it came to *Song of the South*. The use of a mix of live action and animation irked some, with the *New York Times'* Bosley Crowther writing: 'More and more, Walt Disney's craftsmen have been loading their feature films with so-called "live action" in place of their animated whimsies of the past', and by just those proportions has the magic of these Disney films decreased.' Despite criticisms such as that, *Song of the South* out-grossed *Make Mine Music*, hitting $3.3 million at the

North American box office, a third higher than the previous movie.

Neither *Make Mine Music* nor *Song of the South* proved to be either cheap-to-make movies nor the quick successes for which Disney had been hoping. That didn't stop the company producing another three movies in the same Frankenstein stitched-together style: *Fun and Fancy Free* and *Melody Time* (both 1947), and *So Dear to My Heart* (1948), based on Sterling North's novel, *Midnight and Jeremiah*. The best of the two segments that made up *Fun and Fancy Free* was *Mickey and the Beanstalk*, originally intended as a stand-alone Mickey Mouse feature film to follow *Dumbo* – it was the final time that Walt himself would provide the voice for Mickey outside of television's *The Mickey Mouse Club* (sound-effects man Jimmy MacDonald would voice Mickey for the next thirty-eight years until 1977 when he retired). *Melody Time* was a follow-up to *Make Mine Music*, featuring songs from popular 1940s vocalists, among them the Andrews Sisters (on the segment *Little Toot*), Bobby Driscoll (*The Legend of Johnny Appleseed*) and Roy Rogers (*Pecos Bill*). Finally, *So Dear to My Heart* combined live action and animation once more (again as a cost-saving exercise) in telling the folksy, sentimental story of Jerry Kincaid (Bobby Driscoll) who struggles to raise a black wool lamb rejected by its mother in early-twentieth-century Indiana.

A signpost of a future direction for Disney product was the half-hour nature short *Seal Island* (1948), which won that year's Oscar for Best Short Documentary Subject. Walt commissioned travelogue directors Alfred and Elma Milotte to make a film about Alaska, but he was unfocused as to the specific subject matter. Eventually, the focus was narrowed to the life cycle of seals, and the resulting film paved the way for the Disney television nature films of the 1950s and 1960s (although many were exotic, their basic concentration on wildlife recalled for Walt his days on the Marceline farm).

After the war, some of the older Disney animated films were

released abroad, with *Snow White and the Seven Dwarfs* proving a success in Japan and China, and *Bambi* making money across post-war Europe, running for thirty-one weeks in Copenhagen. In the post-war years, Walt Disney found himself to be less the popular artist of Mickey Mouse and *Snow White* and more a conservative businessman looking to run a successful company.

Disney was back on track with *The Adventures of Ichabod and Mr Toad* (1949), another package movie that put together two very different-in-tone feature films already in development, Kenneth Grahame's *The Wind in the Willows* (narrated by Basil Rathbone) and Washington Irving's *The Legend of Sleepy Hollow* (narrated by Bing Crosby). The first story had been under development as an animated feature at Disney since 1938, intended as one possible follow-up to *Snow White*. The war put paid to those plans and the film was put aside until 1945, when Disney returned to the adventures of Toad, Rat and Mole. To fit the post-war Disney plan of releasing anthology films, Walt was going to team up *The Wind in the Willows* with *Mickey and the Beanstalk*, and then when that was used in *Fun and Fancy Free*, the ultimately unmade 'The Gremlins'. Instead, in 1946 he decided to add *The Legend of Sleepy Hollow*, a project that had a running time that was too short for feature release. Combined, the resulting movie ran for sixty-eight minutes, just enough to convince RKO to put it out as a main attraction. It would be the last of the 'package' movies that Roy had urged on Walt as a cost-saving measure. Walt was determined to return his studio to the production of crafted animated fairy-tale feature films for the 1950s.

The return to single-story, fairy-tale animated features by the Disney studio was heralded by the announcement in the 1948 company report that Walt had authorized work to begin on *Cinderella* (1950), a film to be produced on 'a grand scale'. Walt led the story development meetings – something he hadn't done in some years – and the studio's most experienced animators, including Kimball, Larson, Reitherman and Kahl, were put on the project. However, many of his collaborators saw him as less enthused with the art of animation than before, and more concerned with matters such as technical quality, budgets and the business end of filmmaking rather than the artistic and imaginative side. Despite that, *Cinderella* promised a return to the quality that Disney used to be associated with in *Snow White*, *Pinocchio* and *Bambi*. 'Ever since *Snow White and the Seven Dwarfs*,' said Walt, 'I've been eager to make a feature which would possess all of that picture's entertainment qualities and have the same worldwide appeal.' With the problems of the war years now largely behind the studio, *Cinderella* finally gave Walt that opportunity. It would also be the first film in the post-war years to be extensively merchandised, with the spring of 1950 seeing a host of tie-in products and toys hit stores – this was an international revenue stream that the company had sorely missed during the war.

Cinderella was the first proper animated feature from Disney since *Bambi*, and Walt had emphasized to everyone the need for it to succeed. The next feature, *Alice in Wonderland*, was also in production, but if *Cinderella* didn't hit big there'd be no money to fund future projects. By the end of 1949 *Cinderella* was complete, but not entirely to Walt's satisfaction. In interviews to promote the film, he was almost dismissive ('It's just a picture,' he said to one), instead pinning his studio's artistic revival on the forthcoming *Alice in Wonderland*.

The seventy-four-minute *Cinderella* turned out to be just the success Walt had hoped it would be, and that the company sorely needed. It grossed over $7 million during its release in North America. Several factors combined to make the film a hit: it was a well-known, easily sold story (just like *Snow White*), and the animation style was dramatic, with clever supporting characters (the mice Jaq and Gus and the cat Lucifer recalled *Snow White*'s comic dwarfs) that helped prop up the more realistically animated leads. Combined with the classic character voices and a great musical score, *Cinderella* hailed the start of a mini-renaissance for the Disney studio's animated feature films in the 1950s.

The critics, though, had become disillusioned with Disney – thanks partly to the absence of any breakthrough films during wartime and the lacklustre, unambitious 'package movies' the company had put out in the years immediately afterwards. The *New York Times* reported that 'the creators of the picture have leaned rather heavily toward a glamorous style of illustration . . . Disney and his craftsmen have brilliantly splashed upon the screen a full-blown and flowery animation of the perennially popular fairy tale . . . matching the romance of the fable with lushly romantic images.' However, *Variety* complained that 'The cartoon has far more success in projecting the lower animals than in its central character, Cinderella, who is on the colourless, doll-faced side, as is Prince Charming.' *Cinderella*'s dramatic upswing in box-office profits drove Disney into the black in 1950 for the first time in many years.

On Walt's mind since 1933, plans for an animated version of Lewis Carroll's *Alice's Adventures in Wonderland* had been developed and abandoned several times. The problem had always been condensing Carroll's whimsical, picaresque story down to feature length. The latest attempt saw Walt bring in novelist Aldous Huxley (who'd recently scripted Hollywood versions of *Pride and Prejudice* and *Jane Eyre*), apparently in the hope that he'd know how to convert a British literary classic into a viable feature film.

Seemingly confused by the possibilities of animation, Huxley turned in a script at the end of 1945 that combined live action and animated segments to tell the story (although this may have been the result of believing that he was supposed to produce something in line with Disney's then-current projects like *Song of the South*). The script was quietly filed away in a drawer at the Disney studio and forgotten. It wasn't until the return to full-length animated feature films with *Cinderella* that Walt went back to *Alice in Wonderland* as a subject.

Walt cast eleven-year-old English actress Kathryn Beaumont as Alice, and in a break with Disney tradition decided to fill out the many other roles with star names. Comic Ed Wynn took on the central role of the Mad Hatter, with fellow comedian Jerry Colonna as the March Hare. Sterling Holloway was the Cheshire Cat, and fellow English actor Richard Haydn voiced the Caterpillar. In another break with tradition, Walt decided to promote the 'celebrity' voices by crediting them on the film's eventual posters, something he'd previously resisted, preferring the films to stand on their own without cast-name support.

The seventy-five-minute movie was produced by the same writing and animation teams that had worked so well on *Cinderella*, with Ben Sharpsteen supervising. Work began in earnest in late 1949, with around thirteen individual Disney 'story men' (as studio writers were still known) contributing to a script that drew on *Alice's Adventures in Wonderland* and its follow-up, *Through the Looking Glass*. A full-length, live-action version of the film was shot featuring Kathryn Beaumont and other actors in costume as the main characters, with a few key props also used. This acted as a guide for the animation teams, although much of the film was constructed as though it were made up of a handful of discrete shorts, resulting in a rather variable approach to the material. The finished movie cost in the region of $3 million and required in excess of 700,000 individual drawings.

Unusually, the premiere of *Alice in Wonderland* was held in Britain, with London's cinema district of Leicester Square hosting the event on 26 July 1951. Although the film took a total of just over $2 million at the box office, critics were hostile to it and it ended up losing $1 million overall. The *New Statesman* accused the movie makers of 'ineptitude' in their handling of the literary classic, while the *New Yorker* complained of the film's 'shiny little tunes' and 'touches more suited to a flea circus'. The film's prospects had not been helped by the release just days before of French director Lou Bunin's version of *Alice in Wonderland*. Animator Ward Kimball believed Disney's *Alice in Wonderland* suffered from the input of too many directors all trying to outdo one another. Each wanted to 'make his sequence the biggest and craziest in the show'.

Years later, Walt Disney would put the film's relative failure down to 'weird characters' and a heroine who 'wasn't very sympathetic'. His persistence in persevering over decades to get the film made had not been well rewarded by its financial and critical failure, although like many of the Disney movies that failed on their first release, *Alice in Wonderland* would go on to become a favourite, regularly re-released, screened on television (an hour-long version featured as an early instalment of the *Disneyland* television series in 1954) and available for home viewing on videotape and DVD. The bright, colourful approach to *Alice in Wonderland* caught on in the 1960s following the release of the animated *Yellow Submarine* (1968), as it became associated with the period's psychedelic culture that also embraced Disney's *Fantasia*.

Although it failed, *Alice in Wonderland* did have a superb launch with the Christmas Day 1950 screening of the television special *One Hour in Wonderland* on NBC. Essentially a promotional film for the yet to be released movie, the special featured Walt Disney himself (beginning a long association with television; see Chapter 7) hosting a party with an audience of children, including his own daughters and celebrities such as ventriloquist Edgar Bergen and his dummy Charlie McCarthy, Kathryn Beaumont (who voiced Alice and was dressed as her for the special) and Bobby Driscoll. The special included various clips from Disney movies including the party scene from *Snow White*, *Clock Cleaners* (a Mickey Mouse short from 1937), a Br'er Rabbit clip from *Song of the South*, *Bone Trouble* (a 1940 Pluto short) and an advance clip from *Alice in Wonderland* featuring the Mad Hatter's Tea Party. Although seen as a blatant puff piece for the forthcoming movie, *One Hour in Wonderland* was a hint of the Disney studio's future in television and a harbinger of the role Walt Disney himself would shortly take on.

Accompanying *Alice in Wonderland* in cinemas was the third of Disney's new live-action documentary nature shorts, *Nature's Half Acre* (1951), released with the umbrella title 'True-Life Adventures'. The series had followed the success of *Seal Island* in 1948, with a second film, *In Beaver Valley* (1950), released with the live-action film *Treasure Island* (1950, see Chapter 8). The first three won Oscars for Best Live Action Documentary Short, with the later *Water Birds* (1952) and *Bear Country* (1953) also winning in the same category.

True-Life Adventures would eventually comprise a series of fourteen releases between 1948 and 1960, winning eight Oscars, including three for Best Documentary Feature for *Living Desert* (1953), *Vanishing Prairie* (1954) and *White Wilderness* (1958). These and other nature films would enjoy an extended life on television as part of the various regular Disney weekly series between the 1960s and the 1990s. Walt's nephew, Roy E. Disney, gained his first film production experience working on this series, and would later go on to be a pivotal figure in the development of the Disney studio in the 1970s and 1980s (see Chapter 11).

Another long-in-development animated feature film was finally released in 1953. *Peter Pan* had long been a favourite subject for Walt Disney to consider as the basis of an animated movie, and he'd obtained the film rights to the J. M. Barrie play in 1939 for $5,000. In the two years before the bombing of Pearl Harbor much work was done on the project, with the construction of character models and the development of early artwork – a Captain Hook model figure can be seen during the behind-the-scenes tour of the Disney studio in 1941's *The Reluctant Dragon*. The abandoned *Peter Pan* project was finally revived in 1949 as part of a slate of new animated feature films.

Dancer Roland Duprec was hired to perform the role of Peter Pan for a live-action version of the story made as a guide

for the animators (as had happened with *Alice in Wonderland*).
Disney favourite Bobby Driscoll provided the voice, his last
performance in a Disney movie and the first time that the
traditionally female role of Peter Pan was played by a male
performer. Hans Conried voiced both Captain Hook and Mr
Darling, as well as physically playing the roles for the live-
action version. *Alice in Wonderland*'s Kathryn Beaumont
returned to voice Wendy Darling, and radio comic Candy
Candido played the Indian Chief and sang the song 'What
Makes the Red Man Red?'.

Posters for the film promised audiences would 'See The
Land Beyond Imagination Where Adventure Never Ends',
with a variety of artists given the task of bringing Neverland
to the screen. The end result used over 900 background images,
the most employed on a Disney film to that date. Contrasting
nicely with Neverland was the film's romantic depiction of
Victorian London, with the Darling children's flight across the
capital in the company of Peter Pan an undoubted highlight.

Perhaps the biggest challenge for Disney animators was
how to handle the character of Tinker Bell the fairy, usually
represented through the use of a simple spotlight in stage productions. The 'sweet and sassy' Tinker Bell of Disney's *Peter
Pan* would come to be associated with 'the magic of Disney'
in the same way that Jiminy Cricket, 'When You Wish Upon
a Star' or 'Zip-a-Dee-Doo-Dah' were. For a long time it was
believed that Disney animator Marc Davis had modelled *Peter
Pan*'s Tinker Bell after actress and pin-up Marilyn Monroe,
but his actual model was Margaret Kerry, an actress who had
featured in a trio of 'Our Gang' comedy shorts. She acted out
Tinker Bell's actions and used outsize props, allowing Davis to
then animate the character's movements.

Disney faced significant new competition in the animation
arena at the start of the 1950s. United Productions of America
(UPA) had been founded by several ex-Disney animators in
1943 following the exodus of Disney staff in the wake of the
rancorous 1941 animators' strike. Key among them was John

Hubley, who had worked on *Snow White*, *Pinocchio* and *Dumbo*, but had major reservations about Walt Disney's move towards more realistic animation for *Bambi*. He'd worked briefly for Screen Gems and the Army's Motion Picture Unit before joining UPA. In 1949 Hubley created the character of the short-sighted Mr Magoo, which put UPA on the map.

UPA became identified with a distinctively modern, highly stylized and occasionally abstract form of animation, distinct from the dominant Disney style. The studio took the 1951 animation Oscar for *Gerald McBoing Boing* and was lauded with great critical praise for their work. In some ways, UPA's style was the logical conclusion of the experiments in style the Disney studio had tried but abandoned after their series of package movies flopped at the box office. Disney attempted to bring elements of such stylized animation back to some of their shorts with mixed results, as in *Rugged Bear* (1953) and *Donald's Diary* (1954).

The Disney shorts did not prosper in the post-war years. Mickey Mouse was still largely out of favour, only making occasional appearances in films that relied on other characters such as Pluto for their laughs (Pluto's final short for thirty years was 1953's *The Simple Things*, which celebrated the character's twenty-fifth anniversary). Goofy was becoming ever more human-like in his shorts, standing in for the average American man who had trouble coming to terms with innovations in the post-war world. Donald Duck had new co-stars in the form of chipmunks Chip 'n' Dale from 1943, and they seemed to more often than not steal the limelight from the film's supposed 'star'. Disney's shorts unit was losing the battle against innovative and irreverent material from MGM (Tom and Jerry), Warner Bros. (Looney Tunes and Merrie Melodies), and the work of directors like Tex Avery and Chuck Jones, while Mickey Mouse couldn't compete with more anarchic characters like Bugs Bunny and Daffy Duck.

Walt Disney finally reclaimed the Oscar for Best Animated Short once more in 1953, after a ten-year losing streak during which other studios and creative personnel (many of them trained at Disney) had scooped the award. *Toot, Whistle, Plunk and Boom* was an abstract history of musical instruments, a follow-up of sorts to Disney's first 3D cartoon, *Melody* (1953). Ward Kimball directed *Toot, Whistle, Plunk and Boom* using the widescreen CinemaScope process for impact – Disney would also use CinemaScope for the feature film *Lady and the Tramp* (1955).

The ten-minute, award-winning short opens with Professor Owl introducing a history lesson to a schoolroom full of unruly birds. The film then proceeds to chart the development of brass instruments (Toot), woodwind (Whistle), strings (Plunk) and percussion (Boom). It ends with the four elements united in one performance. The short was reissued in 1963 as support to the re-release of *Fantasia*, and in 1994 it was placed at no. 29 in the 50 Greatest Cartoons of All Time, voted for by animation professionals. The short is often still used today in an educational capacity in schools.

Production slowed on the shorts, and key creative people left Disney to work elsewhere, attracted by a spirit of innovation that the original animation-pioneering studio seemed to have lost. The shorts unit eventually ceased production of new films in 1956, with segments from the immediate post-war package features being released instead as 'new' shorts. Occasional 'specials' kept the Disney name attached to short film releases, but they were one-offs such as *The Brave Engineer* (1950), *Susie the Little Blue Coupe* (1952) and *Social Lion* (1954). While the characters of Mickey Mouse, Donald Duck, Pluto and Goofy would endure, their actual theatrical film appearances would be few and far between, with their earlier shorts finding new audiences and keeping the Disney name in front of children thanks to regular television airings from the mid-1950s onwards (see Chapter 7).

Writing to his younger sister Ruth towards the end of 1947, the middle-aged Walt Disney admitted:

I bought myself a birthday-Christmas present, something I've wanted all my life: an electric train! Being a girl, you probably can't understand how much I wanted one when I was a kid, but I've got one now and what fun I'm having. I have it set up in one of the outer rooms adjoining my office so I can play with it in my spare moments. It's a freight train with a whistle, and real smoke comes out of the smokestack – there are switches, semaphores, station and everything! It is just wonderful.

Walt had been fascinated by trains since his childhood days in Marceline. As an adult he regularly visited the Southern Pacific station in Glendale, not far from his Los Feliz home. The vibrating tracks and the hustle and bustle of the passengers, coming and going to their destinations, fascinated him. Owning an electric train set was fulfilment of a childhood dream – since he had become famous and wealthy through the Disney studio, Walt had actually fulfilled very few indulgences. He had some encouragement from a couple of Disney animators who were also train fans: Ward Kimball and Ollie Johnston. They'd join him during the day to 'play' with his train set, but they both had much more impressive set-ups at home. Kimball had a full-size railroad built on his property and Johnston was in the process of constructing a one-twelfth scale steam train. Walt attended the laying of the track at Johnston's place and visited the Santa Monica machine shop that was building the locomotive. It was enough to persuade the studio mogul that he wanted his own full-size railroad set at home.

Walt spent months educating himself, obtaining blueprints from the Southern Pacific Railroad and enlisting the draughtsmen at his studio to draw up plans for his own railway. He was taught woodworking and metalwork by his studio teams and set up a suitable workshop at his home. In 1948, Disney and Kimball took a trip to the Railroad Fair in Chicago, travelling by the Santa Fe Super Chief. The event was a celebration of what had attracted the two men to the railroad in the first place – the pioneering American spirit. It was the development of the railway that truly allowed the conquering of the West, bringing 'civilization' in its wake. At the fair were a Civil War locomotive and Lincoln's funeral train. Many engineers, signalmen and firemen who had been involved in the early days of the railroad were in attendance, some of them for the last time. The trip would help fuel Walt's growing idea of building his own movie-based theme park.

Upon returning home, Walt began to properly plan his own mini-railroad. He had the studio prop shop draw up plans for a one-eighth scale model of a Central Pacific engine, Number 173. Walt himself was hands-on in constructing the sheet-metal work, fabricating the lamps and the smokestack. In looking for a property for a new house with his wife Lillian, Walt insisted that any plot be large enough to encompass his planned mini-railway. While she appreciated the amusement and peace of mind the project was giving her husband, the last thing she wanted for her new home was to have it encircled by a miniature railway. In response, Walt had a mock legal agreement drawn up stipulating that he'd build a new home for the family, as long as he could also build and operate the 'Walt Disney R.R. Co.', his own railroad company. He didn't want his wife and daughters Sharon and Diane reneging on their verbal agreement to allow him to pursue his railway dream at the new house at Carolwood Drive in the Holmby Hills – the parcel of land was big enough for the railway to be some distance from the residence.

The Carolwood–Pacific Railway – as Walt dubbed the resulting track – was the seed that would eventually result in Walt constructing entire theme parks in California and Florida (see Chapter 7). As with his films, he attended to every detail of the project (although, ironically, it meant he was spending less time supervising work at the studio). Studio resources were usurped for Walt's home railroad project, with a 300-foot test track constructed on studio property. The eventual half-mile track was designed to cause minimum disruption to Lillian and their neighbours during operation. A short underground tunnel added to the thrill of any ride on his mini-railway. Walt even dressed the part, wearing an engineer's cap and overalls whenever he rode his miniature locomotive around the grounds. It provided great amusement whenever the Disneys entertained, but the idea for a whole park of such rides open to the public was growing in Walt Disney's mind, although it'd be another decade before it came to fruition.

7

THE MAGIC KINGDOM

Disneyland is often called a magic kingdom because it combines fantasy and history, adventure and learning, together with every variety of recreation and fun designed to appeal to everyone.

Walt Disney, quoted in *The Quotable Walt Disney*
by Dave Smith, 2001

During the immediate post-war years Walt Disney had struggled to get his studio back on course. The wartime work of training films and propaganda had sidelined the studio from its central purpose of creating popular entertainment. The 1950s would see a return to classic animation in feature films, a dramatic expansion into television and the development of the new field of theme parks.

The ideas that eventually coalesced into *Lady and the Tramp* (1955) had been around since the mid-1930s. Disney writer Joe Grant had come up with the character of Lady when he wrote a story based upon his own cocker spaniel. Walt had approved of that as the basis for a film; models were made of the main character and artwork was developed for the two Siamese cats, Si and Am, who featured in the story. Despite that, the film never formally entered production at that time, despite the efforts of contributors such as Frank Tashlin and Sam Cobean. Disney published the tale as an illustrated storybook in 1944, but there was still no movie.

It wasn't until much later that Walt Disney discovered another story that would complement that of Lady. Ward Greene's 1943 *Cosmopolitan* short story 'Happy Dan, the Whistling Dog' focused on an altogether rougher canine than Lady. This suggested to Walt that the combination of the upper-crust Lady with a cynical yet loveable dog from the wrong side of the tracks had the elements of a good shaggy dog story. By 1949 Grant had departed Disney, leaving his work behind, and Greene had produced a screenplay featuring two dogs named Dan and Patsy (later novelized by Greene in 1953 as *Lady and the Tramp: The Story of Two Dogs*).

Disney's most experienced writers contributed to the final screenplay, including Joe Rinaldi and Ralph Wright, although Greene retained final story credit. Lady was the central charac-ter, but the dog she falls in love with had various names during development, including Rags, Homer and Bozo, before Tramp was settled upon. A supporting cast was created, including Trusty, the bloodhound with no sense of smell, and Jock, the Scottish terrier. The local dog pound featured a variety of other ne'er-do-well characters, including a neurotic dachshund, a melancholic Russian wolfhound and a Mae West-inspired Pekinese named Peggy. Voices came from Peggy Lee (Lady's owner and the Siamese cats), Barbara Luddy (Lady), Larry Roberts (Tramp), and comedians Alan Reed and Stan Freberg. Production formally began in 1952, with a budget of $2.5 mil-lion, although the final cost reached $4 million, including the cost of over 150 animators creating two million drawings across almost four years.

Set in 1910, *Lady and the Tramp* attracted Walt Disney's focus in a way that much of the studio's recent work had failed to do: it was a period he identified with strongly, and the story was the first original for Disney not based on a classic tale, so critics could not accuse the resulting film of letting down the source material. Hamilton Luske, Clyde Geronimi and Bill Thompson were the film's directors, supervising the teams of studio animators who worked on the project. They made sure that all the animation emphasized low shots, based on the dogs' perception of the world around them. The story focused on Lady's growing fear that she will be replaced in her owners' affections by the baby they are due to have in a few months, and her growing liking for the rough-hewn scamp known as Tramp.

The CinemaScope format presented the animators with a new set of challenges. The larger screen format required bigger and more detailed backgrounds, while a series of quick cut edits would not work as well as they had previously. This resulted in longer sequences and fewer character close-ups in *Lady and the Tramp* than was usual for most Disney feature films up to that point. A regular version of the film also had to be prepared for cinemas that were not CinemaScope equipped, meaning that much of the animation had to be reworked so that it would be suitable for regular projection.

Lady and the Tramp was heavily promoted on television through Walt's new *Disneyland* series (see below), with items in December 1954 and February 1955. The resulting film was welcomed by *Variety* as 'A delight for the juveniles and lots of fun for adults . . . the first animated feature in CinemaScope . . . each of these hounds of Disneyville reflects astute drawing-board know-how and richly-humorous invention'. Bosley Crowther in the *New York Times* saw *Lady and the Tramp* as 'not the best [Disney] has done in this line. The sentimentality is mighty, and the use of the CinemaScope size does not make for any less awareness of the thickness of the goo. It also magnifies the animation, so that flaws and poor foreshortening are more plain. Unfortunately and surprisingly, the artists' work is below par in this film.'

Crowther's accusation of 'sentimentality' would regularly become attached to Disney product from the 1950s on. Despite this, one scene from the story – when Lady and Tramp share a plate of spaghetti – has become an animation classic, often parodied. The film was re-released in 1971 and again in 1980 for its twenty-fifth anniversary, before reaching videotape in 1987, which grossed $90 million (rated by the *Hollywood Reporter* in 1988 as the highest grossing videotape release to that point). A direct-to-video sequel would follow in 2001.

For most of the 1950s Disney's *Sleeping Beauty* (1959) had been in various stages of production. The story had been written by 1951 with voices recorded in 1952, but animation production took from 1952 until 1958 to complete. The music and songs were recorded in 1957. The film marked a return to the use of classic stories or fairy tales by Disney after the departure of *Lady and the Tramp*. Billed by Walt Disney as his company's 'biggest and finest animated feature', the long-in-production *Sleeping Beauty* would prove to be a massive box-office disaster. It suffered partly due to Walt's distraction with his theme park, television shows and live-action movies.

Many of the delays in making the film came from the fact that it was the first to be made in 70 mm (Super Technirama 70, as distinct from *Lady and the Tramp*'s CinemaScope format – the only other Disney film to use the format would be 1985's *The Black Cauldron*). Additionally, Walt Disney himself was not particularly attached to the project, as animation was now of far less interest to him, especially when he might be seen as simply repeating himself. Ward Kimball said of Walt: 'He never repeated himself. He would say, "We've done that, let's do something new." He'd frighten everyone half to death by challenging them that way, but then you'd get with it and new ideas would come.' Walt delegated much of the responsibility for *Sleeping Beauty* to others, including the four directors: Clyde Geronimi, Eric Larson, Les Clark and Wolfgang Reitherman. Although they were all extremely experienced, as were the film's key animators Milt Kahl, Marc Davis, Frank Thomas and Ollie Johnston, the lack of Walt's supervisory input was felt in the final film.

Part of the problem came from *Sleeping Beauty*'s all-human cast, with few of the 'funny animals' of past Disney productions, such as *Cinderella*'s talking mice and birds. Woodland creatures did feature, but although charming enough they weren't distinct characters with animated antics of their own to amuse younger viewers. Not only were the main cast members all human, they were all somewhat older (apart from Sleeping Beauty herself, Princess Aurora and Prince Philip), especially the three interfering fairies Flora, Fauna and Merryweather, who lacked the charm of *Snow White*'s seven dwarfs. The only character to really catch the audience's attention was the magnificently evil Maleficent, and she was largely a carbon copy of the Wicked Queen from *Snow White and the Seven Dwarfs*.

The story and the music came from Tchaikovsky's *Sleeping Beauty* ballet, adapted by George Bruns. Although the film featured the singing voices of soprano Mary Costa and baritone Bill Shirley as the main characters, it was distinctly lacking in memorable or hummable tunes that would cement the film in viewers' memories. The animation style was also something of a departure, with strong areas of primary colour featured in an attempt to create a more stylized fairy-tale world. The animators also made use of Technirama's super-widescreen process to feature more detailed geometric background paintings, designed and executed by Ken Anderson and Eyvind Earle. Parts of the story drew upon discarded ideas from 1936's *Snow White and the Seven Dwarfs*, including Maleficent's capture of the Prince and his dramatic escape from the castle, giving the entire film something of a second-hand feel to those making it. The fantasy sequence of the lead characters dancing in the clouds had been developed for, but ultimately dropped from, *Cinderella*. The film's climax, which sees Maleficent transform into a huge fire-breathing dragon, however, remains a classic moment of Disney animation.

Released in both traditional 35 mm and widescreen 70 mm prints, *Sleeping Beauty* grossed $7.7 million at the US box office (largely down to elaborate and costly showcase screenings), but at a total cost of almost $6 million it was the most expensive Disney movie to that point, twice as costly as each of the three preceding animated films, *Cinderella*, *Peter Pan* and *Lady and the Tramp*. This, among several other factors such as the cancellation of the *Zorro* and *Mickey Mouse Club* television shows (see below), saw the Disney company produce its first loss in over a decade for the fiscal year of 1960, resulting in a swathe of layoffs throughout the animation wing.

Critics took the movie to task, with the *New York Herald Tribune* claiming the film was the Disney studio imitating itself, badly, while the UK's *Observer* newspaper noted that Disney's newest movie compared poorly (in terms of imagination) with its first animated feature film, *Snow White and the Seven Dwarfs*. That was *Sleeping Beauty*'s main fault: that in trying so hard to repeat the impact of *Snow White*, it failed to do justice to the story of *Sleeping Beauty*. Walt blamed the failure of the film on the audience, regretting 'a considerable leaning on the part of the public towards pictures involving violence, sex, and other such subjects'. *Sleeping Beauty* could easily have been the final animated Disney feature, but as he had done so often before, Walt Disney regrouped, reorganized his company's approach to animation and returned stronger than ever in the new decade of the 1960s with a trio of classics: *One Hundred and One Dalmatians* (1961), *The Sword in the Stone* (1963) and *The Jungle Book* (1967) (see Chapter 9).

Walt Disney was one of the first Hollywood studio moguls to recognize the potential importance of television to their productions and audiences. Most of the other studio bosses saw television as the enemy, a possible threat to their business. Why would people go out to the cinema, if entertainment could be brought to them at home through their televisions, was their short-sighted argument.

Although he had claimed ignorance of the new medium back in 1937 when United Artists had demanded television rights to Disney movies, Walt had kept himself informed of the slow growth of the new medium, especially in the post-war years. In 1945 he had claimed that eventually television would have a 'tremendous impact on the world of entertainment, motion pictures included . . . television is playing a major role in informatively entertaining the masses. It is the most intimate form of communication yet developed.' That same year, the Disney studio had applied for permission to 'build and operate a television station in Los Angeles', although nothing was actually developed. It wasn't until Christmas Day 1950 that Disney made its first foray into broadcast television with the special *One Hour in Wonderland*, promoting the release of *Alice in Wonderland*. This had been followed in 1951 with *The Walt Disney Christmas Show*, seen as a highlight of Christmas Day television and a further boost to Walt's television persona.

Walt's interest in television would lead to a series of anthology shows across all three main US television networks that would run uninterrupted from 1954 to 2008, taking in 1,224 individual episodes, with Walt himself presenting them up until his death in 1966. Initially nervous and hesitant, Walt quickly got used to appearing in front of the camera and came to relish the opportunity to speak directly to his audiences young and old (he was nominated for an Emmy for his presenting efforts). These weekly television appearances, more than almost anything else, would cement the 'Uncle Walt' image of the man in the minds of generations of viewers, and further connect the Disney studio product with wholesome family values.

The series was specifically developed to help promote and fund the Disney theme parks, with the first iteration of the show going under the title *Disneyland* (1954–8). Roy Disney had pitched the idea to CBS, ABC and NBC, the primary three US television networks, and all were initially lukewarm. CBS quickly dropped out, and although NBC – which had aired *One Hour in Wonderland* in 1950 and was the studio's preferred partner – was interested, they wanted to see a 'pilot' episode first. Walt refused to make one. Eventually, a deal was done with ABC, giving the *Disneyland* television series a $500,000 budget and ABC a 35 per cent ownership share in the planned Disneyland park, beginning an association between the station and Disney that has lasted until the present (Disney bought ABC outright in 1995). The deal also saw ABC offer $4.5 million in guaranteed loans to Disney to fund the park development.

Bill Walsh, formerly of the studio's press and publicity office, was appointed to run the company's television shows after he'd set up *One Hour in Wonderland* as part of his promotional duties. The *Disneyland* show featured one of the most memorable title sequences of all time, depicting the fairy Tinker Bell flying across the Disneyland fantasy castle, wielding her wand and trailing magic fairy dust in the air (all in black and white at this stage) to the tune of *Pinocchio*'s 'When You Wish Upon a Star'. Each show would match one of the themed 'lands' from the park: Frontierland, Tomorrowland, Adventureland and Fantasyland. Walsh would later become a prolific writer and producer for Disney's family films of the 1960s and 1970s, until his death in 1975.

The *Disneyland* series launched on ABC in October 1954, introduced by Walt Disney, fulfilling his old ambition of becoming an actor through hosting the show. *Disneyland* featured a mix of older cartoons, excerpts from feature films (live-action and animated), True-Life Adventures wildlife material and occasional educational films. Opening episode, 'The Disneyland Story', recalled 1941's *The Reluctant Dragon* with its tour of the studio, where *20,000 Leagues Under the Sea* and *Sleeping Beauty* were shown in production. The first 1950s series gave rise to the Davy Crockett craze of 1955, with the television dramatization of the American frontiersman's adventures starring Fess Parker also released as two feature films, *Davey Crockett, King of the Wild Frontier* (1955) and *Davy Crockett and the River Pirates* (1956), bringing in a $2.5

million profit for material already seen on television. The theme song 'The Ballad of Davy Crockett' dominated the charts for thirteen weeks, while sales of Davy Crockett-style furry hats went through the roof – all to the evident surprise of Walt.

As part of the series' educational remit, *Disneyland* presented an episode entitled 'Man in Space' in March 1955, produced, written and directed by animator and space enthusiast Ward Kimball. A light-hearted history of rocketry and satellites was followed by an exploration of the practicalities of launching man into space and the dangers that might lurk there. Among those featured on the programme were German space pioneers (now working for NASA) Dr Willy Ley and Dr Wernher von Braun. Around forty million viewers were estimated to have seen the show, which was also released (in an edited form) as a supporting feature to cinemas and was nominated for a Best Documentary Short Oscar. The show spawned two thematic follow-ups in 'Man in the Moon' (December 1955) and 'Mars and Beyond' (December 1957), both directed by Kimball with much artistic freedom. The *Disneyland* series did much to inform a generation about the possibilities of space travel, just as the 'space race' was beginning. The educational trick would be repeated with the *Disneyland* instalment 'Our Friend the Atom', broadcast in 1957, which extolled the virtues of nuclear power.

The opening of the Disneyland theme park (see below) had been covered in the special instalment 'Dateline: Disneyland' on 17 July 1955, hosted by Walt and featuring future US President Ronald Reagan among other guests. In 1958, *Disneyland* was retitled *Walt Disney Presents*, which became a television institution when it was moved to Sunday nights from 1960.

By 1961 the Disney television show had moved to NBC and been retitled *Walt Disney's Wonderful World of Color* to take advantage of colour broadcasting's wider availability. The Disney–ABC relationship had faltered, with the broadcaster selling its stake in the theme park back to the studio in 1960. The show would remain under that title and on NBC until the end of the decade and saw the debut of the first Disney character created specifically for television: Ludwig Von Drake, a German-accented uncle of Donald Duck (perhaps inspired by Wernher von Braun) who introduced an explanation of the principles of colour on the first episode in September 1961.

Although Walt Disney died in December 1966, he had filmed enough introductions for episodes to run through to the end of that year's season, and the studio decided to retain his introductions. Believing that no one could adequately replace Walt as host after twelve consecutive years, the introductions were then dropped. The show was retitled *The Wonderful World of Disney* in September 1969 and continued on NBC (often featuring in the top-twenty list of weekly programmes) until 1979, when the title changed again to *Disney's Wonderful World* and ran until 1981. Occasionally, the show featured Disney movies split into 'episodes' run across several weeks, but the 1961 movie *The Parent Trap* was run in its entirety, a television first for Disney. During the 1970s, the emphasis of the show switched from Disney's animated and live-action movies and shorts to focus on their nature-based True-Life Adventures series. The Disney show ran briefly on CBS – the channel that had been first to reject it back in the 1950s – under the simple title *Walt Disney* between 1981 and 1983, a time of falling ratings for the long-running series and the arrival of a competing dedicated Disney channel on cable.

After a three-year hiatus, the show was revived in a new two-hour format as *The Disney Sunday Movie* on ABC between 1986 and 1988, with the Disney company's then Chief Executive Officer Michael Eisner rather uncomfortably hosting (until 1997 – see Chapter 14). The show then became *The Magical World of Disney* on NBC between 1988 and 1990, and then on the Disney Channel between 1990 and 1997, where it was an umbrella title for a variety of Disney productions. Disney's ownership of ABC saw *The Wonderful World of Disney* return to its original home from 1997 to 2008. The most recent iteration has been *The Magical World of Disney Junior,*

running on the Disney Junior channel since 2012. The weekly
Disney television show remains one of the longest-running
continuous American television series of all time.

As well as the weekly anthology show, the Disney com-
pany diversified in television, first with *The Mickey Mouse
Club*, which ran in various formats intermittently from 1955
to 1996 and introduced the world to 'Mouseketeers' – young
Disney fans who made up the audience in the studio – as
well as a host of child or young performers such as Annette
Funicello, Keri Russell, Christina Aguilera, Ryan Gosling,
Britney Spears and Justin Timberlake. Disney also moved into
television drama with the two-season *Zorro* show (1957–9, on
ABC). Guy Williams starred as the masked avenger created in
pulp magazines by Johnston McCulley, producing a hit theme
song and starting a craze among children for carving 'Z' shapes
everywhere.

A dispute over ownership of *Zorro*, *The Mickey Mouse
Club* and the *Disneyland* series contributed to the collapse of
the deal between Disney and ABC by 1960. Apart from the
regular weekly Disney show (and 1972–4 syndicated compilation clips show *The Mouse Factory*), the company stayed
away from television (preferring to concentrate on home
video releases in the 1980s), until the cable Disney Channel
launched in 1983.

Walt Disney had long thought there should be something in
Hollywood for visitors to the moviemaking capital of the world
to see, and he also felt that general amusement parks failed to
reach their true potential. Both thoughts came together in his
ideas for what eventually became Disneyland, a 'theme park'
based around the Disney studio's various movies and cartoon
characters. He once said to fellow train enthusiast and Disney
animator Ward Kimball: 'You know, it's a shame people come
to Hollywood and find there's nothing to see. They expect to
see glamour and movie stars and they go away disappointed.
Even the people who come to this studio – what can they see?

A bunch of guys bending over drawings? Wouldn't it be nice if people could come to Hollywood and see something . . . ?'

Walt had his oversized toy train set to amuse himself, but what if a movie theme park also contained rides that people could go on, something that would entertain adults and children alike? Attempts to entertain his daughters, Diane and Sharon, at weekends had shown him the failings of American amusement parks. They were untidy, scrappy, horrible places. He recalled taking his daughters to parks after Sunday school and watching the other parents, bored while their children rode on rather dull carousel horses. He wanted an amusement park to be a place 'where I can have fun, too . . . where the parents and children could have fun together'.

His first thoughts about creating his own park had come as far back as the move to the new studio in Burbank in 1939. He dreamt of developing a 'magical little park' within the studio grounds for the use of Disney employees and their families, perhaps opening it to the public occasionally. As well as rides and amusements, the park would contain statues of Mickey Mouse and other Disney characters, as well as magical items such as 'singing waterfalls' and a working locomotive. It wasn't until 1948 that Walt expanded upon his vision. There was a triangular parcel of land opposite the Burbank studio on Riverside Drive that he felt might be suitable for a larger public amusement park that would reflect the values of the Disney studio. It would be called 'Mickey Mouse Park' and would contain an Old West-themed town ringed by a railroad, a waterway with a paddle steamer, a movie theatre (showing Disney films) and shops (selling Disney products). After building his model railway at his new home in Brentwood, he revived his amusement park plans and in 1952 established a personal company, WED Enterprises (for Walter Elias Disney), to make his dream a reality. It would be called Disneyland.

Three Disney studio artists – John Hench, Ken Anderson and Marc Davis – were seconded to WED to design the park, alongside the designer of *20,000 Leagues Under the Sea* (see

Chapter 8), Harper Goff, whom Walt had met in London in a model train shop, and two artists from Twentieth Century Fox, Richard Irvine (who'd worked for Walt on *Victory Through Air Power*) and Marvin Davis. Collectively, the people who created the park (and those who came after them and reinvented it to keep up with new technology) would become known as 'Imagineers'. Disney later said: 'Almost everyone warned us that Disneyland would be a spectacular . . . a spectacular failure.'

Members of the Disney studio board objected to Walt devoting his time to his theme-park 'hobby', but Walt was not to be dissuaded. He had thoroughly researched amusement parks, zoos, circuses, fairs, exhibitions and museums the length and breadth of the US and beyond in his quest to design the perfect movie theme park. 'There's nothing like it in the whole world,' he said of his plans for Disneyland. 'I know, because I've looked. That's why it can be great, because it will be unique. A new concept in entertainment, and I think – I know – it can be a success.' As so often previously, Walt had found a new challenge and he set out once more to achieve something no one had ever done before.

With the studio heavily indebted to the Bank of America, Walt knew he couldn't go there for funding, so he decided to raise the money for Disneyland himself. He sold his holiday home in Palm Springs and borrowed $100,000 against his personal life insurance policy. He invited studio personnel to join him in a group called 'Backers and Boosters', and he even persuaded a few less sceptical banks to put money into developing his theme-park concept. By 1953 Walt had the Stanford Research Institute scouting possible locations for the park, looking to find the best place in Southern California where the attraction could be sited. They settled on a 160-acre site in Anaheim, Orange County, around twenty-five miles outside Los Angeles. It had good road links, being close to the then under construction Santa Ana freeway, and the climate meant that it would always be welcoming to visitors. Attendance, according to the institute's research, could be in the area of up to three million people each year.

Walt's designers put together expansive plans for the park including Main Street, Fantasyland, Frontierland and The World of Tomorrow, and former studio landscape artist Herb Ryman (a veteran of Walt's wartime South American escapades) painted a three-dimensional aerial view showing the topography and layout of the proposed park. The construction was costed at $7 million. In September 1953 Roy Disney pitched the concept to the American television stations, convincing ABC to sign on for the weekly Disney television show and to help fund the park. A publicity brochure prepared by the Disney studio noted:

> Sometime in 1955 Walt Disney will present for the people of the world and children of all ages a new experience in entertainment: Disneyland! The idea of Disneyland is a simple one. It will be a place for people to find happiness and knowledge . . . It will be filled with the accomplishments, the joys, and hopes of the world we live in. And it will remind us and show us how to make these wonders part of our own lives.

With ABC's $500,000, Walt Disney Productions' $500,000, his own $250,000 and a $200,000 investment by the Western Printing and Lithographing Company (who then published Disney comics and books), Walt had the funds to begin work on Disneyland. Digging on the site began in August 1954, as the plans changed and ideas were dropped, including potential attractions Holiday Land, Lilliputian Land and True-Life Adventure Land (some of these would be used in other parks developed after Walt's death). The World of Tomorrow became Tomorrowland and would feature rocket ships and moving walkways.

The construction of Disneyland took almost a year, with 3,000 construction workers on site. Main Street – an idyllic American town from the past, recalling Walt's original hometown of Marceline – was decorated with genuine period pieces, including 100-year-old gas lamps from Philadelphia and original park benches from San Francisco. With an opening date of 17 July 1955 set, work was seriously behind at the beginning of that year, giving Walt pause. He considered abandoning Tomorrowland and building it later, but decided that all four 'lands' had to be ready for opening day. With a total investment of $17 million (well above original estimates), everything was riding on opening on time, yet early on the morning of July 17 plumbers and carpenters were still hard at work preparing the park for the first visitors. Walt himself had spent the night painting part of the '20,000 Leagues Under the Sea' attraction.

A seven-mile traffic jam clogged the Santa Ana freeway as eager visitors attempted to gain entry to Disneyland on that first day. Entry was by invitation only, and 22,000 had been issued to assorted movie stars, civic dignitaries, press representatives and Disney studio employees and their families. Unknown to Walt, a healthy trade in counterfeit invites had been under way for some time, and by 10 a.m. on the first morning an estimated 30,000 people had made their way through the Disneyland turnstiles. Walt would later look back on the event as 'Black Sunday'.

The park opening was broadcast live by ABC as a ninety-minute show called *Dateline: Disneyland*, and featured the opening ceremonies and Walt's address to attendees:

> To all who come to this happy place; welcome. Disneyland is your land. Here age relives fond memories of the past . . . and here youth may savour the challenge and promise of the future. Disneyland is dedicated to the ideals, the dreams, and the hard facts that have created America . . . with the hope that it will be a source of joy and inspiration to all the world.

There were many problems that first day. The park was manned by agency staff, not the specially trained Disney 'cast members' staff that would later be used (often in costume as Disney characters from 1961), and they became belligerent and unhelpful as the queues lengthened and tempers shortened. Some of the rides broke down, while others didn't function in the first place. Overcrowding made the entire experience a misery for many, food and drink soon ran out, litter proliferated, and as the temperature rose, even the newly laid asphalt on Main Street began to melt, sticking to visitors' shoes.

Animators had been recruited to work on developing various rides, including those based around *Snow White*, *Peter Pan* and Mr Toad. Walt's personal favourite was the Peter Pan ride that in its use of suspended cars as floating sailing ships presented the sensation of flying to riders. Walt found his enthusiasm for the theme-park concepts meant he was concerned with the minutest of details, and personaly involved in every decision and development. Among the visitors to Disneyland during 1955 was an eleven-year-old George Lucas, later a filmmaker whose *Star Wars* saga would see him emulate his hero, Walt Disney, in building an empire that encompassed movies, television, merchandise and technology. Other famous visitors to the park in its early days included President Sukarno of Indonesia, the King and Queen of Thailand (given a personal tour by Walt) and the King and Queen of Nepal. One person frustrated that 'security concerns' denied him a visit was Soviet premier Nikita Khrushchev.

In an attempt to resolve the park's problems in the two weeks following the official opening, Walt Disney lived on site at Disneyland in an apartment he'd had built above the Main Street fire station. Walt wanted his own people manning the park: 'You can't expect outsiders to give the courtesy that we want. We want the people who come here treated as guests, not customers.' Seven weeks after opening, in September 1955, new specially trained staff had been recruited, litter was collected regularly and the park cleaned every night, a better management system had been put in for rides and lines, and the overall ambience and visitor experience at the park had been markedly improved. That month saw the arrival of Disneyland's one millionth visitor, and within a year the total would exceed five million, way above the estimate of up to three million per year.

Continual improvement was Walt's mantra when it came to Disneyland. 'The way I see it,' he said, 'my park will never be finished. It's something I can keep on adding to and developing.' It was the methodology he'd taken in approach to many of his animated feature films, continually developing, changing, tinkering with and altering the story, the animation, the length and the technology, until at some point – usually forced by a release date – he had to abandon each film to the public's judgement. Now, with Disneyland, he could keep on improving the visitor experience by revising the park, adding new rides and attractions, retiring others and regularly refreshing the offering Disneyland made to the tourist public. Disneyland would never be finished, but it would exist in a state of continual evolution.

Soon the park was profitable, and Walt was able to add some of the ideas he'd originally had but abandoned. Storybook Land and Tom Sawyer Land arrived in 1956. In 1959 over $7 million worth of work and expansion was done to the park, adding a submarine ride, a monorail system that traversed the park and the fourteen-storey-high Matterhorn Mountain (completed with twin bobsleigh runs). By 1965, the Disney studio had bought out all the other early interests who'd invested in the Disneyland theme park, including taking over Walt's own WED Enterprises, so that it owned this increasingly important asset outright.

While the newspaper coverage of the opening day's disasters chronicled the teething troubles at Disneyland, Walt's ambition overrode all that. It would take a while, but once things settled down, Disneyland would become one of the world's premiere tourist attractions and would lead to other Hollywood studios eventually having their own theme parks and 'studio experiences' taking movie fans behind the scenes of their favourite films. One next-day headline read 'Walt's dream a nightmare', but it was Walt's willingness and ability to bring his big dreams into reality that drove his creativity in his animated and live-action movies and in his ultimately wildly successful attempt to bring the movie experience to the world of amusement parks.

8

DISNEY DIVERSIFICATION

*I suppose my formula might be: dream, diversify and never
miss an angle.*
Walt Disney, *Wall Street Journal*, 4 February 1958

To most, the name 'Walt Disney' simply meant cartoons, but
from the 1950s onwards the Disney studio produced more
live-action movies than animated feature films, all featuring
Disney's 'family values', but with few of them ever matching
the imagination and invention evident in the cartoons.

After the war, Disney found much of the company's revenue
from foreign distribution was frozen due to currency controls and so could only be spent in those countries rather than
returned to the US. Disney's distributor RKO – which also had
money tied up in foreign territories – suggested that Walt could
use the money locked up in the UK to fund his first ever live-
action feature film: there was $850,000 accumulated that could
only be spent in Britain. The notion was an attractive one, and
was certainly more feasible than Walt's first thought of setting
up an animation studio in the UK with all that implied in terms

of time spent training animators. A live-action project could be produced much faster, and Disney needed a way to get product into cinemas quicker.

Disney producer Perce Pearce was dispatched to London to supervise a live-action adaptation of *Treasure Island* (1950), Robert Louis Stevenson's swashbuckling tale of pirates and lost gold. His posting would last for half a decade. The director was Byron Haskin, a former cameraman and special-effects expert who would later be better known for his science-fiction movies *The War of the Worlds* (1953) and *Conquest of Space* (1955). Novelist Lawrence Edward Watkin adapted Stevenson's book, and Disney contract-player Bobby Driscoll – who'd just won a special Oscar for *So Dear to My Heart* and RKO's *The Window* (1949) – was cast in the lead role of Jim Hawkins. He was paired with English stage and film actor Robert Newton as Long John Silver – his portrayal became influential on many later movie pirates and was frequently lampooned. Walt visited the production (using the trip to the UK as an excuse for a family holiday, bringing Lillian, Diane and Sharon with him – this would rapidly become an annual event over the next few years) and was enthused with the ease with which live-action movies were seemingly made, certainly when compared to animation. 'Those actors over there in England, they're great,' he said to his animators upon his return. 'You give 'em the lines and they rehearse it a couple of times, and you've got it on film – it's finished. You guys take six months to draw a scene.'

The production crew on *Treasure Island* was made up of experienced British filmmaking talent, including matte painting artist Peter Ellenshaw, cinematographer F. A. Young and score composer Clifton Young, who used the British Philharmonic Orchestra to record the film's music. *Variety* called *Treasure Island* 'handsomely mounted' and noted that the 'settings are sumptuous and a British cast headed by American moppet Bobby Driscoll faithfully recaptures the bloodthirsty 18th century era when pirates vied for the supremacy of the seas'. The *New York Times* hailed the movie as capturing 'the true

spirit of the novel. It is a tingling, suspenseful diversion ... the
showdown on the island between the captives and the pirates
crackles and sparkles to the sound of musketry and flying cut-
lasses. Pity the heart that is so worn and tired that it will not
respond to the timeless fascination of *Treasure Island*.'

The second live-action movie from Disney was also produced in the UK, again drawing upon the studio's frozen
funds, and written once again by Lawrence Watkin. *The Story
of Robin Hood and His Merrie Men* (1952) was directed by Ken
Annakin and starred Richard Todd as the notorious medi-
eval outlaw Robin Hood, who stole from the rich and gave to
the poor. Joan Rice featured as Maid Marian, and Peter Finch
played the villainous Sheriff of Nottingham. Like Snow White
with the seven dwarfs, Robin Hood's 'merrie men' made up
a group of comical supporting characters, including James
Hayter as the rotund Friar Tuck, James Robertson Justice as
Little John and Elton Hayes as Alan-a-Dale.

Essentially a Western set in Britain's colourful past, *The
Story of Robin Hood and His Merrie Men* began production
at London's Denham Film Studios in April 1951, shooting in
three-strip Technicolor. Walt was getting used to live-action
film production and was able to offer Annakin some direction
as to what he hoped for from the star performances. Richard
Todd was 'wonderful', but Joan Rice, although 'beautiful ...
she will need some help on her dialogue'.

Variety rated the film as 'a superb piece of entertainment,
with all the action of a western and the romance and intrigue
of a historical drama ... Richard Todd proves to be a first-rate
Robin Hood, alert, dashing and forceful, equally convincing when leading his outlaws against Prince John as he is in
winning the admiration of Maid Marian. Although a compara-
tive newcomer to the screen, Joan Rice acts with charm and
intelligence.'

Walt was impressed with Annakin's work, and he set the
director the task of helming two more period-set British-based
movies, once again starring the 'first-rate' Richard Todd.

The Sword and the Rose (1953) was the story of Mary Tudor, younger sister of King Henry VIII, drawn from an 1898 novel called *When Knighthood Was in Flower* by Charles Major. Watkin once more scripted, with Todd playing the Duke of Suffolk opposite Glynis Johns as Mary and James Robertson Justice as Henry VIII. Annakin had travelled to Disney's Burbank studio to work on the script and the storyboards for the movie, all of which benefitted from Walt's direct input.

In the summer of 1952 Walt was back in London, supervising production of *The Sword and the Rose*, keen to ensure that the period detail was as realistic as possible. Despite this, critics in the UK were quick to point out the film's many inaccuracies, such as Mary and the Duke's attempt to set sail for the 'new world' (presumably added to give the film some relevance to Americans). King Henry is portrayed as the traditional over-weight and jolly middle-aged figure of fun he was often seen as in movies (following Charles Laughton's portrayal), although during the period the movie is set he was only twenty-three years old. Peter Ellenshaw once more worked on matte paintings for the movie's backgrounds, as well as designing the studio sets – he was shortly to be signed up as a full-time Disney employee in Burbank.

Richard Todd once again top-lined Disney's fourth UK-produced, live-action feature film, *Rob Roy, the Highland Rogue* (1954), the final Disney film to be distributed by RKO, which was now owned by the eccentric Howard Hughes. Disney wanted to control his own distribution, establishing Buena Vista for that purpose – it was named after the street where the Disney studio was located. Richard Todd, as Scottish leader Rob Roy MacGregor, was reunited with *The Sword and the Rose*'s Glynis Johns as Helen and James Robertson Justice as Duke Campbell. Harold French was the director this time, working from another Lawrence Watkin screenplay. The action scenes were especially good, populated as they were by soldiers from the Argyll and Sutherland Highlanders, just returned from active service in Korea.

This quartet of British-made live-action movies were essentially dry runs for a prestige production that Walt Disney had been contemplating for a while, but now had the confidence to put into action: Jules Verne's *20,000 Leagues Under the Sea* (1954). The idea had grown out of an entirely separate underwater True-Life Adventure project that Walt had hired designer Harper Goff to work on in 1952. Inspired by the Universal 1916 silent version of Verne's tale, Goff had compiled some storyboards that included deep sea divers – the image caught Walt's attention, causing him to read the 1870 novel and acquire the film rights, initially intending to make an animated movie from the adventure story. However, feeling that the four live-action movies the Disney studio had made so far were only scratching the surface of what was possible, he decided to make *20,000 Leagues Under the Sea* as an ambitious live-action, science-fiction movie, a genre gaining in popularity in the 1950s.

Richard Fleischer was hired as director, having completed several accomplished crime thrillers including *Armored Car Robbery* (1950) and *The Narrow Margin* (1952, largely set on a train, so especially appealing to railroad buff Walt). He was also the son of animation pioneer Max Fleischer, an early competitor of Walt's back in the 1920s and 1930s – he'd asked his father for permission to accept the Disney job before committing to the project. Unlike the previous live-action movies, this one would be shot mainly in the US, with additional underwater photography in the Bahamas and Jamaica.

20,000 Leagues Under the Sea would be an expensive movie, financed directly by the studio not through the use of otherwise unobtainable 'locked-in' funds. A new sound stage was built, large enough to include a water tank suitable for underwater photography. The leading actors were all star names who commanded larger salaries than any of the British actors in the studio's recent films or the voice artists used for the animated films. Location work in the Caribbean, detailed effects work, a giant animatronic octopus and huge sets for the *Nautilus* submarine all combined to drive up the cost of making the picture.

Not for nothing was the resulting film billed by Disney as 'The mightiest motion picture of them all!'

Although the film starred James Mason as the enigmatic Captain Nemo, and Kirk Douglas and Peter Lorre as Nemo's unwilling prisoners, the main attraction was the elaborate submarine, the *Nautilus*. Goff designed its distinctive exterior as well as all the interior cabins, including Nemo's quarters (which featured a full-size pipe organ). Goff was partnered with Oscar winners John Meehan as art director and Emile Kuri as set decorator to realize his shiny brass and deep red velvet designs. The miniature effects showing the *Nautilus* in action underwater featured fish and bubble effects created by Walt's old partner Ub Iwerks, animator John Hench and effects specialist Josh Meador. Their work would secure the studio an Academy Award.

Robert A. Mattey, who would later work on *Jaws* (1975), was tasked with building a larger-than-life-size articulated model of a monstrous octopus, a prop that was to give director Fleischer a whole host of production problems. Originally filmed in the new studio tank in lighting that suggested dusk (which revealed to the camera the control wires operating the giant creature) and with calm seas, the sequence in which the octopus attacks the *Nautilus* had to be re-shot (at Walt's suggestion and at great expense), this time in the dark and in storm conditions that not only hid the techniques that made the cinematic magic, but also hugely increased the dramatic impact of the scene. It needed eight full days to complete the new sequence at a cost of $250,000, but it was all worth it as far as Walt was concerned, even if his brother Roy was discomfited by the ever-increasing cost of the project. Originally budgeted at about $3 million, the finished film came in at a cost of $4.2 million.

The film was a huge hit, grossing just over $8 million at the US box office, making it the second highest grossing film of the year just behind *White Christmas* (1954). It proved surprisingly popular with critics, with the *New York Times* critic

Bosley Crowther deciding that *20,000 Leagues Under the Sea* was 'as fabulous and fantastic as anything [Disney] has ever done in cartoons'. *Variety* said that: 'Walt Disney's production of *20,000 Leagues Under the Sea* is a very special kind of picture, combining photographic ingenuity, imaginative story telling and fiscal daring . . . the production itself is the star. Technical skill was lavished in fashioning the fabulous Nautilus with its exquisitely appointed interior. The underwater lensing is remarkable on a number of counts, among them being the special designing of aqualungs and other equipment to match Verne's own illustrations.'

The film's Christmas week release had been boosted by the 8 December seventh instalment of Walt's new ABC weekly television show, *Disneyland*. 'Operation Undersea' was partly a glorified trailer for the forthcoming movie, but there were enough interesting details about the making of the movie to justify the programme, which won an Emmy award for Best Individual Show of the year. The new techniques Disney had developed for underwater filming were explained, while the film's stars were interviewed on location and in the studio. It pioneered the idea of supporting a major film with an accompanying 'making of' documentary that would become commonplace many years later.

20,000 Leagues Under the Sea saw a re-energized Walt Disney return in triumph to the Academy Awards. Having been distant and cut off from his employees, like the movie's Nemo, Walt was now emerging from his post-war funk. The film won two Oscars, one for Best Art Direction/ Set Decoration and one for Best Special Effects. The *Nautilus* submarine enjoyed a healthy afterlife at the Disneyland park, appearing in Tomorrowland between 1955 and 1966, allowing visitors to see the sub and visit the interior in a walk-through exhibit made from recreated sets, littered with authentic props. The later European park, Disneyland Paris, honoured French writer Jules Verne by including the *Nautilus* as part of the park's original design. A 'submarine voyage' ride simulated the experience of diving to the depths of the sea in the *Nautilus* from 1971 until it was dismantled in 1994. Plans to remake the movie are periodically revived, but no one has so far managed to match Disney's original.

Stories of the Old West or the days of the pioneers were to form a major part of Walt Disney's continued live-action film-making throughout the 1950s. Episodes of the *Zorro* television series on ABC were re-edited into two feature films, *The Sign of Zorro* (1958) and *Zorro, the Avenger* (1959), while original productions included the Western-themed *The Light in the Forest* (1957), *Johnny Tremain* (1957) and *Tonka* (1958). Based on a 1953 novel by Conrad Richter, *The Light in the Forest* chronicled the adventures of a boy kidnapped by Indians in the 1760s. *Johnny Tremain* was also drawn from a novel, this one for children, published in 1944 by Esther Forbes. Directed by Robert Stevenson (originally for television, but released theatrically), it told of the early days of the American Revolution, although it received mixed reviews, with the *New York Times* critic Howard Thompson complaining that 'The Boston Tea Party seems more like a musical-comedy frolic'. *Tonka* starred Sal Mineo and followed the adventures of a US cavalry horse following the Battle of Little Big Horn. The earlier *Westward Ho, the Wagons!* (1956) starred television's Davy Crockett, Fess Parker, as the head of a wagon train heading through hostile Indian territory.

The newly revitalized Disney studio also specialized in live-action movies featuring various animals. *The Littlest Outlaw* (1955) followed a runaway Mexican boy who saves a tormented horse from a cruel trainer; *Old Yeller* (1957) was a tear-jerker about a dog infected by rabies that ultimately has to be put down by its distraught owner, Tommy Kirk; and *The Shaggy Dog* (1959), based on a novel by the author of *Bambi*, was a hugely successful comedy caper – Fred MacMurray starred and it grossed $8 million at the US box office – that set the template for the studio's 1960s live-action movie output.

Perhaps closer to Walt's own heart was *The Great Locomotive Chase* (1956). This story of an incident from the Civil War starred Fess Parker as the leader of a group of Union soldiers who steal a Confederate train in Atlanta and take it to Tennessee, destroying as much of the track behind them as they can (the same incident had inspired the 1926 silent Buster Keaton classic, *The General*).

Made in CinemaScope in colour and boasting a star cast, including Jeffrey Hunter and Slim Pickens, *The Great Locomotive Chase* was more an opportunity for Walt to 'play' with a full-size train set than the basis for an engaging movie. Critics were lukewarm towards the film, largely due to its reverence for history and its failure to turn that history into an engaging narrative in the way Keaton had managed thirty years before.

Disney's *Darby O'Gill and the Little People* (1959) is famous now for giving the young Sean Connery an unusual starring role as an Irishman caught up in a battle of wits with a leprechaun. Based upon elements from two books by Herminie Templeton Kavanagh, this was originally intended to be an animated feature film under the title 'The Little People'. Albert Sharpe starred as title character Darby O'Gill, while Irish comedian Jimmy O'Dea played the twenty-one-inch high, 5,000-year-old King Brian of Knocknasheega, the film's leading leprechaun. Shot in Burbank, California, Disney relied upon *20,000 Leagues Under the Sea*'s accomplished matte painter Peter Ellenshaw to create a series of backgrounds that could convince as rural Ireland.

Premiered in Dublin, *Darby O'Gill and the Little People* was not particularly appreciated by local critics. Even Americans were not taken in by this 'overpoweringly charming concoction of standard Gaelic tall stories, fantasy and romance', as the *New York Times* had it. Although the film lost money, it did a service to the future of movies. It was in *Darby O'Gill and the Little People* that Dana Broccoli, wife of producer Albert Broccoli, first saw Sean Connery. She recommended the Scottish actor to her husband, who was in the middle of a search for the right actor to take on the role of Ian Fleming's charming spy James Bond in the movie *Dr No* (1962).

From the post-war years and into the 1950s Walt Disney's life had changed dramatically. At the studio, he had become more of a distant figurehead, apart from the animators and other creative people who worked for him. There was too much material going through the studio for him to be involved in everything. He'd always prioritize animated features above the studio's new factory production line turning out the live-action movies, which often featured anonymous work by journeyman directors. Even then, by the middle of the decade, he was so involved with the developing theme park that everything else at the studio was happening in the background.

His daughters were grown and pursuing lives of their own, although Walt worked his magic on Diane and Sharon's respective husbands, eventually involving them both in the work of his studio. Even Walt and Lillian's thirtieth wedding anniversary was celebrated at Disneyland, further connecting his home life and his work life (or perhaps putting his domestic life a constant distant second to his work). In July 1955 hand-picked guests attended the celebration, enjoying a cruise down the 'Mississippi' on the *Mark Twain*, followed by dinner and entertainment at the Golden Horseshoe saloon.

Thanks to his television appearances, as the 1950s wore on Walt Disney became a recognized face worldwide. His frequent personal visits to the park, where he liked to check up on the staff and the quality of experience on offer to visitors, became more and more difficult as he was frequently mobbed by autograph hunters. He quickly adopted a policy of not giving autographs as, if he did so, he could easily find himself trapped in the park for hours.

Directed by Charles Barton (who'd handled *The Shaggy Dog*), *Toby Tyler, or Ten Weeks with a Circus* (1960) was one of the

string of formulaic kids and animal movies Disney would produce through the 1960s. The star was Kevin Corcoran, who
played the title character, a young boy who runs away to join
the circus and befriends Mr Stubbs, a performing monkey who
made a scene-stealing name for himself in a series of movies
including *Moon Pilot* (1962), *The Monkey's Uncle* (1965) and
Monkeys, Go Home! (1967).

Corcoran reappeared with Tommy Kirk, another regular
Disney juvenile, in Disney's version of *Swiss Family Robinson*
(1960), based upon the Johann Wyss novel of 1812. The tale of
a shipwrecked family, it was a return to British co-production
and featured John Mills. Filmed in Tobago, the Disney crew
had to import a variety of wildlife, including tigers, monkeys,
zebras and parrots, as the island had little indigenous bird and
animal life itself. Filming on location and involving so many
animals made for a long and involved shoot, with the arrival of
the family on the island taking ten days to film and the whole
relatively troubled production finally concluding after twenty-
two weeks and a production cost of around $4 million.

Storms flooded the sets, including an elaborate treehouse,
and much energy and effort had to be expended in managing
the animals. Although a seemingly expensive production, *Swiss
Family Robinson* paid off for Disney, grossing $40 million at
the US box office, taking more than such highly rated movies
as *Psycho*, *Exodus* and Stanley Kubrick's *Spartacus*. 'It's hard to
imagine how the picture could be better as a rousing, humorous
and gentle-hearted tale of family love amid primitive isolation
and dangers,' said the *New York Times*. The iconic treehouse,
central to the film, was said by director Ken Annakin to be
'really solid, capable of holding twenty crew and cast and constructed in sections so that it could be taken apart and rebuilt
on film by the family'. It later formed an attraction at several
Walt Disney theme parks.

Another of Robert Louis Stevenson's classic works was tackled by Disney in a faithful but rather dull version of *Kidnapped*
(1960), starring Peter Finch with James MacArthur as David

Balfour. Over-reverent to the novel, the film was slated by the usually supportive *New York Times*: 'Either Mr Disney, who made a vigorous *Treasure Island* ten years ago, has lost his touch in the intervening decade, or the kids have been spoiled by [TV shows] *Gunsmoke* and *Peter Gunn*. [The] audience was definitely not amused.'

A formula was now established for a series of family-friendly live-action comedies that would in the 1960s and 1970s come to define the Disney studio in audiences' minds almost as much as their groundbreaking animation had previously. This formula featured a light-hearted, easy-going leading man (such as Fred MacMurray) and an unthreatening, happy kid or adolescent (Tommy Kirk or Kevin Corcoran, and later Kurt Russell) caught up in a whimsical caper, often involving wayward animals or a touch of the supernatural.

The Parent Trap (1961) was one such film. Its star, the thirteen-year-old Hayley Mills, had previously appeared in Disney's *Pollyanna* (1960), about a happy-go-lucky American orphan bringing joy to a small town (she was the last to receive the special Juvenile Oscar, despite her English accent), and was the real-life daughter of *Swiss Family Robinson*'s John Mills. For six years she top-lined a series of Disney family movies following her role as mischievous twins Sharon and Susan in *The Parent Trap*. The twins meet at summer camp, initially unaware that they are sisters. They are soon engaged in a project to bring their divorced parents (played by Maureen O'Hara and Brian Keith) back together again. Only a few trick shots were originally intended to depict the two sisters together, but when Walt saw how well the process photography worked he asked for more of the scenes in which Mills played against herself.

Shot all across California, *The Parent Trap* became a breezy family favourite (remade in 1998), with catchy songs – including the title number – from brothers Richard and Robert Sherman, who Walt had brought in as the studio's staff songwriters after a few key contributions to *The Mickey Mouse*

Club on television (they'd be instrumental in the success of films such as *Mary Poppins*, 1964, and the non-Disney *Chitty Chitty Bang Bang*, 1968).

Mills's next Disney film was *In Search of the Castaways* (1962), based on a little-known Jules Verne novel, in which her spirited teenager gathers together an expedition team to go looking for her shipwrecked father. More Sherman songs supported this boisterous adventure that was clearly constructed to capitalize on both *20,000 Leagues Under the Sea* and *Swiss Family Robinson*. *Summer Magic* (1963) saw Mills co-star with Burl Ives and Dorothy McGuire as part of a family that relocates to the country and has to adapt to country ways. More Sherman songs – including the popular 'The Ugly Bug Ball', a song that Walt initially didn't rate – added even more sweetness to this confection.

Growing up on screen, the now almost eighteen-year-old Mills enjoyed a romance in Crete in the light thriller *The Moon-Spinners* (1964, directed by former war photographer James Neilson) and her first screen kiss, courtesy of Peter McEnery. Silent movie star Pola Negri was persuaded out of a twenty-year retirement by Walt to feature in *The Moon-Spinners* (her final film) as a mysterious wealthy woman who provides the key to the adventure. Finally, *That Darn Cat!* (1965, remade 1997) co-starred Mills with Dean Jones in a tale of bank robbery, kidnapping and an interfering feline. All of Mills's Disney films were very popular hits, and came to epitomize a certain perception of Disney's 1960s live-action adventure comedies as wholesome, essentially harmless and perhaps a little sentimental and twee.

Animal movies remained a staple of Disney's productions in this period, with the Oscar-winning True-Life Adventures series heavily influencing the approach of some of the drama productions. Criticized for over-anthropomorphizing the animals in his heavily edited and constructed 'documentaries', Walt felt he may as well go the whole way and make animals central to several fiction features, thus side-stepping any questions of authenticity. *Nikki, Wild Dog of the North* (1961), the 'historical' Edinburgh-set drama *Greyfriars Bobby* (1961) and war-set horse drama *Miracle of the White Stallions* (1963) all put animals at the centre of their stories, at the expense of the human leads. Humans were almost dispensed with altogether in *The Incredible Journey* (1963), which followed three pets – two dogs and a cat – on their quest to return home through the Canadian wilderness (the inevitable 1993 remake *Homeward Bound: The Incredible Journey* gave star voices to the animals' thoughts: Don Ameche, Sally Field and Michael J. Fox).

Fred MacMurray had featured in several Disney movies since *The Shaggy Dog* (including the Paris-set *Bon Voyage!*, 1962), finding his signature role in *The Absent-Minded Professor* (1961), in which his eccentric college chemist Dr Brainard invents 'flubber', an unusually flexible 'flying rubber' that appears to defy gravity. Amid making his car fly and offering extra lift to a basketball team during a vital game, Brainard repeatedly misses his own wedding to Betsy Carlisle (Nancy Olson). Comedian Keenan Wynn featured as an unscrupulous character out to profit from flubber, while Disney regular Tommy Kirk played a pupil. All were reunited two years later for the sequel, *Son of Flubber* (1963), in which Brainard invents 'dry' indoor rain, a side effect of 'flubbergas'. The 1997 Disney film *Flubber* starred Robin Williams and drew on both previous movies. Medfield College, from the Flubber movies, reappeared in the Kurt Russell trilogy begun with *The Computer Wore Tennis Shows* (1969).

From *Old Yeller* at the end of the 1950s, Tommy Kirk had become a regular Disney juvenile. His teaming with MacMurray in the two Flubber movies and in *Bon Voyage!* saw him spun-off into his own high-profile, gimmick-driven vehicles, including as a student inventor (a younger absent-minded professor) in *The Misadventures of Merlin Jones* (1964) and *The Monkey's Uncle* (1965), again with monkey thespian Mr Stubbs. Despite his success, Kirk was fired personally by Walt Disney when it was discovered he was gay – the mother of a teenage boy he was seeing complained to the studio. Kirk noted: 'Disney was the most conservative studio in town . . . The studio executives were beginning to suspect my homosexuality. Certain people were growing less and less friendly. In 1963, Disney let me go. But Walt asked me to return for the final Merlin Jones movie, *The Monkey's Uncle*, because the Jones films had been moneymakers for the studio.'

His firing was kept under wraps and Kirk continued making movies at other studios, until leaving acting in the mid-1970s after a struggle with drug addiction. His situation displayed the innate conservatism at the centre of the Disney studio's live-action movies, and that came from the figurehead at the top of the studio: Walt Disney. Despite this unfortunate history, Kirk joined the roster of Disney Legends – important studio figures recognized for their contribution – in 2006.

Live-action production may have boomed at the Disney studio in the 1960s, but that same decade also saw a return to form for Disney animated feature films.

9

ANIMATION'S SECOND COMING

I make films for the child in all of us, whether we be six or
sixty. I try to reach and speak to that innocence, showing
the fun and joy of living; showing that laughter is healthy;
showing that the human species, although happily ridiculous
at times, is still reaching for the stars.
Walt Disney, quoted in *A Walt Disney Resort Outing*, 2002

At the start of the 1960s, it looked like animation could be a
thing of the past at the Disney studio. *Sleeping Beauty* had
failed miserably at the box office, the live-action films were
taking off and making more money than ever, and animation
was consequently seen as ever more expensive in comparison. Walt even went so far as to tell one of his animators: 'I
don't think we can continue [with animated cartoons], it's too
expensive.' The problem for Walt was his deep affection for
animation as a form and for the animated movies his company
had made. The only way forward would be to find a cheaper
way of making animated feature films.

One Hundred and One Dalmatians (1961), the next Disney

animated cartoon following the failure of *Sleeping Beauty*, would according to Walt Disney 'introduce some technical advancements which, I believe, enhance the work of our fine staff of animators'. The book by Dodie Smith had been published in 1956, read by Walt the following year, and optioned as a film property quickly thereafter. Unlike on previous animated films that were developed by a group of 'story men', Walt assigned this one to just one writer, Bill Peet, as had increasingly been the case for the live-action movies.

Having spent recent years tied up with the development, building and promotion of Disneyland, and in overseeing his television interests (as well as regularly introducing *Walt Disney Presents . . .*), Walt was more detached from his company's animated feature films than ever before. Although he sat in on all the story sessions, as had long been his habit, he concluded that Peet's script was virtually ready to go – the script and the character designs had already met the approval of the story's author.

The 'technical advancement' introduced on *One Hundred and One Dalmatians* was something of which Walt was rather suspicious. Instead of laboriously tracing and inking the animators' pencil drawings – something central to the practice of animation since Walt's earliest days – the drawings could now be mechanically copied using an adapted Xerox process developed by Walt's technical supervisor, Ub Iwerks. The process resulted in thick black lines outlining the key characters, a fault that Walt felt did not match the more finely drawn characters of traditional animation. However, the new process was a major labour- and money-saving device, so had to be adopted as an economic imperative. As a result, the inking department at the Disney studio was closed, reducing the animation staff from around 500 people to about 100. The trick, Walt felt, would be in adapting his studio's traditional animation style to make a virtue of the bolder character outlines that resulted from the Xerox process. The humans in the film are more caricatured and 'cartoony' than those in previous Disney features, yet still work convincingly, especially in relation to the dogs.

Ken Anderson designed the contemporary-set (a first for a Disney animated movie) film in a bright, storybook style, adopting abstract backgrounds, full of pastel colours, against which the heavily outlined characters would play well. The fact that the story was about black-and-white dogs helped enormously in disguising some of the corners now being cut by the Disney studio. Animator Chuck Jones (best known for his Looney Tunes work at Warner Bros. but briefly a Disney employee) felt that using the Xerox process 'helped Disney tremendously. They were able to bring in *One Hundred and One Dalmatians* for about half of what it would have cost if they'd had to animate all those dogs and all those spots.'

That was the biggest problem for the animators: making all the spots on each of the dogs relatively consistent from shot to shot. The film concerned two Dalmatian dogs, Pongo (voiced by Rod Taylor) and Perdita (Cate Bauer), whose puppies are kidnapped by the villainous Cruella de Vil (Betty Lou Gerson) so she can make a spectacular Dalmatian-fur coat. A gang of other dogs, including a deaf sheepdog named Colonel and his tabby cat assistant Sergeant Tibbs, as well as the Twilight Bark gang, are soon on the Dalmatian pups' trail. The dogs' spots were designed as though they were constellations, grouped together in easy-to-duplicate patterns. Overall, Pongo had seventy-two individual spots, while Perdita had sixty-eight and the pups had thirty-two each.

Upon release, critics commented on the different look of *One Hundred and One Dalmatians* without knowing of the technical advancements behind it. *Punch* magazine described the art in the new Disney film as 'far more interesting than usual', while *Monthly Film Bulletin* noted the 'strong and simple lines' denoting the movie's characters, dogs and humans. The usual Disney songs had been kept to a minimum (with just three, and only one of those strongly featured). *Time* magazine described the film as 'the wittiest, most charming, least pretentious cartoon feature Walt Disney has ever made'.

Budgeted at just $3.6 million, well under the cost of recent

animated movies, *One Hundred and One Dalmatians* was a
huge hit, taking $6.4 million at the US box office and helping
transform 1960's studio deficit of over $1 million into a positive
balance of over $4 million by 1961. Its success finally enabled
Walt and Roy to free themselves from having to service the
twenty-two-year-old bank loan from the Bank of America (for
a while at least: there would be new loans). A live-action remake
called *101 Dalmatians* (starring Glen Close as Cruella de Vil)
followed in 1996, with a sequel – *102 Dalmatians* – in 2000,
and an animated television cartoon series, *101 Dalmatians:
The Series*, in 1997 and 1998. An official sequel to the original
animated film, complicatedly titled *101 Dalmatians II: Patch's
London Adventure*, was released to DVD in 2003.

The success of *One Hundred and One Dalmatians* led directly
to *The Sword in the Stone* (1963), the eighteenth Disney animated feature film put into production – twenty-five years
after *Snow White and the Seven Dwarfs* – and the last one to
be released while Walt was alive. The rights to film the T. H.
White novel had been bought by Walt in 1939, just one year
after it had been published, but he was slow to exploit it, fearing that the King Arthur story was not as well known in the
United States as it was in Britain. It was considered again in the
late 1950s in the wake of the Lerner and Loewe stage musical
Camelot, which was based on White's complete story cycle of
The Once and Future King.
  Although the story of the wizard Merlin instructing the
young King Arthur while transforming him into a variety of
birds and animals was well-suited to animation, *The Sword
in the Stone* might have benefitted from the more lavish and
detailed animation style of *Sleeping Beauty*. Instead, the new
economic realities of cartoon animation at Disney dictated the
same cost-saving approach as had been used on *One Hundred
and One Dalmatians*. Bill Peet once again worked alone in
adapting the story, subject to Walt's notes. This film was also
the first to feature a single credited director, rather than a team

of animation supervisors, with Wolfgang Reitherman taking the helm. The Sherman brothers composed the featured songs.

Three people voiced the character of young Arthur – Rickie Sorensen, Richard Reitherman and Robert Reitherman (Wolfgang Reitherman, as director, cast all of his sons – Bruce, Richard and Robert – as leading voices in his movies, including *The Jungle Book* and *Winnie the Pooh*). The powerful and comic wizard Merlin was voiced by Western star Karl Swenson, and the character was handled by animator Milt Kahl. Martha Wentworth, who'd voiced several characters in the previous movie, was the witch Madam Mim, Merlin's rival. The pair feature in one of the most fondly remembered sequences, in which they engage in a magic duel taking the forms of various creatures, from a crocodile and a turtle to a rabbit and a dragon.

The Sword in the Stone did not meet the near unanimous positive critical reception afforded its predecessor. Although the *New York Herald Tribune* described it as 'a thorough delight', one British critic (who perhaps felt a greater sense of ownership of this national myth) complained of 'a lack of exuberance and a fatal lack of imagination . . . as Disney has concentrated more and more on nature films and on children's live action films, bringing the latter to a very high standard, his cartoons have degenerated almost beyond repair'. Hollywood's trade paper, *Variety*, described the latest Disney as 'a tasty confection . . . but one might wish for a script that stayed with the more basic storyline rather than taking so many twists and turns which have little bearing on the tale about King Arthur as a lad'. Despite the misgivings of some critics, *The Sword in the Stone* went on to be the sixth highest grossing film of 1963, taking just over $22 million at the US box office.

The Jungle Book (1967) was the first Disney animated feature film released after Walt Disney's death, and the last to carry his credit as producer. However, his stamp was all over the finished film, as it was another he'd long had under consideration but had never been able to crack the storyline. Based on Rudyard

Kipling's 1894 collection of short stories, Bill Peet worked on the script as he had done for the previous two animated features. However, with *The Sword in the Stone* artistically less successful than *One Hundred and One Dalmatians*, Walt decided the animated features needed more of his time and attention once more. Peet's take had been as dark, dramatic and sinister as the original Kipling tales, but this was not what Walt wanted. Disputing Walt's view, but knowing he'd never win the argument with the man after whom the studio was named, Peet finally left Disney early in 1964.

To solve the story problem, Walt fell back on his former way of working, with him supervising a series of story meetings with a lead writer – Larry Clemmons, a former joke writer for comedians like Bob Hope and Jack Benny – and a varied group of 'story men', including Ralph Wight, Ken Anderson, Vance Gerry and Floyd Norman. Between them they came up with a more straightforward telling of the tales than Peet had managed (although they kept his original character of the orang-utan King Louie), with Walt adding special comic business to engage the animators in their tasks.

Wolfgang Reitherman once more directed, with animators Milt Kahl and Frank Thomas looking after the lead character of jungle boy Mowgli and Bagheera the Panther, while John Lounsbery handled the elephants and Ollie Johnston took responsibility for the break-out character of Baloo the Bear. The voice cast had more impact on the animation in *The Jungle Book* than on any of the previous features. Walt had seen comedian Phil Harris perform at a benefit in Palm Springs and felt he'd be good for the bear. 'In *The Jungle Book* we tried to incorporate the personalities of the actors that do the voices into the cartoon characters,' recalled Reitherman, 'and we came up with something totally different. When Phil Harris did the voice of Baloo, he gave it a bubble of life. We didn't coach him, [we] just let it happen.'

The suggestion of Louis Prima as King Louie came from Disneyland Records president Jimmy Johnson. Prima was a trumpeter, songwriter, singer and actor who'd started out in jazz bands in the 1920s just as Walt Disney was making his first serious inroads into movie animation. He moved with the musical times, getting into swing in the 1930s, the big band sound of the 1940s, becoming a Vegas lounge act in the 1950s, and moving into the pop music of the early 1960s. He performed the movie's hit song 'I Wanna Be Like You (The Monkey Song)' by the Sherman brothers, and contributed to two albums with Phil Harris, released on Disneyland Records. The other main song, Phil Harris's 'Bare Necessities', was Oscar nominated as Best Song in 1967.

Other high-profile actors cast as character voices in *The Jungle Book* included *The Saint* star George Sanders, who brought his smoothly malevolent tones to the role of the villainous Shere Khan, Sebastian Cabot (Sir Ector in *The Sword in the Stone*) as Bagheera, Sterling Holloway as the snake Kaa and Bruce Reitherman as Mowgli, the orphaned 'man-cub' of the movie.

The animators on *The Jungle Book* were worried as they were beginning their work long before the story had been finalized and locked down, an approach that had caused major problems on *Pinocchio* back in 1940. 'As they grew in dimension,' said Wolfgang Reitherman of the characters, 'the story was altered as they interacted with each other. We always leave the plot loose enough so that the personalities meshing together enhance it.' However, under Reitherman's control the animation of each sequence was completed successfully and the continuity of characters was carried off throughout the entire film. Most of the characters were considerably lightened from the Kipling stories, with Walt's comedy business making for a movie that would become – in common with so many Disney productions – a family classic.

Released thirty years after *Snow White and the Seven Dwarfs*, the final Disney animated movie to have major input from Walt Disney himself met largely with critical praise. It grossed just over $26 million, making *The Jungle Book* the company's most profitable animated feature on first release (many, including *Snow White*, made most of their money upon frequent re-releases) to that date. Although the movie drifted far from Kipling's tales, *Time* welcomed *The Jungle Book* as 'thoroughly delightful . . . the happiest possible way to remember Walt Disney'. *Life* magazine saw the new film as 'the best of its kind since *Dumbo*, another short [the movie was only seventy-eight minutes], bright, unscary and blessedly uncultivated cartoon'. The *New York Times* referred to *The Jungle Book* as 'a perfectly dandy cartoon feature', while *Variety* (although largely positive) criticized the film's 'restrained' story development. As with several of the classic animated movies, *The Jungle Book* was remade as a live-action movie in 1994, and expanded upon in several animated sequels and spin-offs.

The Jungle Book could have been the final animated feature film from the Disney studio. With the passing of Walt there was concern about how the studio would fare without his input. It was also felt that with nineteen animated films already made and most unlikely to date thanks to their largely timeless storytelling, there was little point in making anything new – the currently existing films could simply be recycled on an endless re-release programme, capturing new generation after new generation. This view was largely attributed to Roy Disney, concerned as ever by money and business. He argued for the closure of the studio's animation division on the basis that no one other than Walt had ever produced a successful animated film at the studio. There was one other film in development, though, that the animators argued had been fully discussed with Walt before his death, a tale of kidnapped kittens called *The Aristocats*.

Given it was under close scrutiny as the first post-Walt animated feature, inside and outside the studio walls, *The Aristocats* (1970) was very carefully planned so as not to incur any of the costly production rethinks that had affected previous films like *Pinocchio* and *The Jungle Book*. Based on a story by Tom McGowan and Tom Rowe, *The Aristocats* (Disney's twentieth animated feature) told of a family of pampered cats kidnapped by the family butler who hopes to get the inheritance due to go to them, and the alley cat who helps them out.

As a result of studio concern regarding possibly cancelling feature-film animation, *The Aristocats* is a fairly simple, safe movie, produced to meet economic restrictions imposed by Roy that Walt may well have baulked at. Wolfgang Reitherman directed once more, having taken over responsibility for the studio's animated output following Walt's death, but even this thirty-five-year veteran of the Disney studio couldn't liven up this feline farce. 'I think that a little of Walt rubbed off on all of us,' claimed Reitherman, in his defence of continued animation production at the Disney studio.

Five of the most experienced animators (the 'nine old men' of studio legend) worked on *The Aristocats*: Reitherman, Milt Kahl, Ollie Johnston, Frank Thomas, John Lounsbery and Eric Larson. They all endeavoured to do things just as Walt would have done them, although the animation seemed less distinctive and the songs far less catchy than in the most recent animated hits. It took four years to produce the film, at a cost of $4 million; this, despite the need to be economical to please Roy was more than most of the recent films following the adoption of the time- and money-saving Xerox copying system.

Eva Gabor voiced the lead cat, Duchess, with Phil Harris returning from *The Jungle Book* as the helpful alley cat O'Malley. The trio of cute kittens were voiced by Gary Dubin, Liz English and Dean Clark. The rapacious butler, Balthazar, was voiced by Roddy Maude-Roxby, while singer and actor Scatman Crowthers played Scat Cat, O'Malley's best pal. Other voices came from Sterling Holloway, Paul Winchell, Thurl Ravenscroft (who'd voiced many Disney characters since Monstro in *Pinocchio*) and English DJ 'Lord' Tim Hudson as Hip Cat, the English cat.

Despite its obvious deficiencies compared to prime Disney

product, *Variety* praised *The Aristocats* for its 'outstanding animation', while bemoaning the story as 'a series of well-plotted vignettes bracketed by establishing sequences which suggest but don't deliver a sturdy plot line, and finished by a limp run out'. A domestic US gross of $10 million (less than half of *The Jungle Book*) was boosted by an additional $16 million taken in overseas releases. This was enough to prove to doubters, especially Roy Disney, that there could be life in Disney animation beyond Walt.

10

DEATH OF AN ICON

My greatest reward, I think, is that I've been able to build this wonderful organization . . . to have the public appreciate and accept what I've done all these years. That is a great reward.
Walt Disney, interview with Fletcher Markle, *Telescope*, Canadian television show, 25 September 1963

In the mid-1960s Walt Disney produced what many consider to be his crowning achievement. *Mary Poppins* was the Disney movie that was 'practically perfect in every way' in its winning combination of spirited live action and lively animation, but it only appeared after a long, hard struggle between Walt and the author of the original stories, P. L. Travers. It seems Walt was driven to get this film made, and to secure the long-term future of his company, as though he had an inkling that he was living through his final decade. The question asked by many, including those inside the Disney studio, after the death of their founder in 1966, was whether they could survive without him.

The battle fought by Walt Disney to bring *Mary Poppins* to

the screen was a lengthy and exhausting one, but he never gave up, so strong was his belief that P. L. Travers's story was ideal material for a Disney film – even if the author herself strongly disagreed. Walt first came across the two Travers books – *Mary Poppins* and *Mary Poppins Comes Back* (published in 1934 and 1935 respectively) – as far back as the early 1940s, following a recommendation from his daughter, Diane, who had read and enjoyed them.

Travers had been born Helen Lyndon Goff in Queensland, Australia, in 1899, the daughter of a failed bank manager who died aged just forty-three when she was only seven. As an adult she adopted the name Pamela Lyndon Travers and appeared throughout Australia as part of a Shakespearean touring company before emigrating to England in 1924. She took up writing, abbreviating her name to P. L. Travers, and began what would be the first story about magical nanny Mary Poppins in 1933. Travers was an admirer of the work of J. M. Barrie, and her first publisher was Peter Llewelyn Davies, Barrie's adopted son, who had largely been seen as the model for Peter Pan. Sequels to *Mary Poppins*, eventually totalling eight books, were published intermittently until 1989.

At the time Walt read the first two books, Travers was residing in New York with her adopted son to avoid the wartime Blitz on London. In what may have been a tactical error, Walt sent Roy to visit the author and discuss adapting the two books for film. Travers had recently published a third Poppins book, *Mary Poppins Opens the Door*, in 1943. She was resistant to the idea of a Mary Poppins movie, believing that the form would fail to do her characters justice, whether animated or not. Roy wrote to Walt:

Mrs Travers said she could not conceive of Mary Poppins as a cartoon character. I tried to tell her that this was a matter that should be left for future study – that it might be best for *Mary Poppins* to be produced in a combination of live action and cartoon using the animation to get the fantasy and illusion of the Mary Poppins character. I told her we were thoroughly qualified and equipped to produce either medium and, as a matter of fact, are producing such types of pictures.

Regardless, Travers regarded Disney's work to date as mere 'cartoons' and was put off by the fact that Walt didn't deem her work important enough to come and see her himself. He tried to make up for that by following up Roy's trip with an invite to visit the Disney studio to discuss the idea in greater depth. Travers once again declined, and there things rested until the early 1950s.

When Walt was visiting London to supervise the making of his first live-action movies, he realized Travers had returned there after the war. He felt enough time had elapsed that a second attempt, this time in person, to persuade the author to give permission for a Mary Poppins movie would be worthwhile. Surprisingly, filmmaker and author got on rather well when they eventually met, but Travers still stubbornly said 'No' to any movie ideas, despite being charmed by Walt's legendary powers of persuasion. There matters rested for yet another decade, although Walt would occasionally raise the issue again with Travers only to be continually rebuffed.

By 1961, Travers was sixty years old and had fallen on harder times. She needed the potential income a film deal for *Mary Poppins* would involve, but her agent was now asking Disney for $750,000 for the rights. She also laid down strict terms for the deal, which included her becoming a consultant on the movie – Walt was so keen to finally get the project into production that he even agreed to her demand for script approval (an arrangement he'd previously rejected back in 1944), without giving consideration to what Travers's direct involvement in the film might actually mean for the production. Despite her expressed dislike of songs and musicals, one of the first things Walt did was give a copy of the single-volume version of the first two Mary Poppins novels to the Sherman brothers with instructions that they should begin developing songs for the film.

In breaking down the incidents in the books, the Shermans produced the first storyline for the movie, selecting six key chapters to develop and working out some rough song sketches. When they presented this material to Walt, he showed them his copy of the book with the exact same six chapters marked to become the focus of the film. Disney writers Bill Walsh (*The Absent-Minded Professor* and *Son of Flubber*) and Don DaGradi (*Lady and the Tramp*) were put to work on the screenplay, while the Shermans composed the many songs.

In 1961, P. L. Travers took up Walt's long-standing invitation to come and see the studio, determined to exercise her right to 'consult' on the film of her book. She was not the retiring 'English rose' that Walt perhaps imagined, being determined to protect her story and characters from Walt's changes, many of them deemed necessary to make the story work for film. She didn't understand the needs of cinema in adapting a book to the screen, and he didn't know the right way to handle such an outspoken talent. The result was a rocky relationship and an almost titanic battle of wills that threatened to scupper the production of the film entirely. (This would form the basis of the 2013 Disney movie about the making of *Mary Poppins*, *Saving Mr Banks*, starring Tom Hanks as Disney and Emma Thompson as Travers, a film heavily criticized in its own right for compressing and changing elements of the real-life story.)

The Sherman brothers – whose songs for *Mary Poppins* included 'A Spoonful of Sugar', 'Step in Time', 'Jolly Holiday' and the melancholic 'Feed the Birds' – were on the receiving end of Travers's dislike of musicals. 'She hated everything we'd done,' the brothers recalled in their book *Walt's Time*. '[She] disliked it with a passion. For every chapter we developed, she had a definite feeling we had selected the worst one. She started naming the chapters she felt we should adapt, and they were the ones we thought were absolutely unusable!'

When it came to casting, the title role of Mary Poppins was a difficult one to fill, with Walt and his director Robert Stevenson considering Bette Midler and Mary Martin before settling on twenty-seven-year-old English actress Julie Andrews after seeing her as Guinevere in the stage version of *Camelot*. She had played Eliza Doolittle in *My Fair Lady* on Broadway, but had failed to secure the role in the movie (which went to Audrey Hepburn). The title role in *Mary Poppins* would launch Andrews to international fame and play a large part in securing her the leading role in 1965's *The Sound of Music*. She'd originally turned Walt down due to her pregnancy, but he agreed to delay production until 1963 when she'd be available again – after all, he'd waited the better part of two decades to win the film rights to *Mary Poppins* from Travers so another few months wouldn't matter. Walt wrote to Andrews: 'We definitely feel in our own minds that, with your talent, you would create an unforgettable Mary Poppins.'

Andrews's co-star, in the role of Cockney chimney sweep Bert, would be American comic actor Dick Van Dyke, who was enjoying a burst of fame thanks to his popular television show. Walt wasn't aware of Van Dyke, and originally hoped to cast Cary Grant. Van Dyke had first enjoyed success on radio and in theatre in the immediate post-war years, playing on Broadway in the 1950s. From 1961 he starred in the CBS sitcom *The Dick Van Dyke Show* (which would run until 1966), with Mary Tyler Moore playing his wife.

The Banks family visited by Poppins in the movie was headed up by David Tomlinson as the strait-laced bank manager father (inspired by Travers's own father) and Glynis Johns as the suffragette mother (her political activism a new twist added by Disney's writers). Karen Dotrice and Matthew Garber, both of whom had previously appeared in the Disney movie *The Three Lives of Thomasina* (1963) about a magical cat, played the Banks children, Jane and Michael, for whom Mary Poppins serves as nanny. Elsa Lanchester played the previous nanny who quits at the start of the film, and Ed Wynn featured as the mysterious Uncle Albert, who floats when he laughs.

Over Travers's objections, Walt was determined to feature animated sequences in *Mary Poppins* and put Hamilton Luske in charge of developing them. It was Walt's idea that Bert should draw chalk scenes on the pavements (inspired by someone he once saw doing just that in front of London's National Gallery) that then come to life. Walt had authorized Ub Iwerks to spend $250,000 on a new travelling matte process for the animation sequences, to better combine the live-action humans with cartoon backgrounds and antic animated characters. Some of the animation was as a result of late changes, such as the barbershop quartet of singing penguin waiters replacing real waiters only when Walt observed that waiters had always reminded him of penguins. Although the animators would often complain about such late changes, they more often than not recognized that the finished work almost always improved the picture. Walt also knew that his experienced animators relished challenges, and he was more than happy to continue to issue them.

All shot in studio on the Disney Burbank lot, the strangely colourful, artificial world of *Mary Poppins* added some uniquely cinematic magic to the story different from that in the book. Art director Carroll Clark and set decorator Emile Kuri contributed much to the film's distinctive look, where the exteriors appear as unreal as the interiors of the Banks's home or the bank where Mr Banks is manager. Disney's chief matte painter Peter Ellenshaw was stretched by the requirement to provide backdrops not only for the 'exterior' street and park scenes, but also for such sequences as the opening flight over London by Mary Poppins, while special effects experts Eustace Lycett and Robert A. Mattey had to convincingly show Poppins sliding down a banister or conducting a tea party upside down on the ceiling.

Walt was troubled by the fact that as far as production on the sound stage went, *Mary Poppins* was relatively trouble-free. He recalled:

As the original *Mary Poppins* budget of $5 million continued to grow, I never saw a sad face around the entire studio and this made me nervous. I knew the picture would have to gross $10 million for us to break even. Still, there was no negative head shaking, no prophets of doom. Even Roy was happy – he didn't even ask me to show the unfinished film to a banker. The horrible thought struck me: suppose the staff had finally conceded that I knew what I was doing?

It'd be a fine accomplishment after over thirty years in the feature-film business.

Although long in its final running time of 139 minutes (Walt had considered cutting several sequences, but decided to let the film run to its 'natural' length), *Mary Poppins* would prove enchanting to generations of children, despite its Edwardian values and Dick Van Dyke's laughable attempt at a Cockney accent – he came second in a list of 'worst movie accents' in a 2003 poll conducted by *Empire* magazine, beaten only by Sean Connery, who sounds Scottish no matter the role he's playing. Shooting had concluded at the end of the summer of 1963, although it would take another year to complete and integrate the complex animation. Walt had written to his sister Ruth confiding about *Mary Poppins*: 'I think it's going to be one of our best.'

Although she recognized that the film could never capture all the nuances of her books, P. L. Travers was still bitterly disappointed by the Disney film of *Mary Poppins*. 'Books have to undergo some sort of sea-change when they are translated to the screen,' she conceded. 'Magic, conveyed in a book by words and the silences between words, inevitably in a film becomes tricks. The film of *Mary Poppins*, with all its glamour and splendours and the devoted energy of its cast has been a tremendous success. But if we are comparing book and film, the sea-change has been tremendous.'

Travers attended the star-studded premiere of the movie, although she wasn't initially invited. It was to be the first, and probably only, time she was to see the movie. During the film she was seen to weep, leading the Disney staff present – including Walt – to conclude that she had finally been moved by seeing the film and approved of the way it had turned out. According to Travers, she'd cried through the shock of seeing *Mary Poppins* brought to life on the screen, not because she'd been moved by it. Revealing her lack of understanding as to how movies were made, she confronted Walt after the screening saying, 'The first thing that has to go is the animation sequences.' By now tired of dealing with the difficult creator of the 'practically perfect in every way' nanny, Walt responded harshly: 'Pamela, the ship has sailed.'

The *Saturday Review* regarded *Mary Poppins* as 'one of the most magnificent pieces of entertainment to come from Hollywood'. *Variety* claimed Disney had 'gone all out' with this production, which featured 'a spread of outstanding songs . . . For sheer entertainment, a sequence mingling live-action and animation in which [Dick] Van Dyke dances with four little penguin-waiters is immense. Julie Andrews' first appearance on the screen is a signal triumph and she performs as easily as she sings, displaying a fresh type of beauty.' *Time* magazine noted that 'The sets are luxuriant, the songs lilting, the scenario witty but impeccably sentimental, and the supporting cast only a pinfeather short of perfection.'

Mary Poppins would gross $45 million worldwide, resulting in the Disney studio accruing a profit of $4 million for 1965, and it was the most profitable film of the year, reaping $28.5 million above its production and marketing costs, beating Julie Andrews's *The Sound of Music*, James Bond adventure *Goldfinger* and Audrey Hepburn's *My Fair Lady*. The company's stock share price nearly doubled following the success of the film. The movie won five Oscars (out of a total of thirteen nominations including Best Picture, which it lost to *My Fair Lady*) including, Best Actress for Julie Andrews, Best Original Song for the Shermans' 'Chim Chim Cher-ee', Best Score, also for the Sherman brothers, Best Film Editing for Cotton Warburton, and Best Visual Effects for Peter Ellenshaw, Eustace Lycett and Hamilton Luske.

Despite the perception that the success of *Mary Poppins*

might allow Walt Disney to relax and even retire now he was in his sixties, he felt under even more pressure. 'I'm on the spot,' he said, recalling how he felt after the similar success of *Snow White* almost thirty years before. 'I have to keep trying to keep up to that same level. The way to do it is to not worry, not to get tense, not to think "I've got to beat *Mary Poppins*". The way to do it is just to go off and get interested in some little thing, some little idea that interests me, some little idea that looks like fun . . .' Despite his advancing years, Walt had no intention of spending his final days sitting in a rocking chair being nostalgic about the past – he still had hundreds of new projects he was keen to get going on.

During the making of *Mary Poppins*, Walt had also been involved in developing a new art school. The Chouinard Art Institute, founded in 1921, had fallen on difficult times. Its founder, Nelbert Chouinard – whose staff had helped train many of the Disney animators in the studio's earlier days – was in her seventies and an embezzler had caused great financial problems. In the mid-1950s Walt had sponsored two foundation scholarships and helped to finance the school, recalling the days when he considered art education to be a vital requirement among his animators. He'd joined the board in 1956 and had been given an honorary Doctor of Fine Arts degree by the school.

As the 1960s began, Walt brought in Economics Research Associates to establish the viability of the continuation of the institute, resulting in a merger with the similarly troubled Los Angeles Conservatory of Music (founded in 1883). The resulting body was the California Institute of the Arts, known as CalArts, a private university focusing on the visual and performing arts. Walt and Roy donated thirty-eight acres of the Disney Golden Oak Ranch in Placerita Canyon, north of the San Fernando Valley, which had been bought partly as a location for filming, including *Toby Tyler* (1960) – the school would relocate to its present campus in Valencia in 1971. The project was boosted by a presentation made during the premiere of *Mary Poppins*, and was seen by Walt as an 'interdisciplinary school for the arts'. He said: 'I like the idea of a workshop, with students able to drop in and learn all kinds of arts. A kid might start out in art, and end up a talented musician. A school should develop the best in its students.' The Disney connection with CalArts would continue long after the studio founder's 1966 death, and many who passed through the school in the 1970s would make significant contributions to the Disney studio in the future.

Of *Mary Poppins*, writer and film historian Leonard Maltin had written: 'If he had made no other film in his lifetime, *Mary Poppins* would earn Walt Disney the gratitude of the world. As it happens, it was instead the pinnacle of an already fantastic career.'

There were to be many more live-action Disney movies throughout the remaining years of the 1960s, but few of them had the same ambition as *Mary Poppins*, nor the same amount of attention and input from Walt himself – in fact, most were forgettable fare. *Emil and the Detectives* (1964) was an indifferent version of the Erich Kästner novel with no notable stars, while Tommy Kirk continued to appear in a series of light comedies such as the long-planned Disney version of *Babes in Toyland* (1961), *Moon Pilot* (1962) and *The Monkey's Uncle* (1965). Dean Jones headlined such undistinguished fare as *That Darn Cat!* (1965, remade in 1997, again with Jones), *The Ugly Dachshund* (1966), *Blackbeard's Ghost* (1968) and *Snowball Express* (1972).

Jones's biggest success was in the Herbie series that followed the adventures of a sentient Volkswagen Beetle car – perhaps Disney's best late 1960s movies. *The Love Bug* (1968) was the final live-action Disney film into which Walt had any direct input, to which Jones attributed the film's huge success. The idea had originated with Jones for a serious movie about America's first sports car, but Walt had countered with the suggestion of adapting Gordon Buford's 1961 novel *Car, Boy,*

Girl into a humorous caper film. Jones played Herbie's driver Jim Douglas, and the movie followed their adventures in racing and romance. The movie was the third-highest grossing film in the US of 1968, taking over $51 million at the box office. The anthropomorphic car became a star, and a sequel – *Herbie Rides Again* (1974) – was the first of four theatrical follow-ups (the others were *Herbie Goes to Monte Carlo*, 1977; *Herbie Goes Bananas*, 1980; and *Herbie: Fully Loaded*, 2005, starring Lindsay Lohan). Herbie – one of the last Disney characters to have benefitted from the personal touch of Walt – has also made several television appearances (including a short-lived series in 1982, featuring Jones) and remains a popular Disney character today.

Disney's last child star of the 1960s was Kurt Russell, one of the few who would go on to enjoy a successful adult career (he signed a ten-year contract with Disney). He first appeared in *The Computer Wore Tennis Shoes* (1969), a film made for under $1 million that grossed nearly six times that much on first release. *Variety* noted the movie's 'amusing premise', in which a non-academic student is 'boosted' when computer memory banks are transferred to him as the result of an electrical accident. 'Above average family entertainment,' was *Variety*'s verdict. The film shared the Medfield College setting of *The Absent-Minded Professor* series, and spawned two sequels of its own, *Now You See Him, Now You Don't* (1972) and *The Strongest Man in the World* (1975), both starring Russell as upgraded 'human computer' Dexter Reilly (spelt 'Riley' in the later films). Russell also appeared in other Disney productions, such as *Follow Me, Boys!* (1966), *The Barefoot Executive* (1971) and *Charley and the Angel* (1973). The original film was remade in 1995 as a TV movie starring Kirk Cameron in the Russell role.

Walt Disney had obtained the film rights to A. A. Milne's Winnie the Pooh books and characters such as Tigger, Piglet, Eeyore, Kanga and Roo in 1961 from Milne's widow, although the stories themselves dated back to the 1920s when Walt was just starting out in animation. The first film was intended to be feature length and was directed by Wolfgang Reitherman, with the art style based upon the books' distinctive illustrations by E. H. Shepard. The film would acknowledge the source material by featuring the books as an intrinsic part of the narrative (a device often used in earlier Disney films like *Snow White* and *Pinocchio*). Sebastian Cabot was recruited to narrate, with Sterling Holloway voicing Winnie the Pooh. Reitherman's then nine-year-old son voiced Christopher Robin (with an accent that was controversial for British viewers).

Anxiety over the Britishness of the story and style, and the need to stick to the Shepard look, saw the first film fall short of a feature-length running time. A non-Milne character of a gopher was introduced to appeal to American audiences, replacing Piglet. The British *Daily Mail* attacked the decision: 'It appears that in the Very Unenchanted Forest of film commerce, a gopher is worth more than a Piglet!' Shepard himself called the idea 'a complete travesty', while London's *Evening News* film critic Felix Baxter ran a campaign opposed to the change. Piglet was introduced in the second film, alongside Tigger (voiced by Paul Winchell), who became almost as popular as Pooh.

Winnie the Pooh and the Honey Tree (1966, twenty-six minutes) was the first of the three shorts, later collected along with *Winnie the Pooh and the Blustery Day* (1968, twenty-five minutes) and *Winnie the Pooh and Tigger Too!* (1974, twenty-five minutes) as the feature film *The Many Adventures of Winnie the Pooh* in 1977. A fourth film, *Winnie the Pooh and a Day for Eeyore* (twenty-five minutes) followed in 1983, and Pooh and his friends became a part of the growing Disney empire of appealing family characters (later to include Woody and Buzz Lightyear from Pixar, Jim Henson's Muppets, the Marvel comic book superheroes, and the 'galaxy far, far away' of *Star Wars*). Further Pooh adventures would follow as the company continued to grow following Walt's death, with a live-action television series in the 1980s and an animated television show running from 1988 to 1991. *The Tigger Movie* (acknowledging that character's popularity) followed in 2000, with two more spin-off movies in *Piglet's Big Movie* (2003) and *Pooh's Heffalump Movie* (2005). There were other series produced for a pre-school audience and a new animated musical theatrical feature film (the Disney company's fifty-first animated movie released in the US) in 2011, called simply *Winnie the Pooh*, with Monty Python's John Cleese as the narrator. The *Los Angeles Times* described that movie as 'a fitting tribute to one of the last century's most enduring children's tales'.

Since its inception, Walt Disney's pioneering theme park in Anaheim had continued to change and develop. In 1956, two more 'lands' – Storybook Land and Tom Sawyer Island, personally designed by Walt – had been added to the original four – Adventureland, Frontierland, Fantasyland and Tomorrowland – alongside Main Street USA. There was a major expansion in 1959 when over $7 million of additional attractions were installed, including a submarine ride based upon *20,000 Leagues Under the Sea*, America's first complete daily operating monorail system and the Matterhorn Mountain attraction.

Attendance at Disneyland had been climbing year on year from one million visitors in 1955 to five million by 1960, and 6.5 million by 1965, the park's tenth anniversary – the total number of visitors in that first decade was fifty-two million. By 1962, total investment in the park amounted to $42 million. The park continued to be developed with the addition of a mine cart ride through Nature's Wonderland in 1960, and an extension of the monorail system in 1961, connecting the park with the then non-Disney owned Disneyland Hotel. Holidayland had been added to Disneyland in 1957, but was closed in 1961 (and is now thought of as a 'lost land' by Disney park aficionados). New Orleans Square opened in 1966, eventually adding the immensely popular Haunted Mansion (opened in 1969) and

Pirates of the Caribbean ride (opened in 1967, and later a block-buster film series), and in 1970 a seventy-foot-high copy of the *Swiss Family Robinson* treehouse was installed.

Walt's fascination with automata led to the establishment of the Enchanted Tiki Room in June 1963. On a trip to New Orleans several years before, Walt had purchased an antique automaton of a bird in a cage. The 100-year-old toy fascinated the animator and businessman, and he started to search out ways to use the technology in his films and in Disneyland. The end result would be the lifelike robin perched on the finger of Mary Poppins in the 1964 movie.

In his travels through Europe, Walt had made a habit of collecting miniatures, whether of trains or animals, clockwork toys or miniature street scenes. Since the 1950s he'd been engaged in creating his own miniatures, a hands-on hobby distinct from his 'day job' of producing animated and live-action feature films at the studio. One effort followed the film *So Dear to My Heart* (1948), with Walt recreating Granny Kincaid's cabin in miniature. He hoped to produce a whole set of such nostalgic small-town scenes, enhanced with movement featuring human mini-figures that could sing and dance. The technology of the time didn't allow for this, but the vision never left Walt and he was to achieve much of it at full size in his theme parks. His first attempts – a dancing nine-inch man modelled after film taken of Buddy Ebsen in 1951, and a small barbershop quartet that moved and sang 'Sweet Adeline' (actually a recording that played) – laid the foundations for much more ambitious projects.

Nature's Wonderland in the Disneyland park had featured mechanical birds and animals since the beginning, but they were limited in their movements and realism. The idea for a Polynesian tearoom that became the Enchanted Tiki Room incorporated robotic chirping birds amid Polynesian folk art, ferns and bamboo. The birds were animated via a system Walt dubbed 'Audio-Animatronics', as an optical soundtrack tape controlled the birds' movements and voices (with songs by the

Sherman brothers), while the birds themselves were realized through animated electronics. The portmanteau word would eventually be shortened to just 'animatronics' and would come to cover any mechanical or electronic model of a human, monster or creature, most often used in movies, but also in lifelike displays in theme parks like Disneyland.

There were plans for Liberty Square, which would feature a Hall of Presidents to be populated with lifelike animatronic figures of the great American presidents. Eventually, only one figure was constructed – President Lincoln, who was first unveiled as part of Disney's contributions to the 1964 World's Fair in New York. Disney was involved in creating rides and displays for four of the World's Fair commercial shows: Pepsi's 'It's a Small World', a boat ride that later ended up in Disneyland, General Electric's 'Progressland', Ford's 'Magic Skyway' (later adapted as the 'PeopleMover' at Disneyland) and the Illinois Pavilion that originally featured the animatronic Lincoln. The president began sitting down, then stood up and delivered an oration compiled from various speeches recorded by actor Royal Dano. Initially robo-Lincoln failed to operate for the grand opening in front of a crowd of 200 invited dignitaries, but Walt's 'imagineers' had the problems fixed and, within a week, the animatronic president had become one of the major attractions of the fair, with a total of forty-six million visitors (91 per cent of the overall attendance) visiting the Disney exhibits. The Lincoln simulacrum inspired the 1972 Philip K. Dick novel *We Can Build You*, about artificial intelligence and consciousness. Another version of Lincoln was finally installed in Disneyland as part of the presentation 'Great Moments with Mr Lincoln', which has run continuously with some revisions (and technical updates) to the present day.

Although he'd often said there'd never be a second Disneyland, Walt had asked Economic Research Associates to search out a potential second theme-park location as early as 1958, but the plan wouldn't become public until 1965. Aware that the California park was only really easily accessible to half the nation, Walt hit on the idea of placing a second park on the other side of the country in Florida. A major advantage to 'Disneyland East', as the project was originally known, was the climate, which would allow for all-year-round operation. The new freeway planned for central Florida made Orlando the best choice for what eventually became Walt Disney World, which opened in 1971. The new park would later incorporate EPCOT – the Experimental Prototype Community of Tomorrow, a kind of futuristic city concept. 'It's like the city of tomorrow ought to be,' said Walt, 'a controlled community, a showcase for American industry and research, schools, cultural, and educational opportunities.'

Since turning sixty in 1961, Walt Disney had been as busy as he'd ever been maintaining his studio's output of animated and live-action family movies as well as supervising the successful expansion into fresh areas, such as television and theme parks. The company had grown from a storefront studio established by two mismatched brothers in the late 1920s to a major entertainment force in the 1960s, as well as making a personality of Walt himself as television's 'Uncle Walt'. Such was his reputation for showmanship, Walt had been 'Head of Pageantry' for the 1960 Winter Olympics in Squaw Valley, California, producing both the opening and closing ceremonies. His work for the 1964 New York World's Fair had fed into both Disneyland and the new, much more ambitious Florida resort that was under development at his death. In recognition of his innovative work in the field of film and beyond, in 1964 Walt Disney was presented with the Presidential Medal of Freedom, the highest civilian award in the United States, and in 1966 he headed up the Tournament of the Roses parade in Pasadena as Grand Marshal.

A heavy smoker since his First World War service in France, Walt had been careful never to be seen with a cigarette around children or in photographs to preserve his wholesome image (publicity images were regularly airbrushed to remove cigarettes). Tobacco had significantly affected his health, as had an old polo injury to his neck. Preparing for surgery on that injury, after years of irritation, Walt underwent X-rays on 2 November 1966 that revealed a tumour on his left lung. A biopsy five days later confirmed the tumour was malignant and had spread to encompass the entire lung. Walt's lung was partially removed on 11 November, but his life expectancy was said to be about six months to two years.

After spending time with his wife, Lillian, and his daughters in Palm Springs, Walt collapsed at home on 30 November and was taken to St Joseph's Hospital (across the street from his studio) by fire department personnel who'd revived him. The company issued a statement that he was in hospital for post-operative checks. The severity of his illness was kept secret, and Lillian continued to insist that he'd be home soon. However, Walt Disney died on 15 December 1966 at 9.30 a.m., just ten days after his sixty-fifth birthday, of acute circulatory collapse caused by lung cancer. His older brother Roy had been present when Walt died, and according to Walt's daughter Diane, had said something along the lines of 'Well, kid, this is the end, I guess.' At Roy's insistence, the then in-development second park, Disney World, was renamed Walt Disney World in his brother's honour.

Disneyland opened as usual on the day Walt died, but the American flag was lowered in Town Square that evening, accompanied by an announcer revealing: 'Walt Disney, the creator and chief architect of Disneyland, died today', followed by the Disneyland band playing his and the studio's unofficial theme song from *Pinocchio*, 'When You Wish Upon a Star'. Announcing the death of Walt Disney on the CBS *Evening News*, commentator Eric Sevareid said of Walt: 'He was an original. Not an American original, but an original, period. He was a happy accident, one of the happiest this century has experienced, and judging by the way it's been behaving in spite of all Disney tried to tell it about laughter, love, children, puppies, and sunrises, the century hardly deserved him. People are saying we'll never see his like again.'

There was a huge worldwide response to the unexpected death of Walt Disney. From editorial cartoons – many featuring his most famous cartoon characters, like Mickey Mouse and Donald Duck, in mourning – to considered editorial opinions, commentators struggled to understand the man whose films – short and long, animated and live-action – and television shows had done so much to define popular family entertainment in the middle of the twentieth century. In later years some would raise the spectre of Disney's 'dark side', but at the time of his death there was almost unanimous celebration of his achievements. Many in Hollywood, especially those who'd worked with him, expressed their sense of loss, both of Walt as a person and about the movies and television shows that it was expected he would have continued to produce in years to come. In preparing his company to cope with the future, Walt Disney had essentially worked himself to death. For Roy Disney, the loss was personal, but for many around him the question had to be: what now for the Disney studio?

Walt Disney was cremated following a small, private family funeral on 16 December 1966. His ashes were interred at the Forest Lawn Memorial Park in Glendale, California. In the years after Disney's death an urban legend spread claiming that his head had been cryogenically frozen. It was said that Walt had been interested in the subject of cryonics in his later years, and his frozen head had been placed in a vault deep beneath the Pirates of the Caribbean ride at Disneyland. According to the legend, Walt's frozen head would wait for advances in medical science to develop sufficiently so that he could be revived and brought back to life, perhaps with an animatronic body, like the one he'd created of President Lincoln. The story first saw print in the magazine *Ici Paris* in 1969. The first publicly announced real-world cryonic suspension took place just a month after Disney's death, perhaps feeding the bizarre rumour. Whether this story was the result of wishful thinking by a public who didn't want to let go of one of the twentieth century's greatest entertainers or was a posthumous prank by Disney animators (many pointed to the maverick Ward Kimball as being responsible) that got out of hand, it was an entertaining, silly story that Walt himself might have appreciated. His daughter, Diane, tackled the bizarre rumour head-on in 1972, declaring, 'There is absolutely no truth to the rumour that my father, Walt Disney, wished to be frozen. I doubt my father had ever heard of cryonics.'

PART THREE: THE DISNEY LEGACY

11

THE FAMILY FIRM

I only hope we don't lose sight of one thing – that it all started with a mouse.
Walt Disney, 'The Disneyland Story', *Disneyland*,
ABC, 27 October 1954

The immediate post-Walt period at the Disney studio was a time of transition. There were urgent questions needing answers from Roy Disney, Walt's older brother, when he took over as the Disney studio Chief Executive Officer and President. What was the future for the company, now that its creative driving force was gone? Would work on animated films continue or was live action to be the new focus? What about the theme parks, Disneyland and Walt Disney World – how would they be developed now that their originator was dead?

The final two films that Walt had been involved with were released shortly after his death: the animated *The Jungle Book* (1967) and the musical *The Happiest Millionaire* (1967), based on a stage play, with songs from the Sherman brothers and starring Fred MacMurray. *The Aristocats*, in 1970, would be the first Disney animated film to be completed following Walt's death, but even that had been prepared under his influence. It wouldn't be until 1973's *Robin Hood* that the Disney studio would release an animated film that could truly be considered to have been originated post-Walt. Even then, there were a host of projects Walt had been interested in or tried to develop at one stage or another that could provide an almost endless source of new material.

Roy's first job was to reassure the Disney employees, the shareholders, the creative community and even the public that with Walt Disney's passing, it would be very much business as usual at the Disney studio. 'We will continue to operate Walt Disney's company in the way he has established and guided it,' said Roy. 'All of the plans for the future that Walt had begun – new motion pictures, the expansion of Disneyland, television production, and our Florida project – will continue to move ahead. That is the way Walt wanted it to be.' Walt had been asked in a *National Geographic* magazine interview in 1963 what the future would be for the Disney company when he was no longer around. 'Every day I'm throwing more responsibility to other men,' he had said. 'Every day I'm trying to organize them more strongly.'

Walt's oldest daughter Diane had married football player Ron Miller in 1954. After a stint as a draftee in the US Army, Ron played for the LA Rams, before Walt brought him into the family firm, initially as a second unit director and then as a producer in the early 1960s. He had first worked on the *Zorro* television series before becoming involved in *Moon Pilot* (1962), *Son of Flubber* (1963) and other live-action Disney movies throughout the 1960s. After Walt's death he continued in a producer or executive producer role through the 1970s and 1980s, right up to the animated movie *The Black Cauldron* in 1985. It was Walt's intention to teach Ron the 'Disney way' of making family films, and he became a custodian of 'Walt's will' for many of the post-1966 movies. Walt's younger daughter Sharon had married architectural designer Robert Brown in

1959. Walt tried to get Brown to join the Disney organization, but he managed to stay independent until 1963 when he joined WED and got involved in working on the Disney theme parks.

While Roy was nominally in charge of the studio, he was not the creative personality Walt had been, and neither Ron Miller nor Robert Brown had been seriously considered as possible successors to Walt (and, in fact, Brown died just a year after his father-in-law). It was clear to Roy – who had been planning to retire as he was now seventy-three years old – that to secure the future of the company, no one individual could possibly fill Walt Disney's shoes. It was in many ways an unsatisfactory solution, but for the immediate future Roy decided that decisions on the creative business at the Disney studio should be taken by a committee made up of those who knew and had worked closely with Walt. Those people included Ron Miller; Roy's nephew Roy E. Disney; executive and board member Card Walker (who started in the company mailroom in 1938 and had risen through the ranks); producer Bill Anderson; producer and screenwriter Bill Walsh (who perhaps had most claim to be someone who could possibly take on Walt's role); narrator, screenwriter, director and producer Winston Hibler; screenwriter, director and producer Jim Algar; and production manager Harry Tytle. No animators or theme-park personnel were represented – it was down to director Wolfgang Reitherman to make sure Disney animation continued to prosper.

For many making creative decisions in the post-Walt world of Disney, the question they most asked themselves was: 'What would Walt do?' In some respects, this made sense – if they could somehow capture something of Walt's creativity and spirit, then the studio could continue to thrive. However, in another sense, trying to second guess their own creative instincts by referring back to the company founder might prevent new directions being taken and new areas exploited. For the remainder of the 1960s and much of the 1970s, the Disney studio would flounder between these two poles, neither capturing the elusive spirit of Walt Disney in the studio's output, nor being sufficiently fleet of foot to take advantage of new opportunities, creatively, commercially and technologically, that the 1970s offered.

As well as the studio, Roy had to steward Walt's commitment to CalArts – Walt's new art school, to which the younger Disney had left 45 per cent of his estate, amounting to around $28 million – as well as continuing to develop Walt's ultimately doomed attempt to establish a ski resort at Mineral King Springs (legal action, which began in 1969, scuppered that plan and saw the Mineral King area become part of Sequoia National Park). Roy's biggest challenges outside of the studio remained Walt Disney World and the embryonic plans for EPCOT.

In 1967, Roy managed to secure the legal go-ahead to create a special district in Orlando that would have city status. The building of roads and services began soon after, establishing what was dubbed internally at Disney the 'Entertainment Vacation Complex'. Learning lessons from mistakes made with Disneyland, where the company did not secure enough land to build hotels, so allowing other operators to move in and benefit from the park, the Florida venture was conceived as an all-in-one hotel-and-theme-park complex.

Within Walt Disney World was a new version of the original Disneyland idea, called the Magic Kingdom. This included reproductions of many of the West Coast Disneyland attractions, as well as some unique additions, such as Walt's once-planned Hall of the Presidents featuring all the country's presidents, not just Lincoln, and rides such as Space Mountain and a replica of the *Nautilus* from *20,000 Leagues Under the Sea*. The theme park was complemented by hotels, resorts and an area set aside as an island sanctuary for wildlife.

At a total cost of $400 million, Walt Disney World was completed and opened in October 1971. There was a more mixed reaction to the new park than there had been to Disneyland, just over fifteen years earlier. While many marvelled at the imagination and technology on display, the feeling began to grow and spread that the Disney parks were horrendous artificial environments designed to take money from visitors, rather than for any higher purpose. This post-Walt cynicism would soon spread to encompass the Disney studio's feature films and television programmes over time.

Despite these reservations, Walt Disney World was even more successful than the original Disneyland, attracting visitors from all over the US and Canada, and even Europe, with increasingly easy flight options opening up in the 1970s. Within its first year of operation, Walt Disney World saw over ten million people pass through the turnstiles (twice as many as had attended the original Disneyland during its first year) and grossed almost $140 million in revenue. The park has continued to grow and be refreshed regularly, and remains a top holiday destination to this day.

Roy Disney attended the opening of the California Institute of the Arts in November 1971 – a project he'd originally strongly opposed. Within a month, however, the now seventy-eight-year-old head of the Disney studio died, on 20 December 1971, of a cerebral haemorrhage. The obituaries for Roy Disney were almost as effusive as those for Walt five years earlier. His role as the financial brains behind the Disney success was widely reported, and he was acclaimed as the man who'd made Walt's dreams possible across a period of more than thirty years. Now, the studio both men had created and developed would pass into other hands. In some ways, their achievements would never be truly bettered, but – after an extended rough patch – the Disney studio would go on to become one of the biggest entertainment powerhouses of the modern world.

The three figures at the head of Disney following Roy's death were Donn Tatum (the first non-Disney family member to be president of the company), Card Walker and Walt's son-in-law Ron Miller. They'd all been trained by either Walt or Roy and had played key roles in the recent development of the studio.

However, other than Ron, they were not filmmakers, having come from the business and marketing side of the company. By the time of the studio's golden anniversary in 1973, it was becoming clear that without its founding brothers, the Disney studio was underachieving in both animated feature films and live-action production.

There was much hoopla surrounding the golden anniversary of the Walt Disney Company, but its major film of 1973 – the animated feature *Robin Hood* – although successful enough financially and critically, was clearly no *Snow White and the Seven Dwarfs*. The anniversary was celebrated with a television special, a 'Walt Disney Story' exhibit at both Disneyland and Walt Disney World, and a retrospective film festival in New York. There were several lucrative reissues across the year, with *Mary Poppins* grossing a further $9 million almost a decade after its original release. *Fantasia* and *The Sword in the Stone* also did well in re-release, while one of the more popular, relatively recent live-action films – *That Darn Cat!* – also enjoyed a second lease of life theatrically. However, billed as Disney's 'most ambitious cartoon feature ever', it was *Robin Hood* that was the centre of attention.

Ken Anderson had driven the film forward once his initial idea for an animated feature about Reynard the fox (a trickster figure from European folklore) found little favour within the studio. Instead, the British twelfth-century folk hero Robin Hood, who famously stole from the rich to give to the poor, was selected as the hero of the first Disney animated feature film developed since Walt's death. In a hangover from the Reynard project, Robin was portrayed as a fox voiced by Brian Bedford (a role originally offered to British singer and entertainer Tommy Steele), with the rest of the characters also portrayed as anthropomorphic animals. Larry Clemmons wrote the screenplay from Ken Anderson's story with Wolfgang Reitherman once again directing the animation. With so many old hands working on *Robin Hood* – including such experienced Disney animators as Milt Kahl, Ollie Johnston, Frank Thomas and

John Lounsbery – it was hoped that a traditional approach to both the story and the animation would maintain the spirit of Walt in the picture.

There was a curious sense of déjà vu about *Robin Hood*, and not only from the reappearance of well-used Disney voice actors such as Phil Harris (who voiced Little John, depicted as a bear). As the budget for the film was smaller than for many previous Disney animated features, the artists resorted to tracing artwork from previous movies, putting in characters from the new film over the older ones, so that the new movie's dance sequence was made up of scenes already used in *Snow White*, *The Jungle Book* and even the company's most recent animated movie, *The Aristocats*. Many critics spotted an uncanny resemblance to *The Jungle Book* in many of *Robin Hood*'s characters, with Harris's Little John being a strong echo of Baloo the Bear, and hypnotist Sir Hiss – the advisor to Peter Ustinov's Prince John, voiced by Terry-Thomas – recalling Sterling Holloway's snake Kaa.

These cost-cutting gambits and unimaginative repetitions of previous work ultimately did little to damage *Robin Hood*, which was largely well-regarded by critics. *Variety* noted the film's 'return to the phantasmagoria of sight gags of the type that helped make the late producer [Walt Disney] famous as a master of animation production'. In *New York Magazine*, critic Judith Crist saw *Robin Hood* as 'nicely tongue-in-cheek without insult to the intelligence of either child or adult', noting that the film 'has class – in the fine cast that gives both voice and personality to the characters, in the bright and brisk dialogue, in its overall concept'. Vincent Canby, writing in the *Miami News*, confined the appeal of the new Disney movie to younger film fans, commenting that it was 'a good deal of fun for toddlers whose minds have not yet shrivelled into orthodoxy', while being 'charmingly conventional' in animation and general approach. *Robin Hood* certainly made money and by 1974 had grossed in excess of $9 million at the North American box office.

By the mid-1970s, theatrically released animation in the US was taking new, ever more diverse forms. Former Warner Bros. stalwart Chuck Jones had produced an animated adaptation of Norton Juster's *The Phantom Tollbooth* (1970) for MGM, while Bill Melendez produced and directed *Snoopy, Come Home!* from Charles M. Schulz's popular 'Peanuts' comic strip (with music by Disney's frequent collaborators, the Sherman brothers). Director Hal Sutherland and producers Lou Scheimer and Norm Prescott (who'd later be better known for their television work through Filmation) released an animated version of Robert Louis Stevenson's *Treasure Island* (1972, already tackled as live action by Disney in 1950). William Hanna and Joseph Barbera delivered a theatrical feature cartoon of E. B. White's children's classic *Charlotte's Web* in 1973. All these were family-friendly productions, but in *Fritz the Cat* (1972) and *Heavy Traffic* (1973), Ralph Bakshi was innovating X-rated adult animation, while René Laloux's *Fantastic Planet* (*La Planète Sauvage*, 1973) was serious big-screen science fiction that just happened to be animated. Disney, in harking back to its past triumphs in *Robin Hood*, was failing to keep up with developments in the art form the studio had done so much to pioneer.

The sense of cost-cutting in animation at the studio was further reinforced when the next animated feature film, released four years after *Robin Hood*, turned out to be largely made up of three previously released shorts. *The Many Adventures of Winnie the Pooh* (1977) comprised 1966's *Winnie the Pooh and the Honey Tree*, 1968's *Winnie the Pooh and the Blustery Day* and 1974's *Winnie the Pooh and Tigger Too*. The film was wrapped up with a newly produced conclusion, drawn from the final chapter of *The House at Pooh Corner* and based upon Christopher Robin leaving the Hundred Acre Wood as he must begin school and so grow up and leave Pooh Bear behind.

That compilation movie wasn't 1977's only animated feature from Disney. Based on the books by Margery Sharp, *The Rescuers* (1977) followed the escapades of the Rescue Aid

Society, an organization entirely made up of mice located within the buildings of the United Nations in New York. Alerted by a message in a bottle, timid janitor Barnard (voiced by comedian Bob Newhart) and the refined Miss Bianca (Eva Gabor) set out to rescue Penny (Michelle Stacey), an orphan held captive by avaricious treasure-hunter Madame Medusa (Geraldine Page).

For the first time, the studio's older hands were combined with newer talents recruited from Walt's CalArts training programmes. Reitherman once more directed, with help from Lounsbery and *Peter Pan* animator Art Stevens (he'd started at the studio in 1940 as an in-betweener, filling in the drawings between the main animators' work). The film saw the last joint effort of several of Walt's 'nine old men', including Milt Kahl (who animated Madame Medusa), Ollie Johnston and Frank Thomas, who all retired afterwards – some would teach or guest lecture at CalArts. Among the newcomers who contributed towards *The Rescuers* was Don Bluth, who'd had a previous short stint at Disney in 1958 as an in-betweener on *Sleeping Beauty* before working at television animation house Filmation for several years. Bluth would be involved in the live-action/animation hybrid *Pete's Dragon* (1977), before leaving Disney in 1979 and setting up on his own. Other new character animators who started on *The Rescuers* and would be instrumental to the revival of the art form at Disney in the 1980s included Glen Keane, Ron Clements and Andy Gaskill.

Writing in the *New York Times*, critic Vincent Canby described *The Rescuers* as:

> efficiently short, charming, mildly scary in unimportant ways, and occasionally very funny. [It] moves quickly and without fuss from one episode to the next, never creating a sense of any real dread or fear. The animation is pretty in a conventional fashion that may be as fascinating to children as the bold innovations of someone like Ralph Bakshi are to the rest of us. [It is] a reminder of a kind of slickly cheerful, animated entertainment that has become all but extinct.

Re-released in December 1983, *The Rescuers* was accompanied by twenty-six-minute Dickens spoof *Mickey's Christmas Carol* (1983). This was the first theatrical appearance by Disney's signature character Mickey Mouse for almost three decades (it also featured Clarence Nash's final vocal performance as Donald Duck and cameos from many classic Disney characters). It was directed as a loving tribute to many of Walt's signature characters by Burny Mattinson (who would still be at the studio for its ninetieth anniversary in 2013). *The Rescuers* was later followed by a successful Australian-set sequel, *The Rescuers Down Under*, in 1990.

Much changed from the novels upon which its story was based (the script was the work of multiple Disney 'story men' including Larry Clemmons and Ken Anderson), *The Rescuers* was hugely successful, grossing over $16 million in North America, against a production cost of around $1.2 million, and broke the record for biggest opening for an animated movie, which it held until Don Bluth's *An American Tail* in 1986. Overseas takings of $31.2 million saw the studio's annual revenues for 1977 boosted by almost a third. It would be over a decade before Disney enjoyed the same success with an animated feature, with the release of *The Little Mermaid* in 1989 and the start of the 'Disney renaissance'.

During the 1970s, Disney produced two hybrid movies, part animation, part live action, in the style of *Mary Poppins* (1964): *Bedknobs and Broomsticks* (1971) and *Pete's Dragon* (1977).

Very much *Mary Poppins Part 2*, *Bedknobs and Broomsticks* was directed by Walt's regular live-action filmmaker Robert Stevenson, with a screenplay by Bill Walsh and Don DaGradi based upon Mary Norton's fantasy books about the exploits of apprentice witch Eglantine Price (played by Angela Lansbury). During the London Blitz, the Rawlings children are evacuated to the countryside and placed in her care. There, they enjoy a variety of magical adventures and help defeat a Nazi raiding party that lands on the coast.

Packed with songs and eccentric British characters, as well as an appearance by Mary *Poppins*'s David Tomlinson and distinctive songs from the Sherman brothers, the similarities to the Julie Andrews film were marked – indeed, some of the sequences and songs seen in *Bedknobs and Broomsticks* had been originally planned for *Mary Poppins*, and the rights to Norton's books had been secured by Walt as a back-up if negotiations with P. L. Travers did not pan out.

The animated sequences were directed by Disney veteran Ward Kimball, and as with *Robin Hood* they featured some distinctive echoes of *The Jungle Book*, especially in the soccer scene that once again includes a Baloo-like bear and a lion that resembles Shere Khan. While much of the character animation was done by Milt Kahl, Kimball became concerned enough about inconsistencies in the work of various personnel to send a memo to all animators and assistants outlining a new 'pre-touch up check point' under Charles Williams. Kimball noted: 'The co-operation of all concerned is solicited in order to insure [sic] the quality of imagery that is tantamount to the success of any Walt Disney picture.' Kimball's actions showed some anxiety about the animators' ability to maintain quality in the years after Walt's death. Floyd Norman, who'd returned to Disney to help out on *Bedknobs and Broomsticks*, noted: 'The one thing this motion picture really lacked was Walt Disney. The Disney studio without Walt was sadly never the same. The Old Maestro's touch was clearly missing.' Walt himself may have gone, but the old guard at Disney were determined to do everything that they could to protect his cinematic legacy.

Cut down from a lengthy two-and-a-half hour running time at the film's premiere, *Bedknobs and Broomsticks* was issued originally at a trim ninety minutes, losing a subplot starring Roddy McDowall and several Sherman brothers songs and most of the 'Portobello Road' dance number. A reconstructed, almost two-hour version was issued by Disney in 2001 to mark the movie's thirtieth anniversary. Vincent Canby in the *New York Times* wrote of the original 1971 version that it was:

a tricky, cheerful, aggressively friendly Walt Disney fantasy
for children who still find enchantment in pop-up books,
plush animals by Steiff and dreams of independent flight . . .
The loveliest part of the film – and the section that can renew
one's appreciation of the special gifts of the Disney people – is
the live-action-plus-cartoon sequence in Naboombu featuring, among other things, a tumultuous soccer game, played
by cartoon animals and refereed by Tomlinson, and an underwater ballet in which Miss Lansbury and Tomlinson dance in
slow-motion surrounded by cartoon fish. It recalls the best of
Disney, going all the way back to the first Silly Symphonies.

Others weren't as enthusiastic, with *Films Illustrated* calling
the movie 'a computer-built entertainment designed to pick up
where *Mary Poppins* wisely left off', and *The Times* critic John
Russell Taylor dismissing the film with the faint praise that
'the same as before is better than before'.

The film won the 1971 Oscar for Best Visual Effects, largely
due to the combined animated and live-action sequences.
Although the movie grossed a very respectable $17.5 mil-
lion in North America, production costs of over $20 million
meant that *Bedknobs and Broomsticks* was marked down as a
financial failure for Disney. Ironically, the only way in which
Bedknobs and Broomsticks couldn't emulate *Mary Poppins* was
at the box office.

The other hybrid movie from Disney in the 1970s was *Pete's
Dragon* (1977), the story of a boy (played in live action by Sean
Marshall) and his dragon friend Elliott (voiced by stand-up
comedian Charlie Callas). The unpublished short story by Seton
I. Miller and S. S. Field from which the film was ultimately
drawn had been purchased by Disney in the 1950s for use in
the *Disneyland* television series. Instead, the later film was
scripted by Malcolm Marmorstein, a writer for television's
spooky soap opera *Dark Shadows* (1966–71), and directed by
Don Chaffey, a British film and television director then best
known for large-scale adventure films such as *Jason and the
Argonauts* (1963) and Hammer's *One Million Years BC* (1966).

Ken Anderson created Elliott, modelled after Eastern interpretations of dragons, and made the character tubby and not always graceful in his movements, while Don Bluth took charge of animating the character. *Pete's Dragon* was the first animated Disney feature film not to feature the work of any of Walt's original 'nine old men'. Among the animators working on the project as an assistant to Bluth was Don Hahn, who would later go on to combine live action and animation more effectively in *Who Framed Roger Rabbit* (1988).

The biggest issue with this typically sentimental Disney production was the failure to composite the animated dragon in a convincingly realistic way with the live-action participants, who included Helen Reddy, Jim Dale and Mickey Rooney. Partly this was down to an attempt to innovate – something of which Walt would no doubt have approved, in theory – by using a sodium screen (an early form of the 'green screen' technique) to combine up to three images simultaneously, including a live-action foreground and background with an animated middle ground.

If the animation and live-action combination was unconvincing, it seems as though the characters were more so, at least according to *The Times*'s critic who regarded Elliott the dragon as 'gorgeous . . . in a ghastly sort of way'. *Variety* dubbed the movie 'an enchanting and humane fable which introduces a most lovable animal star (albeit an animated one) . . . Elliott, the dumpy, clumsy, 12-foot tall mumbling dragon with the ability to go instantly invisible and the misfortune of setting the idyllic Maine town of Passamaquoddy even further back into the early 20th century, is a triumph.' *Pete's Dragon* was never going to be one of Disney's finest films, but it was a favourite of many children growing up in the late 1970s, so much so that in 2013 the movie was announced as being 'reinvented' for a modern audience by David Lowry (director of crime drama *Ain't Them Bodies Saints*, 2013) and his writing partner Toby Halbrooks for Disney.

The following year, 1978, saw Mickey Mouse's fiftieth

anniversary, a milestone the studio couldn't let pass unmarked. Events – largely parades – in Disneyland and Walt Disney World celebrated the mouse's golden anniversary, as did a ninety-minute television special on NBC called *Mickey's 50th*. Fittingly, Mickey Mouse became the first animated character to be commemorated with a star on Hollywood Boulevard's Walk of Fame. Card Walker, by then Disney's Chief Executive Officer and President, made a forward-looking statement upon Mickey's significant birthday: 'Clearly, Mickey is 50 years young, with all the vigour he has always enjoyed . . . there could be no better present for him than the solid proof . . . that Walt Disney Productions continues to maintain the same kind of youthful vigour . . . We have already begun to raise the curtain on a new generation of Disney entertainment.'

Since 1970, the Disney studio had continued to produce many family-focused live-action films, usually two or three each year, and usually fairly forgettable, indistinguishable and unremarkable outside of the decade-spanning Herbie franchise. Amid dramatized 'animal adventure' films, such as 1970's *King of the Grizzlies* and 1972's *Chandar, the Black Leopard of Ceylon*, came lame family comedies like *Superdad* (1973, addressing the 'generation gap') and *The Apple Dumpling Gang* (1975, about Gold Rush orphans – it spawned an unnecessary sequel, *The Apple Dumpling Gang Rides Again*, in 1979).

However, there were some entertaining gems, such as the 1976 comedy double bill of *The Shaggy DA* and *Freaky Friday*. The first was a belated sequel to *The Shaggy Dog* (1959) that saw Dean Jones step into the Tommy Kirk role as a grown-up version of Wilby Daniels, the boy who could shape-shift into a dog. Now a district attorney, he gets caught up in a crime caper. A television movie, 1987's *The Return of the Shaggy Dog*, would tell a story placed chronologically between the two theatrical films – there were also remakes of the original, one for television in 1994 and another for the cinema in 2006, starring Tim Allen. Better was *Freaky Friday*, starring Jodie Foster as a teenage girl who is granted her wish to swap places with her mother for just one day. This enduring body-swap formula has since reoccurred in various films, notably *18 Again!* (1988) and *Vice Versa* (1988), as well as in the 1995 Disney made-for-television *Freaky Friday* remake and the 2003 feature film remake.

However, there were moves throughout the decade by Disney executives to diversify the studio's live-action offerings into areas such as science fiction and horror, and to bring in technical innovations – the kind of challenges Walt would have relished. *The Island at the Top of the World* (1974) was a Jules Verne-flavoured airship escapade that failed to replicate the impact of *20,000 Leagues Under the Sea*, but has been better regarded in recent years. Disney explored the vogue for horror movies (following *The Exorcist*, 1973, and *The Omen*, 1976) with the frightening but teen-friendly *The Watcher in the Woods* (1980). Based on a 1976 novel, this troubled production needed two directors to bring it to the screen: John Hough and Vincent McEveety. Following a poor initial reception, the film was withdrawn in 1980, re-edited with a revised ending and then re-released in 1981. Made in the UK, largely at Pinewood Studios, the film featured Bette Davis and was made under the direct supervision of Walt's son-in-law, Ron Miller. Despite the problems, *The Watcher in the Woods* marked an interesting possible new direction for the usually more family-friendly Disney.

It was, however, the studio's attempts at science fiction that were to cause the most problems. *Escape to Witch Mountain* (1975) featured a pair of telepathic siblings who go on the run from a millionaire called Bolt who is obsessed with the paranormal. The central characters are eventually revealed to be aliens who escaped to earth from their dying planet in the company of a larger community, but were the only ones to survive. The movie led to a sequel, 1978's *Return from Witch Mountain*, and a television remake in 1995 as well as a theatrical continuation in 2009's *Race to Witch Mountain*, starring Dwayne Johnson.

Other family-friendly 1970s science-fiction influenced comedy films from Disney included 1975's *One of Our Dinosaurs is Missing* (featuring Peter Ustinov) and 1978's *The Cat from Outer Space*, in which a visiting alien takes the form of a domestic earth feline. However, it was Disney's attempt to compete head-on with the newest kind of big-budget, blockbuster science-fiction films like George Lucas's *Star Wars* (1977) and Steven Spielberg's *Close Encounters of the Third Kind* (1977) that saw the studio come a cropper.

Although in development at the studio before the release of *Star Wars*, the success of the George Lucas film spurred Disney on in creating its ill-fated space epic, *The Black Hole* (1979). The project had been started under the title 'Space Station One', planned for release by Christmas 1978. It proved to be a bigger, more complex undertaking than initially envisioned, resulting in the release being put back one year and the title changing to 'Space Probe'. Insiders began promoting the film as Disney's 'most ambitious motion picture' yet, and with a huge budget (for the time, and this studio) of $17 million, the delayed film entered production in 1978 under the final title of *The Black Hole*.

Disney's light science-fiction comedies like *The Cat from Outer Space* (1978) and *Unidentified Flying Oddball* (1979) could not have prepared the studio for *The Black Hole*, and neither could the relatively serious science-fiction drama of *Escape to Witch Mountain* (1975). The studio had never produced a 'space picture', but in the wake of the Lucas and Spielberg productions outer-space science-fiction epics were the new 'big thing' in Hollywood and beyond, and Disney wanted a share of that lucrative box-office action.

Director Gary Nelson, whose previous work consisted of workmanlike instalments of episodic television series such as *Gunsmoke*, *Gilligan's Island* and *Happy Days*, as well as Disney's *Freaky Friday* (1976), was handed responsibility for *The Black Hole*. Working from a script by Gerry Day (a television writer) and Jeb Rosebrook, Nelson was able to attract an unusually 'starry' cast for Disney, including *Psycho*'s Anthony Perkins, Robert Foster, Maximilian Schell, Ernest Borgnine, Roddy McDowall (as the voice of robot VINCENT) and Yvette Mimieux.

The film followed the crew of the spaceship *Palomino* who discover a black hole, orbited by the long-lost craft the USS *Cygnus*. Exploring the apparently abandoned vessel, the *Palomino* crew find the ship's commander, Dr Hans Reinhardt (Maximilian Schell), and his sinister, angular red robot, Maximilian. Reinhardt plans to fly his ship directly into the black hole, resulting in a battle between the two ships' crews and robots. The film concludes in the style of *2001: A Space Odyssey* (1968), with a near-incomprehensible sequence in which a probe ship and several characters apparently journey through the black hole and seemingly emerge changed into a new universe.

Originally, Disney planned to employ George Lucas's special effects company Industrial Light & Magic (ILM) to work on *The Black Hole*, but they proved too expensive and couldn't take the work on to meet Disney's schedule. That meant the company developing its own in-house special effects camera systems and techniques, although they had the benefit of the expertise of four visual effects Oscar winners in Peter Ellenshaw, Eustace Lycett, Art Cruickshank and Danny Lee (even if their experience was on the like of *Mary Poppins* and *Bedknobs and Broomsticks*, rather than futuristic space epics).

In an indication of the turmoil behind the scenes, the writers, director and cast had no idea of how the film would end when production began. Several endings were considered, and multiple options were reportedly shot, before the *2001: A Space Odyssey*-like mystical conclusion was chosen. During production, Disney's PR department attempted to spin this confusion into a positive by claiming that the story was under wraps as it was 'top secret', in an attempt to create a buzz around the project. 'Nearly everything about this mammoth undertaking,' ran an early Disney PR release, 'sets it apart from our efforts of the past'. One thing that definitely set *The Black Hole* apart was its PG rating, the first in the Walt Disney company's long history. *The Black Hole* prefigured Disney's later move into adult-focused filmmaking with subsidiaries like Touchstone Pictures (from 1984) and Hollywood Pictures (1989–2007).

The cost of *The Black Hole* eventually came in at $20 million, making it the most expensive Disney production to that date (even before a further $6 million was spent on promotion and advertising). Disney branded the film as 'A Journey that Begins Where Everything Ends' in the hope of catching science-fiction fans who were well served in 1979 with the first of the *Star Trek* movies, *Star Trek: The Motion Picture* (another space film with a mystical subtext), and the space horror of Ridley Scott's groundbreaking *Alien* (a film that spawned a franchise still going strong). Although regarded as a failure (certainly when compared to *Star Wars* and its 1980 sequel, *The Empire Strikes Back*), *The Black Hole* nonetheless grossed $36 million at the North American box office, making a small profit for the studio.

Critics had great fun at Disney's expense, ridiculing the company's move into space epics. Several admitted to being baffled by the film's oddball conclusion, which appeared to be a stylized depiction of heaven and hell (or like something out of *Fantasia*), with one wag noting he'd not have been surprised if the *Palomino* crew had discovered Mickey Mouse on the other side of the black hole. The film's blatant similarities to *Star Wars* (especially in the bickering comedy robots, VINCENT and 'Old Bob') were highlighted, although in the late 1970s and early 1980s Disney was not alone in the field of *Star Wars* rip-offs (among the most accomplished were Roger Corman's *Battle Beyond the Stars*, 1980, and the Italian movie *Starcrash*, 1978).

The *Chicago Sun-Times* critic Roger Ebert complained that Disney's *The Black Hole* 'takes us all the way to the rim of space only to bog us down in a talky melodrama whipped up out of mad scientists and haunted houses'. The ship, he notes, is 'inhabited by a crew that's borrowed from gothic thrillers and *Star Wars*. There are strange, hooded, zombie-like figures that mope about all over the place. At the movie's end there is a sensational visual pay-off, but somehow it comes too late: the events leading up to it have been so trivial and cliché-ridden that the movie doesn't earn its climax.'

Variety dubbed *The Black Hole* 'sometimes talky but never dull', while Janet Maslin in the *New York Times* noted that 'The special effects are fancy, and the design even more so . . . Peter Ellenshaw borrows from painters like Chagall and Mondrian to achieve a decorative, dated modernism.' The result was two Oscar nominations, for Best Visual Effects and Best Cinematography. Although the movie failed in Disney's aims of capturing the *Star Wars* audience and appealing to a more adult audience, it did score a big win in one area. The soundtrack by James Bond composer John Barry was one of his best and has, in the minds of many fans, far surpassed the movie itself.

In the decade and more since Walt Disney's death and that of his brother Roy, the Disney studio had prospered more through its two theme parks than it had in the world of movies, animated or live-action. *Robin Hood* and *The Rescuers* had not been classics, although they both had their fans, while hybrids like *Bedknobs and Broomsticks* and *Pete's Dragon* appeared curiously old fashioned. The live-action films, despite brave and experimental forays into science fiction and horror, were doing little more than treading water. If the 1970s had been a decade of business as usual for the Disney studios, the 1980s would be a time of near continuous turmoil, but one that would end with an artistic renaissance in animation from the venerable studio.

12

DISNEY IN DECLINE

A person should set his goals as early as he can and devote all his energy and talent to getting there. With enough effort, he may achieve it. Or he may find something that is even more rewarding.

Walt Disney, quoted in *Walt Disney: Magician of the Movies* by Bob Thomas, 1966

The 1980s kicked off for the Disney studio with the fall-out from an exodus of disillusioned animators. A trio of the company's newest recruits called it quits in September 1979, walking out on the company and leaving the production of the animated feature film *The Fox and the Hound* (1981) in disarray. Don Bluth, Gary Goldman and John Pomeroy were quickly followed out the studio door by eleven other discontented Disney animators. The replacement of Disney's 'nine old men' with a batch of younger, cutting-edge animators was not off to a great start.

Begun in 1977, *The Fox and the Hound* – based on a novel by Daniel P. Mannix – was supposed to mark the official handover from the Disney old guard to a bright new generation of animators schooled (many at CalArts) by the studio's old hands in the ways of Walt. The movie, changed dramatically from the novel, follows the lives of two canines, the orphaned Tod whose mother is killed by a hunter, and his childhood best friend Copper. As they become older, however, their destinies drive them apart: Copper is a dog raised to hunt, and his prey is Tod, a fox.

The feature animation programme begun by the Disney studio in 1976 at CalArts was a formal effort to bring on board younger talent who could be shaped to produce animation the Disney way. Among those enrolled in the programme who would have a major impact on the future of Disney (and the wider Hollywood community) were Tim Burton, John Lasseter, John Musker, Ron Clements and Glen Keane. 'We all got into the business wanting to do *Pinocchio*,' animation director Tom Sito told *Variety*. 'We didn't want to do *Toot, Whistle, Plunk and Boom*, we wanted to get back to what we thought was the really cool stuff.'

At the beginning of the project, the old guard were firmly still in control. Wolfgang Reitherman was producing (with Ron Miller), while the story was adapted by old hands Larry Clemmons and Ted Berman and other traditional Disney 'story men'. Directing the individual sequences were Art Stevens (co-director of *The Rescuers*), Richard Rich (one of several Disney employees who'd started in the mailroom) and Ted Berman (who'd started at Disney in the 1940s, contributing towards *Bambi*, *Peter Pan*, *Mary Poppins*, *Lady and the Tramp*, *Alice in Wonderland*, *Bedknobs and Broomsticks* and *The Rescuers*). The main characters were designed by Frank Thomas and Ollie Johnston, their final work for Disney.

Don Bluth, who worked on the project alongside CalArts-sourced newcomers Henry Selick and Brad Bird, had become increasingly disenchanted with the direction of Disney animation. Bluth started as John Lounsbery's assistant on *Sleeping Beauty* in 1955, but left two years later to focus on other pursuits. He returned to the studio in 1971 and worked on *Robin Hood*, *Winnie the Pooh and Tigger Too* and *The Rescuers*, before directing the animation on *Pete's Dragon*. Increasingly, Bluth came to feel that the studio was not living up to the quality mantra in animation that Walt Disney had always insisted on. Corners were being cut, the quality of the work was in decline, the wrong subjects were being chosen for movies and he could see little chance of things changing. On his forty-sixth birthday in 1979, he left the studio, taking over two dozen others with him to set up on his own. The result was Don Bluth Productions, whose feature animation programme was kicked off by *The Secret of NIMH* (1982) and would later include such movies as *An American Tail* (1986, with Steven Spielberg producing) and *All Dogs Go to Heaven* (1989), as well as the groundbreaking animated arcade game *Dragon's Lair* (1983). His animators – who numbered up to 160 at one time – were all employed on a profit-sharing basis, and Bluth set out to recreate in exile the 'classic' animation style once pursued by Walt Disney.

The breakaway of the Bluth group caused major problems for Disney, and not only on the immediate production of *The Fox and the Hound*. The company had lost almost 20 per cent of its entire animation staff overnight, a major blow for the studio at a crucial time. There was no way the movie would be ready for the original Christmas 1980 release date, as teams of new animators had to be recruited, schooled in the Disney style and production restarted. As a result, *The Fox and the Hound* was delayed until summer 1981. What the studio failed to do was take note of the criticisms of Bluth and the others – it appeared that even the loss of such a significant group of animation talent was not enough to make the studio executives change direction. For a few more years, it would be business as usual, but even the mighty Disney studio could not resist the sea change in animation the 1980s would bring.

When it finally opened, *The Fox and the Hound* – featuring the voices of Mickey Rooney, Kurt Russell, Corey Feldman and Jeanette Nolan – was a financial success, taking just under $40 million at the North American box office. Critics perceived the darker tone of the source material in the finished film, with *Variety* noting that 'the darkish, subdued backgrounds probably represent the artistic highlight', while Richard Corliss in *Time* magazine called the film 'a movie that confronts the Dostoyevskian terrors of the heart'. Roger Ebert in the *Chicago Sun-Times* felt that:

> for all of its familiar qualities, this movie marks something of a departure for the Disney studio, and its movement is in an interesting direction. *The Fox and the Hound* is one of those relatively rare Disney animated features that contains a useful lesson for its younger audiences. It's not just cute animals and frightening adventures and a happy ending; it's also a rather thoughtful meditation on how society determines our behaviour.

The highlight of the animation was seen as Glen Keane's work in the climactic fight between Copper, Tod and an antagonistic bear. A direct-to-video prequel – *The Fox and the Hound 2* (2006) – filled in details of Tod and Copper's earlier years.

Card Walker's years at the top of Disney had not been successful, especially in the field of live-action production. His refusal to expand the studio's filmmaking to take in PG- and R-rated movies held it back and resulted in other studios producing films such as *Raiders of the Lost Ark* (1981) and *E.T. the Extra-Terrestrial* (1982), both films that director Steven Spielberg wanted to do originally with Disney. Walker retired in 1983, but continued to serve as a consultant and board member throughout the 1980s and 1990s. Ron Miller took over as the head of Disney, but the studio was already in a near-fatal tailspin.

Worse was to come in 1985, with *The Black Cauldron*, dubbed by the entertainment press 'the movie that almost killed Disney animation'. Don Bluth had begun working on the movie's earliest stages before his departure, but the film continued what he'd identified as a downward spiral of quality in modern Disney animation. Bizarrely, cost-cutting was not the problem here, as at an official figure of $25 million (later estimates put the actual production cost at nearer $40 million), *The Black Cauldron* was the most expensive animated film made by the studio to that point.

Disney had been under new management since 1984 with the arrival of Michael Eisner and Jeffrey Katzenberg and the return of Roy E. Disney (see Chapter 14), but the idea of adapting Lloyd Alexander's *The Chronicles of Prydain* books had been around for at least a decade. Both the film and the novels draw upon Welsh folklore, which featured legends of various magic cauldrons. The film depicts the Horned King (voiced by John Hurt) and his quest for the cauldron, and Taran (Grant Bardsley) and Princess Eilonwy (Susan Sheridan), who set out to thwart his attempt to rule the world with an army of the undead. *The Fox and the Hound* directors Ted Berman and Richard Rich handled the new film, with many hands contributing to the final story. John Huston was recruited as the narrator of the movie.

Under a shake-up of company responsibility, Walt's nephew Roy E. Disney was now in charge of the studio's animated projects. He was a champion of *The Black Cauldron*, even though the project had no connection with either his father, Roy, or his uncle's time at the studio (it was optioned around 1971). The younger Roy had resigned from Disney back in 1977, believing that 'creatively the company was not going anywhere interesting. It was very stifling', a charge echoed by the animators who departed two years later during the making of *The Fox and the Hound*. However, he retained a seat on the board, which became very important in 1984 when he spearheaded a campaign that resulted in Walt's son-in-law Ron Miller being ousted from the company and replaced by Eisner, Katzenberg and Frank Wells (see chapter 14). Roy was able to fend off hostile takeover bids from other companies, investors and hedge

funds determined to asset strip the organization. Having
won the battle, Roy returned to the studio full time as Vice-
Chairman of the Board of Directors and took responsibility
for the studio's animation output.

During the time *The Black Cauldron* was in development,
early concept art by Mel Shaw was used in brochures, flyers
and advertisements to recruit new trainee animators to the
CalArts course sponsored by Disney. *The Black Cauldron*
promised a return to the animation style of 1937's *Snow White
and the Seven Dwarfs*, a lush form of cartooning that had long
been absent from the studio's output. Part of what had driven
Roy E. Disney, Bluth and the other animators away from the
Disney studio years earlier was Ron Miller's continual delaying of *The Black Cauldron* on the grounds that the company's
animators were not yet up to the task (oddly, echoing Walt's
concerns about his animators' ability with human figures for
Snow White, and realistic animals for *Bambi*, in the 1930s). It
was the threat of Bluth's *The Secret of NIMH* stealing Disney's
thunder that finally saw *The Black Cauldron* enter production.

Part of the intention of the new project, according to producer Joe Hale, was to attract older teenagers, who had
outgrown the comedy fare the studio had produced towards
the end of the 1970s, back to Disney's films. 'Disney had its
ups and downs with its teenage crowds,' recalled Hale. 'No
respectable teenager would be caught dead watching a Disney
movie. We were making movies like *That Darn Cat!*, *The Cat
from Outer Space*, and *Robin Hood*, and movies had changed
a tremendous amount . . . [They were] getting more into the
adult type films, and the Disney type movies just weren't going
over.'

The tabletop fantasy role-playing game Dungeons and
Dragons had broken out of hobby shops and into the mainstream in the early 1980s, while sophisticated adventure fare
like *Raiders of the Lost Ark* (1981) did not shy away from
darker material (such as the depiction of the melting face of a
Nazi villain at the movie's climax). *The Black Cauldron* was

Disney's first PG-rated animated feature. The material certainly seemed tailor-made for animation, but the studio was still in transition during production so there was no single forceful creative director to keep everything on track. One of the animators giving *The Black Cauldron* a darker edge was a young Tim Burton, who would shortly also leave Disney in frustration after making the macabre short *Vincent* (1982) and the original version of *Frankenweenie* (1984) for the company. 'We parted ways at that point,' recalled Burton of his Disney exit. '[They] have a nice revolving door policy! It was a "Thank you very much, but you go your way and we'll go our way" kind of thing.'

The Black Cauldron was notable for another reason – it was the first animated film to make use of computer-generated imagery (CGI), a technique that would in time come to dominate movies, whether live-action or animated. Among the animators driven away from Disney during production was John Lasseter, a champion of the use of computers in animation, who'd later return during Pixar's takeover of Disney (see Chapter 15). The depiction of bubbles in water, a sequence featuring a boat and even – in some scenes – the magical cauldron itself were all realized in animation with the help of computers, marking the beginnings of digital animation at Disney. Many of the problems that remained with the released version of *The Black Cauldron* came about because the film was caught up in the regime change that took place at the studio. Katzenberg, as an incoming executive, attempted to re-edit the movie, delaying the release from Christmas 1984 to summer 1985 (repeating almost exactly the delay that had befallen the release of *The Fox and the Hound* five years before).

Altogether, twelve minutes were chopped from the film, including material featuring the 'cauldron born', the Horned King's army of the undead (which featured some of Burton's work), as Disney executives feared it might be too frightening, even in a PG-rated movie. Some of the missing material, among other unseen sequences, would be reconstructed and featured on a twenty-fifth anniversary DVD release in 2010. Having cost over $40 million to produce, *The Black Cauldron* rivalled such notorious live-action failures as 1963's *Cleopatra* and 1980's *Heaven's Gate* as examples of very expensive films that then went on to spectacularly fail at the box office. *The Black Cauldron* grossed only $21 million at the North American box office (which made the film a flop even against the Disney-claimed production cost of $25 million). The film played better in Europe and elsewhere outside the US, but nowhere near well enough to avoid the company taking a huge loss on the project.

Critics were not kind either, especially as early hype had suggested *The Black Cauldron* would be a new *Snow White*. *Time Out* magazine saw the movie as 'a major disappointment', missing 'the charm, characterization and sheer good humour' of earlier Disney films. *Variety* said that 'By any hard measure, the $25 million animated *Cauldron* is not very original. The characters, though cute and cuddly and sweet and mean and ugly and simply awful, don't really have much to do that would remain of interest to any but the youngest minds.' Meanwhile the *New York Times* noted:

This is the 25th full-length animated feature from Walt Disney studios, and professionally put together as it is, many of the ingredients may seem programmed to those who have seen some of the others . . . Quite possibly, the little kids for whom the people at Disney work will find the sort of magic in *The Black Cauldron* that their parents found in *Sleeping Beauty* and (can it be so long ago?) that their grandparents found in *Snow White and the Seven Dwarfs*.

For his part, Roger Ebert of the *Chicago Sun-Times* went against the critical flow and admitted to having enjoyed the movie: '*The Black Cauldron* is a rip-roaring tale of swords and sorcery, evil and revenge, magic and pluck and luck . . . a new Disney animated film in the old tradition. By the end I was remembering, with something of a shock of nostalgia, the strength and utter storytelling conviction of the early Disney animators. *The Black Cauldron* is a return to the tradition.' That, perhaps, was a step too far, but many years after its release – in common with some of the earlier Disney movies deemed to have 'failed' at first – *The Black Cauldron* does have its fans and it would appear to better fit the cinematic landscape of the twenty-first century than it did that of the mid-1980s. Unlike *The Black Hole*, *The Black Cauldron* didn't make any lists of potential Disney modern remakes, although some felt that in the wake of Peter Jackson's *The Lord of the Rings* and *The Hobbit* that Pixar could make something of the original source material, for which Disney still held the rights.

Just as the new regime at Disney was struggling to solve the problems of animation throughout the 1980s, there were mixed messages about what exactly Disney's live-action movies should be and who they should be aimed at. Following *The Black Hole*, Disney had released a second PG-rated movie in the comedy *Midnight Madness* (1980) – in which teams of college students search for clues in a scavenger hunt – further indicative of the studio's overdue move into making films for adults. Although it flopped, it was followed by another PG movie, *The Devil and Max Devlin* (1981), in which Bill Cosby's Devil tempts Elliott Gould's Devlin. This move into PG-rated material would eventually lead to Ron Miller establishing Touchstone Pictures in 1984 as a 'boutique label' for the release of mainstream adult movies produced by Disney – although it would be Eisner and Katzenberg who'd reap the rewards.

More mature fantasy themes were explored in *The Watcher in the Woods* (1980) and *Dragonslayer* (1981), which were attempts on the part of Disney to compete with the fantasy-driven adventure films of Steven Spielberg and George Lucas such as *Raiders of the Lost Ark* (1981). *Dragonslayer*, in particular, had the potential to be a hit, featuring a fantastically well-realized dragon (created by Lucas's ILM, it wiped out memories of the poorly animated *Pete's Dragon*) and a Dark Ages-set coming-of-age drama built around Peter MacNicol's trainee wizard, Galen. Co-produced with Paramount (who'd released *Raiders of the Lost Ark*, which beat *Dragonslayer* to the Best Visual Effects Oscar), *Dragonslayer* confused audiences expecting a more family-friendly film from Disney, rather than director Matthew Robbins's more mature and thoughtful take on the topic. Walt's late-in-life obsession with animatronics was at last rewarded with the depiction of the forty-foot dragon Vermithrax, with a ninety-foot wingspan, realized with sixteen different models – some miniatures – each specializing in a different physical movement.

Fantasy also featured in both *Something Wicked this Way Comes* (1983), a dark, nostalgic drama about a weird carnival based on a Ray Bradbury novel (Bradbury and Walt Disney became friends late in the filmmaker's life and bonded over Walt's plans for Disneyland and EPCOT) and *Return to Oz* (1985), a belated and much darker sequel to *The Wizard of Oz* that drew upon L. Frank Baum's lesser known Oz stories.

Disney's big breakthrough in the 1980s – although few realized it at the time – was *Tron* (1982), an innovative film from director Steven Lisberger that would give rise to a long-running franchise. A thriller largely set in the interior fantasy world of a mainframe computer, *Tron* combined live-action material with some early computer animation (particularly in the 'Light Cycles' sequences) to create a unique cinematic environment. Not a hit at the time, *Tron* became a cult film over the years, inspiring the almost-thirty-years-later sequel *Tron: Legacy* (2010, directed by *Tron* fan Joseph Kosinski) and an animated television series on Disney XD. While the story in *Tron* may have been swamped by the film's style, the film had a huge cultural impact over a long period of time. It was *Tron* that ex-Disney employee John Lasseter pointed to as being the proof that computers could be used successfully in animation, eventually leading to the establishment of Pixar and the *Toy Story* blockbuster movies. 'Without *Tron*, there'd be no *Toy Story*,' said Lasseter.

Families were served by comedies *Popeye* (1980, starring Robin Williams and a co-production with Paramount Pictures), *Condorman* (1981, starring Michael Crawford) and 1986's *The Flight of the Navigator*, which saw a young videogames enthusiast recruited to fight in an alien space war. The formula finally came together in *Honey, I Shrunk the Kids* (1989), which starred Rick Moranis as an *Absent-Minded Professor*/ Fred MacMurray-style scientist who accidentally miniaturizes his family, resulting in them battling for survival amid giant creatures in their own backyard. The successful film spawned two similar sequels in *Honey, I Blew Up the Kid* (1992) and *Honey, We Shrunk Ourselves* (1997), and a television series that ran between 1997 and 2000.

Of course, Disney couldn't escape its identification with animal movies and continued to produce them throughout the decade, ranging from *Never Cry Wolf* (1983), about a biologist studying the caribou, to the Depression-set *The Journey of Natty Gann* (1985), about a twelve-year-old girl searching for her father in the company of a wild wolf. There was also *Benji the Hunted* (1987), about a domestic dog surviving in the wilderness; Australian horse-drama *Return to Snowy River* (1988); and *Cheetah* (1989), a Kenyan-set drama that featured the phrase 'Hakuna Matata' eventually popularized by *The Lion King* (1994).

The immediate result of the debacle over *The Black Cauldron* was for Disney's animators to be exiled from the main Disney studio lot. From the end of 1984, they were housed in an industrial warehouse in Air Way, Glendale, previously used as the home of the Imagineers who masterminded the attractions at Disney's theme parks, a workplace many of the animators came to resent (they'd return to Burbank in 1995, in the middle of the 'Disney renaissance'). The innovative home of animation now had no place within the studio grounds for its own creative teams. Apart from anything else, the blow to their morale was huge, and it was little wonder that the work they produced over the next few years was generally sub-par. However, there was a change on the horizon.

No one argues that the animation produced by the Disney studio in the mid-to-late 1980s came anywhere near the material that made the studio's name back in the 1930s and 1940s. However, the work was enough to keep the remaining animators together and working until conditions were such that the entire division could reclaim something of its past glory towards the end of the decade. Disney now had a top-flight competitor in Don Bluth Productions, with many of the animators there benefitting from the training they'd had at the Disney studio and CalArts. Disney's next animated films aimed to compete with the likes of *The Secret of NIMH* (in fact, Disney and Bluth productions would go head to head at the box office in 1986 and 1988), but the cost-cutting that had driven Bluth and company away from the studio continued, so the quality of the animation suffered. The one ray of light was that a Disney – in the shape of Walt's nephew, Roy – was still in charge of the company's animation.

The Great Mouse Detective (1986) was based upon the *Basil of Baker Street* series of novels by children's author Eve Titus, published between 1958 and 1982, telling of the adventures of a mouse inspired by Sherlock Holmes. The production was given the go-ahead on the understanding that it would be made cheaply and fast: the whole thing took only a year to make and that was after the budget was cut by more than half, reduced from $24 million to just $10 million by Michael Eisner, a man in charge of a studio famous for its cartoons but who did not understand animation. The pressure was on for those who remained with Disney to prove that they could produce distinctive animation in a cost-effective way. A film based upon a mouse version of Sherlock Holmes seemed tailor-made to begin a proper artistic comeback.

Burnett 'Burny' Mattinson, who produced and co-directed *The Great Mouse Detective*, had started work at Disney in 1953 as a storyboarder and in-betweener. It was Disney's *Pinocchio* that had encouraged Mattinson to seek a career in animation, and the first film to which he contributed was 1955's *Lady and the Tramp*. He assisted on *Sleeping Beauty* and *One Hundred and One Dalmations*, then worked as Eric Larson's assistant on *The Sword in the Stone*, *Mary Poppins*, *The Jungle Book* and *The Aristocats*, before graduating to become a character animator on *Robin Hood* and the Winnie the Pooh shorts. He produced and directed 1983's *Mickey's Christmas Carol* – a tribute to almost the entire history of Disney animation in one short – which was seen as a test run for the job of supervising a feature-length project. He'd resisted the lure of joining the renegade Bluth faction, and was rewarded with the job of bringing *The Great Mouse Detective* to the screen – after all, he had years of Disney experience to draw upon. It was Roy E. Disney who put Mattinson in place, following the departure of Ron Miller.

Working with Mattinson was a group of younger animators who would go on to make significant contributions to the Disney renaissance that began in the late 1980s. Dave Michener, and the team of Ron Clements and John Musker – who'd been taken off *The Black Cauldron* to start work on this movie – co-directed with Disney veteran Mattinson. Animation was handled by Mark Henn, Glen Keane, Robert Minkoff and Hendel Butoy – and they were set the task of re-establishing the quality values of Disney's famed 'nine old men', to whom they all looked as mentors and examples of what Disney animation could be.

Some technological innovations helped in keeping the costs down, including video pencil tests, and the use of newly cheaper computers to aid 'layout' (the camera angles and positioning of characters in the frame) broke new ground. Computer-generated imagery – still in its infancy and used on *The Black Cauldron* – was brought to bear on a chase scene that took place in the interior of Big Ben. The clock gears in the scene were created on a computer as 3D wire-frame images. '[Theme park Imagineer Ted] Gielow and I were locked in the same room for months, slaving over a hot computer,' recalled character-animator Phil Nibbelink. For him, the contribution of computers had to be filtered through artists to succeed:

> [The Big Ben] sequence represents a hybrid of what the computer does best and what animators do best. A computer is adept at creating precise, geometric shapes or inanimate objects. If an animator tries to draw a gear or a car or a house, it's imperfect. What we do best is fluid organic character animation. By combining the two, we get the best of both worlds and hopefully create a more believable and exciting world for the characters to interact in. We completely rebuilt the inside of the Big Ben clock with the help of our new computers. With traditional animation, we would have been forced to stick with a single moving trajectory, from left to right. The computer, however, has given us the possibility to perform a rotary motion around the clock mechanism.

With such small, halting steps began the digital revolution in animation and filmmaking.

The title of the source novel *Basil of Baker Street* was dropped by Eisner as he worried it was too 'English' (Walt had the same concerns about the Arthurian legend as the basis for *The Sword in the Stone*), and the rather more straightforwardly descriptive *The Great Mouse Detective* was used instead. This provoked a satirical memo circulated by some mischievous Disney animators renaming some of the studio's classics in a similar style. The results included such reductive titles as 'Seven Little Men Help a Girl' for *Snow White and the Seven Dwarfs*, 'Colour and Music' for *Fantasia*, 'The Little Deer Who Grew Up' for *Bambi*, and 'Puppies Taken Away' for *One Hundred and One Dalmatians*.

Within one month of release the 'quick and cheap' *The Great Mouse Detective* had grossed almost $18.5 million at the North American box office, against a final production budget of $14 million, proving that Disney animation could still be profitable (the film's lifetime North American theatrical gross, including

a 1992 reissue, reached $38.6 million). If the critics were any-
thing to go by, the company had also successfully managed to
produce a decent film, even with a simplification of the animation. *Variety* said, 'The animation is rich, the characters
memorable and the story equally as entertaining for adults as
for children', which was no doubt music to Disney executives'
ears. The Moriarty of the film, Professor Ratigan (voiced by
Vincent Price), caught the attention of *Time Out*'s critic: 'it is
the villain who steals the heart and one is rooting for in the
breathtaking showdown high up in the cogs and ratchets of
Big Ben'.

In 1975, Disneyland was twenty years old and the Florida
park, Walt Disney World (which had been open for four years),
finally completed its first phase of development. Finally, Walt's
late-in-life dream of establishing a 'city of the future' in the
form of EPCOT – Experimental Prototype Community of
the Future – would go ahead, but not quite as Walt had originally envisaged it. Walt agreed to the development of the
second theme park in Florida in the hope that he could build
EPCOT on the back of it – he didn't really want to develop
another theme park, as he'd done that and was always looking for the next new challenge, rather than simply repeating
himself. In the late 1960s, for Walt that challenge was EPCOT,
a truly futuristic city to be lived and worked in by up to 30,000
people. 'It's like the city of tomorrow ought to be,' Walt said
to the *Chicago Tribune* of his concept. 'It will be a controlled
community, a showcase for American industry and research,
schools, cultural, and educational opportunities.'

    EPCOT, as seen by the company's mid-1970s heads Card
Walker and Donn Tatum, would not be a real, lived-in city,
but merely a theme-park-style model for cities of the future,
'a community system oriented to the communication of new
ideas, rather than serving the day-to-day needs of a limited
number of permanent residents', according to Walker. The
'EPCOT Future World Theme Center' would feature pavilions

dedicated to advances in 'community', 'science and technology' and 'communications and the arts'. At the same time, plans were put in place for the first overseas Disneyland park in Tokyo, Japan, which eventually opened in 1983, and was later followed by Euro Disney/Disneyland Paris in 1992.

The success of Disneyland and Walt Disney World had been part of the problem for Disney as a movie studio. With more income coming from the theme parks than from the actual movies, those against continuing new production – especially in animated form – had solid ammunition to back up their arguments. There were endless amounts of material in the Disney studio's back catalogue to provide a source for new rides and attractions for years to come, although many within the company also believed that new film production was the only way both to generate new ideas, stories and characters as well as theme park rides, and to keep Disney alive and vital.

The Disney company would come some way to establishing Walt's idyllic town envisioned in EPCOT with Celebration, Florida (near Walt Disney World), a 5,000-acre town opened in 1996. Designed in the style of an early-twentieth-century American town, Celebration fulfilled the part of Walt's vision for the future of city planning and community life in EPCOT (which was itself eventually established in 1982 as a 'permanent World's Fair'), while also harking back to his early life in Marceline.

Co-director and animator John Musker said, 'The foundations of Disney are likeable characters in a good story and *The Great Mouse Detective* has that', but the animation division was still having to prove itself. After all, the 1985 re-release of *One Hundred and One Dalmatians* had brought in $33 million (making it the most successful Disney re-release to that point) with minimal prints and marketing outlay. With numbers like that, asked Eisner, why does the Disney studio ever have to produce any new animated films? Four months after the debut of *The Great Mouse Detective*, the Don Bluth studio released *An American Tail*, another story about mice heroes, which quickly became the highest grossing non-Disney animated movie released to that time, taking $22 million more than Disney's film at the North American box office. Internal doubts and ever stronger external competition threatened the very existence of any future for Disney's animated movies.

Bizarrely, it was Eisner's partner Jeffrey Katzenberg who came to the rescue. After his ill-fated tampering with *The Black Cauldron*, Katzenberg had put himself through a crash course in animation history and had found a new appreciation for his new company's classic animated output. There was one good reason why the studio should continue to develop brand new animated feature films: 'The fact is, for this company [Disney], animation has a value that is way beyond the specific profits that you measure for a film itself,' said Katzenberg in 1986. 'We create new characters, these characters will come to life in our theme parks and in our merchandising, and have a longevity and a value in many other aspects of this corporation that are totally unique.'

The Disney studio had purchased the rights to Thomas M. Disch's children's tale *The Brave Little Toaster* not long after its 1982 publication, recognizing in the story of the adventures of anthropomorphic kitchen appliances source material that would fit the Disney animation style. The title caught the attention of two of Disney's newest recruits, John Lasseter and Joe Ranft. Lasseter was keen to develop the use of computer animation in movies further than the minimal efforts thus far. Inspired by Disney's *Tron* (1981) – after seeing the 'Light Cycle' sequence as a work-in-progress by Jerry Rees and Bill Kroyer – he suggested the studio should tackle *The Brave Little Toaster* as its first attempt at a fully animated film using computer animation rather than hand-drawn cels.

Knowing the technology was not quite ready, he and Glen Keane developed the idea of working with almost 3D computer-generated backgrounds, with traditionally animated characters in front of them as a compromise. The pair developed a short test reel based on Maurice Sendak's *Where the Wild Things Are* (later filmed by Spike Jonze in 2009). Keane was put to work on *The Great Mouse Detective*, so Lasseter continued his development work with Thomas L. Wilhite. However, as the development of computer animation was short-sightedly thought to be of no benefit to Disney, Lasseter was fired for spending too much time working on it. 'At the time,' said Lasseter, 'Disney was only interested in computers if it could make what they were doing cheaper and faster. I said, "Look at the advancement in the art form. Look at the beauty of it." But, they just weren't interested.' Lasseter found a new role in the computer graphics division of Lucasfilm, which would later become Pixar.

The Brave Little Toaster was made, but in Taiwan (where animation was cheaper) and in traditional 2D animation. The film was a co-production between Hyperion Pictures (established by Wilhite and fellow ex-Disney staffer Willard Carroll) and the Kushner-Locke Company, and released through Disney (so it doesn't count as a purely Disney animated movie). Two direct-to-video sequels followed: *The Brave Little Toaster Goes to Mars* (1998) and *The Brave Little Toaster to the Rescue* (1999).

While developments in computer animation were taking place elsewhere, Disney's twenty-seventh animated theatrical release would be the traditionally produced *Oliver & Company* (1988). Inspired by Charles Dickens's *Oliver Twist*, the movie followed the exploits of Fagin's gang of thieves (who are dogs) and orphan Oliver (who's a cat) on the streets of contemporary New York. Originally suggested as a sequel to *The Rescuers*, the movie was instead spun off on its own. Despite the Disney studio's seeming antipathy to computer animation, *Oliver & Company* was to make the most extensive use of the technique in any of the studio's films to date. Skyscrapers and vehicles, including taxis and trains, were created on computers, as was the climatic chase sequence that takes place in New York's subway system. As a result, somewhat belatedly,

Disney finally established a dedicated computer graphics department in-house. It was to be too little, far too late ...

Oliver & Company would be the first of Disney's animated films to be fully produced under the Eisner–Katzenberg regime, and it showed a more modern commercial approach. Real-world product placement came to Disney's animated feature films for the first time, with the inclusion of real product brand names such as Coca-Cola, *USA Today* and Sony. There was also a new approach to music. The new executives had pushed for *The Great Mouse Detective* to include more contemporary musical numbers, but the film was too far advanced for much to be done. For *Oliver & Company* modern American singers such as Billy Joel and Huey Lewis were hired to sing the songs, alongside older musical star Bette Midler. It was a sign of things to come.

The movie was released on 18 November 1988, the exact same day that Don Bluth's *The Land Before Time* opened. By the end of 1988, *Oliver & Company* had taken $40 million at the North American box office, with a final figure of $49.4 million for its full theatrical run. *The Land Before Time* enjoyed a bigger opening weekend (its $7.5 million record-breaking take beating *Oliver & Company*'s $4 million and embarrassing the Disney studio), but over the longer term Bluth's move fell behind, taking a total of just $42 million overall. Nonetheless, the opening weekend defeat caused a panic at Disney. Once again the question was asked: why bother with new animation? There was a new mood at the studio, however, following the reactions to both *The Great Mouse Detective* and *Oliver & Company*. The one sure-fire way to defeat the competition at the box office was for the Disney studio to raise its game in animation. The Disney animation renaissance was just around the corner.

13

DISNEY RESURGENT

*Around here, we don't look backwards for very long. We
keep moving forward, opening up new doors and doing new
things, because we're curious . . . and curiosity keeps leading
us down new paths.*

Walt Disney, quoted in the end credits of
Meet the Robinsons, 2007

The period from 1989 to the turn of the century has become
known to animation fans and Hollywood as the 'Disney
renaissance', a time when the studio found its mojo once more
and began producing top-notch animated feature films, as well
as finding a way to produce adult-oriented mainstream movies
through Disney studio sub-labels such as Touchstone Pictures
and the purchase of independent studio Miramax (see Chapter
14).

The groundwork was laid with 1988's *Who Framed Roger
Rabbit*, a film that harkened back to the likes of *Mary Poppins*
and *Bedknobs and Broomsticks* in successfully combining
live action and animation, but in a tale that at its core was

concerned with cartoons, their history and their impact on popular culture.

Disney had first purchased the rights to Gary K. Wolf's novel *Who Censored Roger Rabbit?* in 1981, seeing in its unique world – in which famous comic-strip characters of the past and human beings mixed together – the basis for an innovative movie. Although Ron Miller had initiated the project, and despite hiring screenwriters Peter S. Seaman and Jeffrey Price to adapt the book and considering an approach from later *Back to the Future* (1985) director Robert Zemeckis to helm the film, it had remained in development until after his replacement by Michael Eisner and Jeffrey Katzenberg. They revived the plans for the movie in 1985, approaching Steven Spielberg's Amblin company to co-produce the film with Disney. The budget was set at $50 million, a sum Disney didn't want to shoulder alone in case the film should fail at the box office. The budget was reduced to just under $30 million, which would still make *Who Framed Roger Rabbit* the most expensive animated movie to that point.

Katzenberg saw the new hybrid movie as a way of keeping the animation department at Disney active until new fully animated projects could be devised. The film was an unusual deal for Disney, but given the dire straits the company's legacy of animation was now in, the new management were willing to take the risk. They handed creative control over to Spielberg as producer and Zemeckis as director, convinced that their prestige would make the film work. Disney retained the merchandising rights, in the hope that if the film fell short of blockbuster status at the box office, they could recoup some of the cost through associated toys and products.

It was Spielberg's Hollywood clout that proved instrumental in convincing many other studios and copyright holders to give permission for their classic animated characters to be used in *Who Framed Roger Rabbit*. Among those agreeing were Warner Bros., for the Looney Tunes and Merrie Melodies characters; Fleischer Studios, for Betty Boop; Felix the Cat Productions,

who'd long ago assumed control of the Pat Sullivan charac-
ter; and Walter Lantz Productions (now part of Universal), for
Woody Woodpecker. The results included a scene in which
Donald Duck appeared alongside Warner Bros.'s Daffy Duck
as duelling pianists and Disney's signature character Mickey
Mouse shared a scene with Warner Bros.'s key character Bugs
Bunny. Despite these deals the rights to use several classic
characters – Caspar the Friendly Ghost, Tom and Jerry and
Popeye – could not be obtained in time for the movie.

Supervising the animated portions of the film was Richard
Williams, a Canadian animator who handled the London-
based production unit. Born in Toronto, Williams had been a
long-term London resident, best known for his then uncom-
pleted animated film of *The Thief and the Cobbler* (begun in
1964 and finally finished in 1993). He'd animated various cartoon title sequences for live-action movies, including *What's
New Pussycat?* (1965), *The Charge of the Light Brigade* (1968)
and two of the later Pink Panther movies. Zemeckis insisted
on hiring Williams, whom he dubbed 'the best animator in the
world', even though Williams preferred to remain in London
rather than relocating to Los Angeles. This worried the Disney
executives, as a major part of the production would be out of
their daily supervision and control.

Zemeckis also wanted to move his camera during scenes featuring animated characters, which complicated things for the
animators in combining the live-action and animated characters in motion, one of several issues that saw the cost of the film
balloon during production to $40 million. Eisner threatened to
close the project down, but was persuaded that the bad blood
that would create with Spielberg would cause even more problems down the line. Zemeckis got his way and used VistaVision
cameras, with rubber figures of the animated characters used
in live-action scenes with leading actors like Bob Hoskins (as
Toontown detective Eddie Valiant) and Christopher Lloyd
(as the literal cartoon villain Judge Doom) as reference for the
animators. Kathleen Turner provided the sultry voice for the

slinky animated femme fatale, Jessica Rabbit. Comic actor
Charles Fleischer (no relation to the Betty Boop Fleischers)
was the voice of the main animated protagonist, Roger Rabbit.

While seven months was spent on shooting the live-action
portion of the film at Elstree Studios in the UK, it took over
a year for the animation to be completed. This was before
widespread use of computer animation and sophisticated compositing techniques, so all the animation was done by hand in
the traditional cel animation method, then combined using
optical compositing with the real-world footage. Keeping
the animated characters in proportion and moving alongside
the live-action people was the main challenge for Williams's
unit. Special effects house Industrial Light & Magic in the US
combined the animated and live-action sequences together, as
seamlessly as was possible in 1988.

The finished film ran into trouble with the Disney executives when both Eisner and, more especially given his family
heritage, Roy E. Disney complained to Zemeckis and Spielberg
about what they perceived as risqué material in the movie, especially in the relationship between Roger and Jessica, resulting
in the film being released as a Touchstone movie rather than
a family-friendly Disney movie. Despite that concern, *Who
Framed Roger Rabbit* became the second highest grossing
movie of 1988, just behind the Tom Cruise vehicle *Rain Man*.
After an $11 million opening weekend, the film went on to
gross a total of $156 million in North America and $173 million internationally, for a global box office take of $329 million.

Almost as important, especially to Disney's new management, was the critical reaction. Roger Ebert in the *Chicago
Sun-Times* hailed the movie as 'not only great entertainment
but a breakthrough in craftsmanship . . . the first film to convincingly combine real actors and animated cartoon characters
in the same space in the same time and make it look real'. The
Washington Post suggested, 'If you don't like *Who Framed
Roger Rabbit*, have your pulse checked . . . Robert Zemeckis'
multi-dimensional free-for-all, where cartoon figures bump,

quip and cavort with flesh-and-blood characters, is not only a technical tour de force, it crackles with entertainment.' For animation fans, the movie was packed with in-jokes and references to old characters, many of whom appeared in blink-and-you'll-miss-them background cameos.

Three theatrically released Roger Rabbit animated shorts followed (the first shorts from Disney since Goofy's *Freeway Troubles* back in 1965); rides and attractions soon appeared at Disney parks worldwide; and the film won four Academy Awards, including a special Oscar for Richard Williams and his animation team. Plans for a sequel which would have put Roger and co. in the Army, actively pursued by Eisner for many years, have yet to come to fruition. However, more than *The Great Mouse Detective* or *Oliver & Company*, it was *Who Framed Roger Rabbit* that paved the way for the great Disney animation renaissance.

Like many of the animated features produced by Walt Disney himself during the 1940s and 1950s, the idea for an animated feature film of the Hans Christian Andersen tale *The Little Mermaid* (1989) dated back decades. It came closest to production during the era of Disney's post-war 'package' films when consideration was given to producing an anthology film of several Hans Christian Andersen stories, including this and *The Snow Queen* (eventually made by Disney as *Frozen* in 2013).

After *The Great Mouse Detective*, director Ron Clements revived the idea of *The Little Mermaid*, keen to make a film that featured underwater sequences while also harking back to the classic fairy-tale days of Disney animation. When Katzenberg was soliciting suggestions as to how Disney might follow *Oliver & Company*, Clements submitted a two-page memo that was essentially a story treatment for a modern version of *The Little Mermaid*. Having studied Walt's approach to animation, Katzenberg recognized the key elements in Clements' proposal, as well as the ideal framework to produce a full-on Broadway-style musical film, something he'd been keen on for a while and had only partially achieved with his use of contemporary music in *Oliver & Company*.

Lyricist Howard Ashman and composer Alan Menken had contributed a song to *Oliver & Company*, so they were tasked with developing the musical structure of *The Little Mermaid*. They set the musical style of the film – which told the story of a mermaid who longs to be human – and composed the film's entire score. With the composers installed at Disney's Glendale animation facility, the interaction between them and the animators recalled that of the Sherman brothers and Disney's animators back in the 1960s. A secondary animation facility was established within the newest Disney-MGM Studios theme park at Walt Disney World in Orlando, Florida, during the production of *The Little Mermaid*.

In a return to another practice from the past instigated by Walt, live actors were filmed playing the parts of mermaid Ariel and other characters. Broadway actress Jodi Benson provided the speaking and singing voice for Ariel, but Groundlings improvisation group member Sherri Lynn Stoner physically acted out much of the film (with many scenes involving the use of a pool), providing the animators with a physical reference for the mermaid's key scenes. Again, as in Walt's day, animators were charged with handling specific characters, with Glen Keane and Mark Henn handling Ariel, while other newcomers to the Disney fold took on other main characters.

The underwater settings of much of *The Little Mermaid* provided the Disney animators with their biggest special animated-effects challenge since *Fantasia* in 1940 (much of the 'bubble' work was sub-contracted to an animation house based in China). Even the by-then ancient original Disney multiplane camera was taken out of mothballs for use on *The Little Mermaid*, but was discovered to be in such poor condition it could not be utilized. An alternative multiplane set-up at an outside animation house had to be co-opted instead.

From story, through music, to animation style, it was clear that all the effort put into *The Little Mermaid* was an attempt to return the studio to something approaching the techniques used by Walt Disney to produce the classics from the 1930s and the 1940s, the kind of production approach that the Disney studio had long ago abandoned. As well as a new beginning for Disney animation, *The Little Mermaid* would be a final outing for traditional animation techniques such as hand-painted cels (a computer assisted form of cel colouring was in use from *Rescuers Down Under* onwards). CGI was used in several scenes, including the climactic sea battle and shots of Eric and Ariel in a carriage. CGI would come to dominate animation in the future, although Disney would attempt to maintain the production of traditional hand-animated feature films for many years.

Perceived by some Disney executives as a 'girls' film' that would inevitably make less money than *Oliver & Company*, *The Little Mermaid* surprised them by taking $84 million at the North American box office, 64 per cent up on the previous release. A 1997 reissue and overseas earnings just under $100 million pushed the film's overall theatrical gross to date to $211 million – pretty big numbers for a mere 'girl's film'. Critical reaction was also positive, with Roger Ebert concluding that *The Little Mermaid* was 'a jolly and inventive animated fantasy – a movie that's so creative and so much fun it deserves comparison with the best Disney work of the past'. The *New York Times* called the movie 'the best animated Disney film in at least 30 years', while *Variety* said, 'Borrowing liberally from the studio's classics, *The Little Mermaid* may represent Disney's best animated feature since the underrated *Sleeping Beauty* in 1959. That should come as no surprise to admirers of *The Great Mouse Detective*, writer-director collaborators John Musker and Ron Clements' 1986 animation feature that helped salvage the art form at the studio after it had nearly sunk into *The Black Cauldron*.'

Variety was right to connect the new film to *Sleeping Beauty* as that had been the last time that Disney had simply adapted a well-known fairy tale for an animated movie. In that and so

many other ways, *The Little Mermaid* was a return to form
for the struggling studio that set the road map for the way
ahead for the now resurgent Disney animation. The studio's
'cartoons' were no longer seen by Eisner and other sceptical
executives as a waste of time and money – there was huge profit
to be made in animation, especially Disney-branded animation,
but only if it was done right. Overshadowed by the profitable
theme parks, television productions and cheap, fast and now
successful live-action movies, animation was finally seen as a
potential profit centre in its own right once more. New animators would be recruited and new outposts established not
only in Florida, but also in Montreuil in France, where Walt
and Salvador Dalí's long unfinished collaboration on *Destino*
would finally be completed.

Almost as important as the animation were the music and
songs of *The Little Mermaid*. The 'Broadway show' approach
of Katzenberg, combined with the talents of Ashman and
Menken (who as producers had a huge effect on the story and
depiction of key characters), not only echoed the classic award-
winning songs from the Disney animated feature films of the
past, but also offered a way of updating such seemingly 'old-
fashioned' concepts for 1990s audiences. *The Little Mermaid*
was the first fully animated Disney movie since *The Rescuers*
in 1977 to be Oscar-nominated, with two wins for Best Score
and Best Song, 'Under the Sea', sung by Samuel E. Wright. The
soundtrack album would go on to win two awards at the 1991
Grammys – it sold over two million copies, far more than any
animated film soundtrack had ever done before.

The Little Mermaid set the template for the next few projects.
For the next decade, Disney feature animation would be met
with the kind of acclaim the studio had not seen since the
early days of Walt's original successes. A canny combination
of easily recognizable stories, combined with the knock-out
musical combination of Ashman and Menken, produced a
series of blockbuster animated films that both looked back to

Disney's classic days and ahead to a future that envisaged new stories and new technology to tell them with.

With *The Little Mermaid* trouncing ex-Disney animator Don Bluth's *All Dogs Go to Heaven* (which opened the same weekend) at the box office, and surpassing Bluth's *The Land Before Time*'s record for the highest-grossing opening weekend for an animated feature film, it was obvious that Disney was back on top. Creatively, the studio was clearly heading in the right direction, if only the executives could settle on the next story to tell for the landmark thirtieth Disney animated feature film ...

With Roy E. Disney keeping the animators busy working on his sequel/remake of *Fantasia* (partially funded from the fifteen million copies of the original *Fantasia* sold on VHS), which he'd envisaged since 1974, Katzenberg was working with animation designer Richard Purdum (*A Christmas Carol*, 1971) – who'd been recommended by *Who Framed Roger Rabbit* animation supervisor Richard Williams – on producing a non-musical version of the French fairy tale Beauty and the Beast. Walt had explored this fable as a possible follow up to *Snow White and the Seven Dwarfs*, and again in the 1950s, but his writers had failed to crack the story.

To propel the project forward, and in order to fulfil Eisner's money-making requirement that the Disney studio now release a new animated feature every year to eighteen months, Katzenberg pulled Ashman (who'd recently discovered he was dying from complications of AIDS) and Menken from developing their pet project – a musical version of 'Aladdin and the Magic Lamp' from the *Arabian Nights* stories – and put them to work on *Beauty and the Beast*. The film was now to be reconfigured as another Broadway-style musical extravaganza, a decision that saw Purdum leave the project, taking his British animation team with him. Eisner, who had doubts about the viability of Ashman's *Aladdin* movie due to its Middle East setting, wanted *Beauty and the Beast* to begin with a screenplay, rather than it being developed from storyboards in the long-traditional Disney manner. Linda Woolverton, a writer for television animation, was hired to draft the initial screenplay.

Another unusual feature of this project was that a pair of directors was brought in from outside Disney to handle the film. *The Little Mermaid*'s Ron Clements and John Musker had been offered the job, but claimed they were burnt out and couldn't start a new movie so quickly (they remained involved as producers). Instead, Eisner and Katzenberg turned to Kirk Wise and Gary Trousdale (he'd been an in-betweener on *The Black Cauldron*), who'd never handled an animated feature before but had directed the animated segments of a short film, *Cranium Command*, for the Disney EPCOT park attraction.

Following the style of Rogers and Hammerstein, Ashman and Menken further entwined their music and songs with the narrative of Beauty (voiced by Paige O'Hara) and the Beast (Robby Benson), making for a satisfying whole. With the news of Ashman's precarious health, pre-production of the film was relocated to New York, where he lived. Scriptwriter Woolverton and producer Don Hahn reworked the screenplay with the directors and the songwriters, lightening the original dark fairy tale, adding more than just the two characters the original featured, and opening up the world of the movie. Storyboards were developed – with animators and illustrators put up in a New York hotel for the duration – for each of the film's major set-piece sequences, including the scenes in which the castle kitchen's inanimate objects come to life – an idea from Ashman. More than before, CGI would be strikingly used, particularly in developing the film's detailed backgrounds and in the celebrated ballroom sequence.

By early 1990, *Beauty and the Beast* was deep into production, but Howard Ashman would never see the finished version. He died in mid-March 1991, aged forty, shortly after a rough cut of the film had been assembled and screened, and after he and Menken had nearly completed their work on the score of the next Disney animated feature, *Aladdin* (1992). Eight months later, in November 1991, *Beauty and the Beast* opened to great acclaim and huge box office, but Jeffrey Katzenberg worried that with the death of lyricist Ashman, Disney had lost one of the major contributors towards the studio's animation renaissance.

For many critics, the new Disney movie was on a par with some undoubted classics of the past, such as *Snow White* and *Pinocchio*. Roger Ebert, of the *Chicago Sun-Times*, wrote, '*Beauty and the Beast* reaches back to an older and healthier Hollywood tradition in which the best writers, musicians and filmmakers are gathered for a project on the assumption that a family audience deserves great entertainment, too.' Janet Maslin, in the *New York Times*, noted that 'Disney has done something no one has done before: combine the latest computer animation techniques with the best of Broadway.'

In North America, *Beauty and the Beast* grossed almost $146 million, with international box office bringing the film's total take to almost $425 million. It was the third most successful film of 1991 (of any type), behind *Terminator 2: Judgment Day* and *Robin Hood: Prince of Thieves*, becoming the most successful Disney film to that point and the first animated film to cross the $100 million barrier at the North American box office. Later IMAX and 3D re-releases added further to the film's lifetime takings.

Disney undertook a subtle Oscar campaign for *Beauty and the Beast*, screening the film with unfinished animation to critics, press and other Academy voters as well as playing it as a 'work in progress' at the New York Film Festival and an 'out of competition' screening at the 1992 Cannes Film Festival. The effort paid off, with not only an Oscar win for Ashman and Menken's song 'Beauty and the Beast' and for Best Score, but nominations for two other songs from the film and – in a first for the Academy – an Oscar nomination as Best Picture (it was beaten by thriller *The Silence of the Lambs*). The film did scoop the Best Motion Picture – Musical or Comedy at the Golden Globes. *Beauty and the Beast* would go on to become the first of a long line of Disney movies adapted as theatrical stage productions, including *The Lion King*, *Tarzan* and *Aladdin*.

As a result of the success of both *The Little Mermaid* and *Beauty and the Beast*, a brand new animation building was constructed on the Disney lot, so returning the long-suffering animators from their exile in the soulless warehouse in Glendale back to the Burbank studio. While Disney would release several run-of-the-mill productions – *Duck Tails The Movie* (1990), *The Rescuers Down Under* (1990), *A Goofy Movie* (1995), *Doug's 1st Movie* (1999) and *James and the Giant Peach* (1996) among them – the focus in theatrical animation now was in continuing the success of the Broadway-musical approach with both *Aladdin* (1992) and *The Lion King* (1994).

Clements and Musker returned to directing for *Aladdin*, with a screenplay developed from Howard Ashman's original 1988 story outline, developed by the directors and the writing team of Ted Elliott and Terry Rossio (who would go on to script the *Pirates of the Caribbean* blockbuster movies). Lyricist Tim Rice was paired with Menken to complete the songs unfinished at the time of Ashman's death. In an usual move, Disney cast star comedian Robin Williams as the genie, building the character around his typical stand-up comedy performance and animating it in Williams's likeness, even allowing him to ad-lib during recording sessions. As a result, Williams dominated the movie at the expense of Scott Weinger's Aladdin and Jonathan Freeman's villain, Jafar.

Released in November 1992, *Aladdin* beat *Beauty and the Beast*'s record-breaking box office, taking over $504 million worldwide. The use of adult humour (largely from Williams) combined with the fast pace of the film made the movie equally attractive to adults and the more traditional Disney audience of children. For Chuck Jones, former Warner Bros. Looney Tunes animator, Disney's *Aladdin* was 'the funniest feature ever made'. Peter Travers, writing in *Rolling Stone* magazine, commented that *Aladdin* was 'so funny and scrappy you don't need to drag a kid along . . . Besides the in jokes, the animation and the score supply enough glorious entertainment to hold even brats and cynics in thrall.' In the *Washington Post*, Desson Howe felt that 'There's a good chance you're going to enjoy *Aladdin* more than the children . . . Disney's 31st animated feature carries young and old on its magic carpet. A cornucopia of visual splendor, it's also a comic riot, thanks to Robin Williams.' Two Oscars – both for the music – were only the first of many awards for *Aladdin*, including five Grammys.

Largely due to the success of the animation division, the Disney company posted a record $1.4 billion profit for 1992, numbers that Walt Disney could never have dreamed of in the post-war years of financial struggle. Eisner ensured that much of the credit went to Roy E. Disney, whose father's centenary was in June 1993. 'Roy understood,' Eisner noted in a letter to Disney shareholders that year, 'that animation, done right, was magic. And magic is the essence of Disney.' The faces at the top may have changed, but the creators of Disney's animated movies had finally rediscovered the spirit of Walt and Roy in their work.

The following film, *The Lion King*, was based upon Katzenberg's idea of a coming-of-age story featuring animals (like Walt's *Bambi*), but with an African setting. In a run of well-crafted, critically acclaimed and deeply affecting animated movies from Disney in the 1990s, *The Lion King* would top them all. A starry voice cast brought life to this Shakespearean tale of a lion cub growing to kinghood, including Matthew Broderick (as Simba), Jeremy Irons (Scar, Simba's uncle and usurper to the throne, recalling *Hamlet*) and James Earl Jones (Mufasa, Simba's father). The breakout characters, though, would be Simba's sidekicks, the comic duo of meerkat Timon and warthog Pumbaa, voiced by Nathan Lane and Ernie Sabella.

After a series of films focusing on human or humanoid heroes and villains, *The Lion King* was a departure for many of the newer Disney animators and something of a return to the past in featuring realistic, but not anthropomorphized, animals as the featured characters. Rather than Los Angeles Zoo – as with *Bambi* back in the 1940s – these animators took a trip to Kenya's Hell's Gate National Park to see the required animals in action in their natural settings. Roger Allers (an animator at Disney since *Oliver & Company*) and Rob Minkoff (who'd been with Disney since *The Black Cauldron* and had directed two Roger Rabbit theatrical shorts) directed *The Lion King*.

What had originally been intended as a more straightforward and serious, almost documentary tale was reshaped once more by Katzenberg to fit his Broadway-musical formula, which he was determined to continue even without Howard Ashman (Tim Rice continued to sub for him on lyrics). He was worried that a new direction might not work as well as this proven mix already had. There was also concern that *The Lion King* was an original story, not based on a known fairy tale or folk story that potential audiences would recognize. In addition, many of the animators on the project were doing their first work as supervisors or in depicting animals rather than humans. Overall, during an extensive and troubled production (there were frequent script rewrites, even while animation was under way), *The Lion King* was seen as far from being a sure-fire hit.

The box-office grosses of the film following its June 1994 release surprised everyone, with the eventual worldwide total almost doubling that of *Aladdin*. North American receipts of nearly $423 million and almost $565 million overseas pushed *The Lion King* to a colossal $988 million worldwide, making it the eighteenth highest grossing film of all time and the second highest grossing animated film of all time (behind Pixar's *Toy Story 3*, distributed by Disney). *The Lion King* was the biggest film worldwide in 1994, and Disney reportedly earned an additional $1 billion in revenue through licensed tie-in products and toys.

Critical response was less straightforwardly positive than it had been for most of the recent Disney films, with some suspecting that a sense of calculation had crept into the studio's new filmic formula. The *New York Times* noted that 'nobody beats Disney when it comes to manufacturing such products with brilliance, precision and loving care'. It was a positive reaction, but Disney's films were 'products' that had been 'manufactured'. The *Washington Post*'s Hal Hinson described *The Lion King* as 'an impressive, almost daunting achievement, spectacular in a manner that has nearly become commonplace with Disney's feature-length animations . . . more mature in its themes, it is also the darkest and the most intense. Shakespearean in tone, epic in scope, it seems more appropriate for grown-ups than for kids.' To *Entertainment Weekly*:

> Disney animators may have figured there was no way to take the comic possibilities of cartoons much further [than in *Aladdin*]. And so they've moved in the opposite direction, toward the primal-pop emotionalism of *Bambi*. In essence, *The Lion King* is a leonine remake of that 1942 masterpiece . . . *The Lion King*, more than any of the recent wave of Disney animated features, has the resonance to stand not just as a terrific cartoon but as an emotionally pungent movie.

In terms of quality, critical reaction and box-office largesse, the Disney renaissance had reached its peak with *The Lion King*.

In the tradition of the films immediately following *The Lion King*, *The Hunchback of Notre Dame* (1996), *Hercules* (1997) and *Tarzan* (1999) all returned to pre-existing sources for their traditional storylines and featured human characters, but Disney animated features were entering a period of diminishing returns. Victor Hugo's novel about the deformed bell-ringer of Notre Dame was a leftfield choice, but did include the traditional Disney story focus on overcoming disadvantage and heroes discovering their own virtues. The original idea for the film was reputedly inspired by the Classics Illustrated comic-book adaptation of the novel.

Trousdale and Wise returned from *Beauty and the Beast* to

direct a well-known voice cast including Tim Hulce, Demi
Moore and Kevin Kline. The film matched the Gothic stylings
of *The Black Cauldron* and the then-airing Disney animated
television series *Gargoyles* (1994–7). The religious content of
the novel was, however, watered down, as was the ending,
which was given a trademark Disney makeover. It didn't help
at the box office, where a clearly inferior film (in comparison
to its predecessors) limped to just over $100 million in the US
and Canada, with international releases bringing in a further
$225 million, for a respectable overall total of $325 million,
but about a third of *The Lion King*'s gross. It wouldn't have
been so concerning for Disney executives if the film's production costs hadn't exceeded $100 million where *The Lion King*,
including studio overheads, had cost just under $75 million to
make.

Disney was no longer the only significant animation force
in Hollywood, with its recent successes spurring others to
compete head-on. Katzenberg had quit Disney in 1994 following a falling-out with Eisner (see Chapter 14), and had
been replaced by Joe Roth. Katzenberg joined with director
Steven Spielberg and record-label mogul David Geffen to
create DreamWorks, a rival studio that would have a strong
focus on animation. DreamWorks would soon enjoy great success with the *Shrek* (2001–2010) series, whose 'Lord Farquaad'
was reportedly Katzenberg's revenge on the diminutive Eisner.
Don Bluth had continued to be an equally strong competitor to Disney, filling the fairy-tale and fantasy niches with
films such as *Thumbelina* (1994, based on a Hans Christian
Andersen story) and *Anastasia* (1997, a $140 million box office
hit). Ex-Disney animator John Lasseter's Pixar was beginning
a meteoric rise with 1995's *Toy Story*, the first fully computer-
animated feature film (it took $362 million upon first release).
Although this was a collaboration with Disney, the reflected
glory was entirely Pixar's, and it began a chain of events that
would lead to an eventual merger between the two companies
in 2006 (see Chapter 15).

Greek mythology was behind Clements and Musker's *Hercules* (1997), a film that continued the drop-off in box office, taking just $99 million in North America and reaching a global total of just under $253 million in all. The film attempted to recreate Robin Williams's success in *Aladdin* with Danny DeVito as young Hercules's tutor, Philoctetes, while James Woods gave voice to the villain, Hades.

Under the inventive headline 'Is It High Noon for Toon Boon?', Hollywood trade paper *Variety* reported, 'There may be trouble brewing in toon town. *Hercules* is on track to become Disney's least-successful animated feature in eight years. In fact, since the high water mark of 1994's *The Lion King*, which grossed a mighty $312 million Stateside, the Mouse House's animated pics have seen a steady decrease in US ticket sales.' The piece pointed out the rise of Disney's newest animation rivals – including big studios like Twentieth Century Fox (Bluth's *Anastasia*), DreamWorks (*The Prince of Egypt*) and Warner Bros. (*The Quest for Camelot*) – and the declining trend in the box office of their animated features.

Among the causes for the downturn, *Variety* suggested a parental backlash against the Disney merchandising machine (featured as unsubtle in-jokes in *Hercules*), as selling toys had become almost as important as the films; the increasing costs of quality animation; and the increasing competition from top-end live-action movies (including Disney's own, through Touchstone) and new film franchises. Max Howard, president of feature animation at Warner Bros., noted, 'Animation has been cyclical; it had its early heyday and then Walt Disney died and there was very little material for 20 or 30 years. The recent era began with *The Little Mermaid*. One wonders if this is a cycle that's coming to an end.'

Disney's *Tarzan* (1999) did little to stop such doom-laden speculation. Drawn from Edgar Rice Burroughs's pulp loincloth-clad jungle hero, *Tarzan* saw two more seasoned modern Disney animators take the helm. Chris Buck was a CalArts graduate who'd worked at the Disney studio since *The Fox and the Hound*, while Kevin Lima – another CalArts graduate – had joined the studio on *Oliver & Company* and had directed *A Goofy Movie* in 1995 (he was also married to Brenda Chapman, the co-director of *The Prince of Egypt*, the 1998 film from Disney's rival, DreamWorks). A technical innovation, called Deep Canvas, that created CGI 3D-style backgrounds that looked traditionally painted, was developed for *Tarzan* (it won its creators a Technical Achievement Oscar in 2003), and would play a prominent role in subsequent movies like *Atlantis: The Lost Empire* (2001) and *Treasure Planet* (2002). However, Tarzan's production cost of over $130 million meant the domestic gross of $171 million was hugely disappointing, even if the global overall total reached $448 million.

Disney soldiered on, more or less ignoring the growing competition. A trio of films set out to address the criticisms Disney had received over its depiction of ethnic minorities in several movies (largely *The Lion King* and *Aladdin*) by including more diversity. *Pocahontas* (1995) – based on historic Native American characters – failed to avoid such criticisms and took $140 million at the domestic box office. *Mulan* (1998) – drawn from Chinese legends – starred Eddie Murphy, and didn't escape criticism for ethnic and gender stereotyping, and only grossed $130 million domestically (and a further disappointing $304 million worldwide). Finally, Disney gave up making movies in this vein and instead imported *Princess Mononoke* (1999) from Studio Ghibli, Japan's Disney studio. The English-language dubbed version of the film fell foul of the Miramax–Disney imbroglio (see Chapter 14) and was little advertised or promoted, taking only $2.3 million at the box office.

Disney's renaissance ended with the realization of a dream for Roy E. Disney with the completion and release of the revised *Fantasia 2000* (1999). In production for the better part of a decade (against the resistance of both Eisner and Katzenberg), the film was Roy's way of fulfilling his uncle's wish that *Fantasia* could be updated and reissued with new animated sequences and new music. In the event, the Mickey Mouse-starring *The Sorcerer's Apprentice* was the only section that appeared in both movies. The new music included works by Beethoven, Gershwin, Shostakovich, Elgar (whose *Pomp and Circumstance* was included at Eisner's insistence), Stravinsky and Saint-Saëns. Several directors, including Pixote Hunt, Eric Goldberg, Joe Grant and Don Hahn, contributed sections.

Although broadly critically welcomed, *Fantasia 2000* was not seen as innovative, as its predecessor had been. Nonetheless, the film achieved a worldwide gross of just over $90 million (equalling the production costs), not bad for such a specialist interest release, lacking in mermaids, lions, genies or hunchbacks. 'What better way to recognize the vision of one man who began building on a dream in the twentieth century than by sharing the magic with everyone as we enter the new millennium,' said Roy Disney of *Fantasia 2000* in tribute to Walt Disney's earlier achievements.

14

FROM EISNER TO IGER

Courage is the main quality of leadership, no matter where it is exercised. Usually it implies some risk – especially in new undertakings. Courage to initiate something and to keep it going, pioneering and adventurous spirit to blaze new ways . . .

Walt Disney, quoted in *The Disney Way Fieldbook*, 2000

Disney after Walt was a different place. There was no way it could be the same, no matter who took over. For a short time, Walt's brother Roy carried the torch, but with his death in 1971, the company had passed into the control of a trio of old Disney hands: Card Walker, Donn Tatum and Ron Miller. Miller was as close to being a Disney as anyone could be, and he supervised the studio's output in much the same way Walt did. The only problem was that he wasn't Walt.

Card Walker had risen through the Disney ranks in the post-war period, from Vice President of Advertising and Sales through to the Board of Directors in the 1960s; Tatum also came from the business side of the company, and at various times both were President, CEO and Chairman of the company. Ron Miller was the only creative figure at the top of the company during the difficult period that ran from Walt's death through to 1984.

The running of the lucrative theme parks was left to those already in charge, so they continued to produce income that helped the overall Disney company survive the commercial ups and downs of both their live-action and animated film business: by the early 1980s, the theme parks accounted for up to 70 per cent of the company's total annual income. Changes in the film business in the wake of Spielberg's *Jaws* (1975) and *Close Encounters of the Third Kind* (1977) and Lucas's *Star Wars* (1977) had left Disney behind, with the creative figures running the studio unsure of how to respond. *Midnight Madness* (1980) had been no *Animal House* (1978), while *The Watcher in the Woods* (1980) had failed to herald a move by Disney into the lucrative horror-film market. Despite everyone's best efforts, *The Black Hole* (1979) had been no *Star Wars*.

The first few years of the 1980s even saw that television perennial, *The Wonderful World of Disney*, come off the air (it finished in 1979, returned for a single season in 1986, and then again for a successful fifteen-year run from 1994). Even the theme parks saw their attendance drop off slightly in the early 1980s, suggesting that they needed refreshing and an influx of new characters and new attractions if they were to keep drawing in tourists – but the Disney studio hadn't produced anything new of any significance that caught the attention of the public like Mickey Mouse or Donald Duck once had.

Although largely seen as a period of decline, Ron Miller's management of Disney did provide a few pointers towards the future, but it would be his successors who were able to take full advantage of innovations he originally presided over. Ron was the driving force behind the *Who Framed Roger Rabbit* project that did so much to put classic animation and classic characters back on the American cultural map, following a period when they'd been out of favour. He indulged precocious talents, like Tim Burton – when he realized that Burton's sensibilities didn't suit working on *The Fox and the Hound* or *The Black Cauldron*, it was Ron who gave the auteur the opportunity to make his Disney shorts *Vincent* (1982) and *Frankenweenie* (1984, remade in 3D stop-motion animation as a feature film for Disney in 2012), although it wasn't enough to keep Burton at the company.

Ron Miller supervised the initial development of computer animation at Disney, but fumbled the ball badly with *Tron* (1982) and the company's handling of John Lasseter. He developed the idea of a dedicated Disney cable television channel. He also came up with the concept of Disney developing Broadway shows, although the first – *Total Abandon* (1983), starring Richard Dreyfuss – had not been built around solid Disney successes as the later shows like *The Lion King*, *Beauty and the Beast* and *The Little Mermaid* would be.

It was Ron Miller who established Touchstone, the Disney sub-label that allowed the studio to properly branch out into the production of mainstream movies for audiences other than children and the family. Films like *The Black Hole*, *The Devil and Max Devlin* and *Tron* had sat uneasily under the Disney banner. The answer was Touchstone, not a separate company but a branding under which films that didn't match the popular widespread conception of what a 'Disney' film should be could be easily released.

The first Touchstone release was *Splash* (1984), a live-action, PG-rated fantasy about a mermaid starring Tom Hanks and Daryl Hannah. A brief shot of Hannah's naked back and some occasional un-family-friendly language was enough to earn *Splash* its PG rating, although overall the film was fairly inoffensive. It was a big box-office hit, bringing the company $68 million at the domestic box office. Ron Miller, however, would not survive long enough at Disney to enjoy the reflected glory and others would benefit from his work.

*   *   *

By 1984, Disney was truly in the doldrums, economically and creatively. It looked like a tired company, past its best and ripe for a takeover, friendly or otherwise. There was still much value attached to the Disney studio in 1983, even if it had produced nothing of significant note since the death of the founder seventeen years earlier. The film library, for one thing, had immense potential value attached to it. New areas of distribution were beginning to emerge in the mid-1980s, with the rise of home video and cable television. Although many of the films had been cannibalized by the various Disney television shows, it had usually been in truncated versions, often just highlights or specific scenes. The theatrical re-release value of the main animated hits had been maintained, and potential purchasers of the studio knew there would be amazing demand to own films like *Snow White and the Seven Dwarfs* and *Pinocchio* on videotape.

After a decade on the Board of Directors, Walt's nephew Roy E. Disney had resigned his executive position in 1977: no longer would the 'idiot nephew' (as some in the company had referred to Roy) be a punchbag for those who refused to listen to his criticisms that the studio had creatively lost its way. The years following 1977 seemed to do little to disprove Roy's contention that 'the company was not going anywhere interesting'. In March 1984 – incidentally on the same day that *Splash* was released – Roy finally also left the Board of Directors, paving the way for a wholesale change of creative management at the venerable company. Following Roy's departure, takeover rumours saw the stock price of Disney soar – which simply made it even more attractive to potential purchasers (who were rumoured to include Coca-Cola and Rupert Murdoch) – while the company arranged an additional line of credit from their long-term backers, the Bank of America, as well as over half a dozen other banks and financial institutions.

Financier Saul Steinberg had initially made his money in his twenties through a computer-leasing company, Leasco, in the 1960s. He'd succeeded in a reverse takeover of the Reliance

Insurance Company in 1968, and then attempted to take over the Chemical Bank in 1969. By 1984, Steinberg had the Disney company in his sights, intending to buy up a majority of the shares and then split the company up, selling off the most lucrative parts individually, a process known as 'asset stripping'. Over the month of April, Steinberg started buying up Disney shares, gradually increasing his shareholding above Roy's almost 5 per cent.

The attempted hostile takeover was resisted by Disney's board, who bought up Steinberg's 11.1 per cent holding (his plan called for him to gain 25 per cent, then 49 per cent) of Disney shares for more than $325 million – a process known as 'greenmail', essentially paying a potential corporate raider to leave the company alone. Legal suits between company shareholders (who felt they'd been denied potential income from a lucrative sale), the Disney studio and Steinberg would continue until 1989, with both companies eventually compensating the shareholders by paying out $45 million.

The attempted takeover by Steinberg – although it had been resisted – had simply raised the profile of Disney as a potential target for other corporate raiders. The board, however, wanted investment that would enable the company to continue intact, to produce new films for the new era. Oil man Sid Bass came to the rescue of Disney, buying almost 25 per cent of the shares, and so becoming the largest shareholder in the company, a position he would maintain until the stock market crash of 2001. It was Roy E. Disney who put together the consortium led by Bass (known in financial circles as 'white knights') that saved Disney.

There was a price to be paid for Roy riding to the rescue of the company: the removal of his cousin's husband, Ron Miller, as CEO. Roy, Bass and fellow Disney director Stanley Gold ousted Miller, bringing into the company a trio of successful Hollywood executives, Paramount's Michael Eisner and Jeffrey Katzenberg, and Frank Wells, then at Warner Bros. They arrived in September 1984 and were to be the future of the Disney studio.

Roy E. Disney (who bore an uncanny facial resemblance to his uncle, Walt Disney) rejoined the board as Vice Chairman, and took responsibility for the studio's animation division. He felt he had an obligation to protect the Disney family legacy, which he saw as specifically connected to the animated movies, while understanding he had to allow the newly arrived executives the opportunity to modernize the company and make Disney an all-round multimedia entertainment company fit for the new millennium.

Michael Eisner had a strong television background, having worked variously at all three major American networks: NBC, CBS and ABC. In 1976 he'd become CEO of Paramount, and during his time the studio produced such popular hits as *Saturday Night Fever*, *Grease*, *Raiders of the Lost Ark*, the *Star Trek* movie series and *Beverly Hills Cop*. Jeffrey Katzenberg was in marketing at Paramount in the mid-1970s when he met Eisner after he was given the task of reviving the then-dormant *Star Trek* television franchise as a movie series, leading to *Star Trek: The Motion Picture* (1979), a film that competed with Disney's *The Black Hole*. He eventually became President of Production at Paramount, under Eisner. The third member of the new management team, Frank Wells, had worked his way up through the executive ranks at Warner Bros., starting in the late 1960s until arriving at the position of Vice Chairman. Having left Warner Bros. in 1982, Wells was directly recruited by Roy E. Disney to take up the role of Chairman and Chief Operating Officer at the newly revitalized Disney company.

In 1984 Eisner was confident he'd succeed Barry Diller as head of Paramount, but he was passed over. He was looking for a new position at the same time that Disney and Wells were looking for new management figures. When Eisner signed up with Disney, he then brought Katzenberg from Paramount with him, giving him specific responsibility for the motion-picture division (including animation), while Eisner developed the company's broader interests.

Eisner and Katzenberg inherited a company that was already beginning to turn the corner, and they were able to harness innovations brought in by Ron Miller and make the most of them. In particular, they paid special attention to the Touchstone label, allowing the Disney studio to move into more adult fare. Following the success of *Splash*, Touchstone had several notable successes. A film like *Pretty Woman* (1990) could never have been released under the Disney label, even though the originally intended grittier prostitution drama had been softened into a romantic comedy that launched Julia Roberts, who co-starred with Richard Gere. This revision, to make the story more of a fairy tale (in the long-standing Disney tradition), came from Katzenberg. Disney's first R-rated film had been the Touchstone release *Down and Out in Beverly Hills* (1986), a reworking of the French drama *Boudu Saved from Drowning*. Touchstone also struck a long-running deal (1993–2014) with Jerry Bruckheimer for a series of action-driven films, such as *Con Air* (1997), *Armageddon* (1998, Touchstone's highest grossing movie) and *Pearl Harbor* (2001). This separation of family-friendly fare under the Disney label, and more adult drama and comedy under the Touchstone (and later Hollywood Pictures and Miramax Films) label, was behind much of the studio's box-office success in the 1990s and beyond.

Katzenberg was a driven executive who believed that hard work counted for more than creative inspiration. His first few years at Disney produced high-grossing offbeat successes such as *Ruthless People* (1986) and *Three Men and a Baby* (1987), which took over $100 million at the box office. Based on a French film, and with 'stars' who originated in television like Ted Danson and Tom Selleck, *Three Men and a Baby* offered a new model of low-cost, high-impact film production that Disney would pursue aggressively through Touchstone. The simultaneous expansion into television brought the pay-cable Disney Channel five million subscribers by 1990, making it instantly profitable.

While the Tim Burton stop-motion animated film *The*

Nightmare Before Christmas (1993) was released through Touchstone – as it was seen to be too different from the regular Disney animated fare – the Disney studio continued to produce many family-friendly live-action films through the 1990s and into the twenty-first century. Their traditional animal films continued, such as 1991's *White Fang* (and a 1994 sequel), while family-focused sports movies were represented by *The Mighty Ducks* (1992, followed by two sequels).

The Disney forte in live action during this time was in fantasy adventure films such as *The Rocketeer* (1991), a period thriller in the mould of Paramount's Indiana Jones films; witchcraft comedy-drama *Hocus Pocus* (1993); and *Mighty Joe Young* (1998), a remake of a *King Kong*-inspired 1940s original. The studio even produced a selection of special interest documentaries looking back at its own history, including *Frank and Ollie* (1995), about Disney animators Frank Thomas and Ollie Johnston; *The Hand Behind the Mouse: The Ub Iwerks Story* (1999); *The Boys: The Sherman Brothers' Story* (2009), about Walt's musical collaborators; and *Walt and El Grupo* (2009), about Walt's 1940s South American adventures. There was a feeling of a company becoming more comfortable exploring its own legacy, now that it had a solid future.

The decade from 1984 to 1994 was a boom time in business for the Disney studio, with various interests in the theme parks (a new one, the Disney-MGM Studios Theme Park, opened in Florida in 1989); an increasing presence in television (in animation and live action, such as comedies like *The Golden Girls*); a vibrant successful series of animated features (see Chapter 13) that returned some of the lost lustre to the studio; an expansion in themed Disney retail stores; and a growing success in mainstream live-action filmmaking. During the first four years of Eisner's term as CEO, the studio had risen from last place out of the eight major Hollywood studios in terms of annual box office to first place. The Disney back catalogue of animated classics was slowly becoming available on videocassettes and generating huge revenues, almost pure profit from pre-existing assets (although this would limit future theatrical re-release prospects for the same material). With a hugely profitable company, Eisner and Wells were the highest paid American corporate executives in 1988. However, all was not well behind the scenes of these remarkable corporate achievements.

In 1993 the Disney studio further expanded its mainstream adult-movie presence with the purchase of indie film outfit Miramax Films from founding brothers Bob and Harvey Weinstein. Miramax had grown since its establishment in 1979 to become one of America's most successful independent film studios, making award-winning dramas such as *Pulp Fiction* (1994) and *Shakespeare in Love* (1998), while distributing other independent productions and European or Asian films in the US. Harvey Weinstein built a reputation as both a hugely successful Oscar campaigner and an opinionated producer not afraid to re-edit his directors' movies. Disney bought the company for $60 million and allowed the Weinsteins initially to continue to run it as a wholly independent subsidiary within the larger Disney company.

This led to a series of conflicts, often over specific films that Disney did not want to release, such as Larry Clark's *Kids* (1995), a drama that featured teen sex and substance abuse; Kevin Smith's religious satire *Dogma* (1999); and the 2004 Michael Moore anti-Bush political documentary *Fahrenheit 9/11* (which the Weinstein brothers eventually distributed themselves independently). *Fahrenheit 9/11* was the final straw for Disney. The company fully absorbed Miramax, ousting the Weinsteins in the process, with the once proud independent studio reduced to little more than a distribution label, just like Touchstone, by 2010. The brand and its assets (mainly the 700-item film library) were then sold off for $663 million to a group of investors (which included the Weinstein brothers' new outfit, the Weinstein Company).

At Easter 1994, Disney's Chief Operating Officer Frank Wells was killed in a helicopter crash when returning from a ski trip to Nevada's Ruby Mountains, depriving Jeffrey Katzenberg of his strongest ally in defence of the company's animation output against Michael Eisner. Katzenberg made a bid to replace Wells as Disney Chairman, but he was turned down by Eisner. Their increasingly fractious relationship came to a head, with Katzenberg quitting Disney (he joined Spielberg and Geffen at DreamWorks) and launching a series of lawsuits against his former employer. Eisner brought in 'super agent' Michael Ovitz – he'd founded talent agency CAA in 1975 – to be Disney President in 1995, replacing Katzenberg. After a troubled year in which his responsibilities remained unclear and his relationship with Eisner collapsed, Ovitz was sacked in January 1997, leading to more lawsuits.

During this turmoil the company continued to expand, getting into book and record publishing, as well as sports teams, hotels and even a cruise-ship line, while also purchasing the ABC television network in 1995 – the same network that had once invested in the original Disneyland and launched Walt Disney as an international television personality. Under Eisner, the Disney company had become a truly modern, diversified entertainment and leisure conglomerate.

Eisner eventually overplayed his hand, thinking of himself as the new Walt Disney – he even took to hosting the *Wonderful World of Disney* television show in the late 1980s (during the 1986–7 season, and again in 1994–7), but he was no 'Uncle Walt', however hard he tried to be. Although successful in many respects, Eisner had lost his way after the death of Frank Wells, mishandling the departures of both Katzenberg and Ovitz, and becoming ever more controlling as time went on, just as Disney's quality of product was starting to fall off once more and the successes of the Disney renaissance in animation began to fade.

The revenues from the theme parks were hit by a collapse of tourism to America in the wake of the 2001 terrorist attacks, while a wider recession saw a collapse at the box office and a downturn in ratings (and so advertising revenue) at ABC.

In 2001 almost 4,000 staff were laid off from what was now officially called the Walt Disney Company, with the organization suffering a massive $158 million loss in net income. The releases of films like *Mulan* and *Hercules* (see Chapter 13), both failures from the animated features division, hit the company hard, and Eisner's autocratic leadership of the now widely diversified company was seen as a liability. Even as it became the first Hollywood studio to report over $3 billion in worldwide receipts in 2003 (largely due to the *Pirates of the Caribbean* movie franchise and the increasingly successful Pixar movies; see Chapter 15), the Disney company seemed trapped in another unavoidable period of downturn as the twenty-first century began.

There was one person who felt that such a downturn could be avoided: the by then seventy-two-year-old Roy E. Disney (he was the same age his father was when he took the reins at Disney following Walt's death). Eisner attempted to consolidate his power within Disney by demanding the resignation of Roy from the Disney board, claiming he was past the mandatory retirement age (in reality, he seemed to regard the last involved Disney as a threat). In support of Roy, Stanley Gold resigned and called on other board members to fire Eisner. The irony was that it had been Roy Disney and Gold who had brought in Eisner to 'save' Disney in the first place (a largely successful venture), and they were now agitating, as they saw it, to save the company from him.

In 2003, Roy E. Disney stepped down from the Board of Directors (just as he'd done in 1984) and left his position as the head of the Walt Disney Feature Animation unit (where he'd been a huge contributor to the 'Disney renaissance' of 1988–2000; see Chapter 13). In a parting shot he accused Eisner of 'micromanagement' to the wider detriment of the company, of the mismanagement of the ABC television company, of responsibility for a number of movie flops from the year 2000 onwards (most recently *The Alamo*, 2004, and *Home on the Range*, also 2004), and of refusing to plan for his succession.

Contributing to Eisner's downfall at this time was his failure to successfully handle negotiations with Pixar, bringing to an end their twelve-year distribution relationship with Disney (see Chapter 15). An uninvited takeover bid from Comcast in 2004, valued at $54 billion, added to Eisner's troubles. He was forced to relinquish the position of Chairman of the Board, and at the March 2004 Disney shareholders' meeting 45 per cent of shareholders (in a move organized by former board members Roy Disney and Stanley Gold) withheld their proxy votes that would have re-elected Eisner to the board. The position of Chair went to former senator George J. Mitchell (a position he held until 2007), but the board did not make an immediate move to terminate Eisner's employment.

Eisner's eventual successor in 2005 was Robert 'Bob' Iger, who'd started at ABC in 1974, rising through that company. He was responsible for ABC broadcasting David Lynch's groundbreaking 1990–91 television series *Twin Peaks* and had become President of the company in 1993. By 1999, following the Disney takeover of ABC, Iger had become President of Walt Disney International, overseeing the company's international interests, while still chairing ABC. As President and Chief Operating Officer, Iger had been Eisner's effective deputy since 2000, replacing Joe Roth. In taking over from Eisner as head of the company, Iger brought Roy Disney back into the Disney studio fold as a 'director emeritus' and company consultant, reinforcing the last connection remaining to the days of Walt Disney himself.

For his part, Roy had not always seen eye-to-eye with Iger, mainly due to his role as Eisner's deputy since 2000. However, he came to be an ardent supporter of Bob Iger's activities as the head of the company, seeing him as the man likely to take Disney animation (in particular) into a new era, when Disney and Pixar eventually merged in 2006. Roy stated: 'Animation has always been the heart and soul of the Walt Disney Company and it is wonderful to see Bob Iger and the company embrace that heritage by bringing the outstanding animation talent of the Pixar team back into the fold. This clearly solidifies the Walt Disney Company's position as the dominant leader in motion picture animation and we applaud and support Bob Iger's vision.'

In Eisner's final years and as Iger got to grips with running the company, Disney live-action production had come to be dominated by a variety of ongoing film series. The most successful was the *Pirates of the Caribbean* films (starting in 2003, reaching four films by 2011 with more in production), based upon a theme park ride at Disneyland; the *National Treasure* (2004, 2007, with a third planned) heritage adventure films starring Nicolas Cage; the *High School Musical* trilogy (starting in 2006); and the C. S. Lewis Narnia films (with the early entries co-produced with Walden Media as part of a bigger Walden–Disney package), begun with *The Chronicles of Narnia: The Lion, the Witch, and the Wardrobe* (2005).

Animation had rather lost its way during this period, with the misconceived likes of *The Emperor's New Groove* (2000), which had been a troubled production with Eisner heavily involved in the eventual buddy-comedy revamp (recounted in the controversial documentary *The Sweatbox*, 2002), which failed at the box office. The high-concept adventure duo of *Atlantis: The Lost Empire* (2001) and *Treasure Planet* (2002) failed to recapture the magic of *The Lion King* or *Beauty and the Beast*, while the likes of *Brother Bear* (2003), *Home on the Range* (2004), *Chicken Little* (2005) and *Meet the Robinsons* (2007) were all critical and commercial misfires.

Eisner and Katzenberg had saved the Disney studio from what in the mid-1980s looked like an unstoppable drift into irrelevance. Walt's nephew, Roy E. Disney, had stood four-square behind traditional Disney animation (although it was increasingly augmented by the use of computers) throughout the Disney renaissance. However, it would be their replacement at the top of the company, Bob Iger, who would do even more to transform the Disney studio into the biggest pop-culture creator on the planet.

15

DISNEY GOES DIGITAL

Fantasy, if it's really convincing, can't become dated, for the simple reason that it represents a flight into a dimension that lies beyond the reach of time.
Walt Disney, quoted in 'The Rides of Passage', *Via*, July 2005

Born almost sixty years after Walt Disney, John Lasseter has perhaps the biggest claim to be the inheritor of Disney's mantle as the world's most creative and successful name in animation. His first ever job was with the Walt Disney Company, where he was taught animation skills at CalArts by three of Disney's original 'nine old men' – Eric Larson, Ollie Johnston and Frank Thomas. Fired from Disney by animation supervisor Ed Hansen, John Lasseter would, within three decades, find himself Chief Creative Officer of not only the wildly successful Pixar, but also of Walt Disney Animation Studios – essentially, Lasseter would become the Walt Disney of the twenty-first century.

An animation fan from a young age, John Lasseter read books about the history of Disney animation and was confirmed in his career ambitions following a viewing of Disney's 1963 film, *The Sword in the Stone*. He quit his intended course at Pepperdine University in California to enrol in a programme at the newly established California Institute of the Arts. Walt had described CalArts as his ideal arts school: 'I want to have a school that turns out people that know all the facets of film-making. I want them to be capable of doing anything needed to make a film – photograph it, direct it, design it, animate it, record it.'

In 1975, Lasseter became only the second student to sign up for the new Character Animation course taught by ex-Disney animator Jack Hannah (other Disney-related teachers at CalArts included Marc Davis and Thornton 'T.' Hee). Among those joining in the following years were Tim Burton and Henry Selick (*The Nightmare Before Christmas*, 1993), John Musker (*The Little Mermaid*, 1989), Brad Bird (*The Incredibles*, 2004), Michael Giaimo (art director on *Frozen*, 2013) and Gary Trousdale (*Beauty and the Beast*, 1991), among many others. The Disney studio recruited directly from the school, which made the end-of-year presentations a hugely competitive event. It would be mainly animators who graduated from CalArts, many based in the now notorious windowless Room A113 (there are 'shout-outs' to the room in *Toy Story*, *Finding Nemo* and *Cars*, among other Pixar and Disney films), who would mastermind the Disney renaissance, build Pixar and contribute to the huge growth of cinematic animation beyond Disney in the 1990s. In some ways, the CalArts recruits simply represented too much young talent for the Disney studio to contain.

When Lasseter joined Disney, he was soon working as an animator at Walt Disney Feature Animation in 1982. However, he'd arrived at the studio at a time when animation was suffering something of a creative downturn. For Lasseter, Disney 'animation had reached a plateau with *One Hundred and One Dalmatians* (1961). Somehow, I felt that the films after that, while they had wonderful moments and characters, overall, they were just the same old thing.'

His brief involvement with Disney's *Tron* (1982), a partly computer-animated movie, gave him a glimpse of the future, but it was a future Disney was not at that time interested in pursuing. As mentioned, although he managed to dabble in developing computer animation at the studio, he was eventually 'let go' when it became clear his ambitions didn't match those of the executives in charge at the time, Walt's son-in-law Ron Miller and animation supervisor Ed Hansen. Within a few years, Miller would be gone and a new regime would be more open to the future that Lasseter saw in computer animation.

Pixar, Lasseter's original studio, had begun life as the computer-graphics department of George Lucas's company, Lucasfilm. Following 1977's blockbuster, *Star Wars* – the film to which Disney responded by creating *The Black Hole* (1979) – Lucas had innovated technology that changed the way films were made, paving the way for the digital era. Special effects house Industrial Light & Magic had been established to fill a gap in the market and to create the effects Lucas needed for his movies. ILM developed motion-control cameras, made innovations in computer graphics in movies and created photorealistic digital characters. Lucasfilm's Graphics Group pioneered computer effects in movies such as *Star Trek II: The Wrath of Khan* (1982) and *Young Sherlock Holmes* (1985), where they created the 'stained glass knight' character.

In February 1986, the Graphics Group was sold off for $5 million to Steve Jobs, who'd recently left Apple Inc., the company he'd founded. Investing a further $5 million, Jobs reshaped the group into Pixar, retaining founding figures Edwin 'Ed' Catmull and Alvy Ray Smith in key positions. The company initially developed computer hardware, such as the Pixar Image Computer that was sold to the Disney company as part of their Computer Animation Production System (CAPS), first used on *The Little Mermaid* (1989) and then rolled out on other Disney animated feature films.

After being fired by Disney in the early 1980s, John Lasseter had continued to pursue his interest in computer-aided animation. He'd come into contact with Catmull and Smith while they were at Lucasfilm, and worked with them on the 1984 fully computer-animated short *The Adventures of André and Wally B*. Simple and straightforward, this two-minute film was a harbinger of bigger things to come. 'It became the first *real* animation that the computer had ever done,' said Lasseter. '*André and Wally* was very cartoony, and people loved that. I remember one guy, who worked with a computer graphics company, coming up to me after a screening to ask what software I used to get the humour in! It really brought home to me how much it was seen as science at the time.'

Lasseter was part of the team that formed Pixar when Steve Jobs bought Lucas's computer graphics division. He'd faced a choice: to stay at Lucasfilm with ILM and work in special effects, or to leave and become part of Pixar, or as Lasseter himself put it, to become 'a storyteller'. The first computer-animated film Lasseter directed, the two-minute *Luxo Jr.* (1986) – in which parent and child desk lamps play with a ball – demonstrated to Lasseter that he'd achieved a storytelling breakthrough. 'The thing that was pivotal is that straight afterwards a pioneer in computer science came up to me and said, "Can I ask you a question?",' Lasseter told *Total Film*. 'I thought he was gonna ask me about the software or the soft shadowing algorithm or something like that. But he goes, "Was the big lamp the mother or the father?" At that moment I realized that we'd achieved something, for the very first time in computer animation history, the story and the characters were the thing that was entertaining the audience.'

Just as with Walt Disney back in the 1930s, it was John Lasseter's ambition to be able to produce an animated feature film, but using computers rather than traditional hand animation and cels. Just like Walt back in the 1930s, Lasseter would spend several years working out all the kinks of his new medium in a series of influential shorts, including *Tin Toy*

(1988, winner of the Short Film Oscar), *Knick Knack* (1989), and a variety of television commercials that provided 'proof of concept' opportunities. Steve Jobs, recognizing the importance of the Walt Disney Company in the history of film animation, wanted the Pixar feature-film project to be done for them, but they initially turned him down. Disney then attempted to lure Lasseter back, especially after his Oscar win. He faced another choice, one that this time – according to a discussion he had with Ed Catmull – was easy: 'I can go to Disney and be a director, or I can stay here and make history.'

It was only after Disney released Tim Burton's *The Nightmare Before Christmas* (1993) that the company opened their doors to developing film projects with outsiders. For Lasseter, the idea behind *Toy Story* (1995) was to produce an anti-Disney animated film. 'We actually made a list of what we wanted our movie *not* to be,' he admitted. 'We didn't want it to be a musical; we didn't want it to have a good guy and a bad guy, and sidekicks, all that stuff, because that was all Disney's thing. We started to look at different kinds of film genres and we landed upon the buddy picture.'

Just as back in the 1930s, when Walt Disney was concerned whether a cinema audience would be prepared to sit through an animated feature film of ninety minutes in length, so the company was sceptical in the mid-1990s that modern audiences would take to a fully computer-animated film of that same length. The Disney view seemed to be that computer animation was all right for shorts and as a tool to augment traditional animation, but was unlikely to succeed at feature length. It was down to Lasseter to show them otherwise. There was yet another echo of Walt's original struggles making *Snow White and the Seven Dwarfs* in *Toy Story*: Lasseter knew animating human figures would be a problem, while such 'artificial' characters as plastic toys would be far easier. 'The humans in *Toy Story* really became very secondary,' Lasseter said, 'because we always knew they would look a little clunky.'

* * *

There was a mutual need at play in the uneasy alliance between Disney and Pixar. Disney needed an effective way of getting to grips with the new technology of computer animation, and its in-house efforts to date had been mostly expensive failures. Pixar was in a poor economic position and close to bankruptcy (at least according to Walter Isaacson's biography of Steve Jobs). Negotiations over *Toy Story* were fraught, with each side looking to maximize their advantage: Katzenberg wanted an ownership share for Disney of Pixar's technology, while Jobs wanted to share revenues on video rights and sequels, and share ownership of the characters Pixar created. It took almost a year from the beginning of discussions to the middle of 1991 for agreement to be reached. The deal gave Disney ownership of the characters and story, and Pixar 12.5 per cent of ticket revenues – the contentious details of the deal would contribute to its unravelling almost fifteen years later.

In a mantra that Disney seemed to have all but forgotten before the advent of the 'Disney renaissance' beginning in 1989 with *The Little Mermaid*, Lasseter and his team put their emphasis on storytelling rather than the medium. The technology used was almost incidental – for the Pixar team computer animation was simply another animation tool to be used to tell stories that could engage audiences. The characters of Woody, the old-time Western cowboy doll, and Buzz Lightyear, the cutting-edge futuristic astronaut (essentially Roy Rogers versus Buck Rogers), became the basis for a buddy movie concerning a group of lost toys who struggle to get back home to their owner.

It was 1993 before *Toy Story* had a script that met with the approval of Jeffrey Katzenberg and other Disney executives. Lasseter had always conceived of Woody being voiced by Tom Hanks, but they felt obliged to try out other actors, including Billy Crystal. Tim Allen – who would later star in Disney's 2006 theatrical remake of *The Shaggy Dog* – was signed to voice Buzz Lightyear. A screening of the work in progress (in the form of 'story reels', where the audio is matched to semi-completed sequences or still artwork) for Disney executives towards the end of 1993 was quickly dubbed 'Black Friday' by those involved. Following a huge amount of micromanagement regarding the characters of Woody and Buzz by Katzenberg, Pixar's project had been blown off course and the characters had become, in the words of Tom Hanks, 'jerks'.

Those within Disney, mainly head of animation Peter Schneider, who were against bringing in 'outsiders' to make Disney films, seized their opportunity. Production on *Toy Story* was shut down and Lasseter and co. were given three months to retool the movie, make it 'fun' and re-present their project to Disney. 'It just isn't working,' Schneider told Lasseter, according to *Entertainment Weekly*. 'The movie was horrible,' admitted Lasseter. 'The characters, especially Woody, were just repellent! Woody was just awful. I was embarrassed, because it wasn't the movie we set out to make. Disney actually wanted to shut the production down and lay people off. We went back and said, "Let us do one more cut. Let us see what we can do ourselves." We decided to make it the kind of movie we wanted to make . . .'

By February 1994 a new, lighter approach to *Toy Story* had been agreed and the principal cast members recorded new dialogue the following month. As the animation was refined and the film began to look more complete, those at Disney and at Pixar (even Steve Jobs, who'd had his doubts in the middle of production) began to feel that *Toy Story* really could revolutionize the animation industry. The only question now for all involved was how would American audiences react?

Toy Story premiered in November 1995, by which time Disney feature animation was back on its feet with a string of hits, from *Beauty and the Beast* (1991) to *The Lion King* (1994). Beyond the looming threats in theatrical animation from the newly formed DreamWorks (Katzenberg had left Disney in 1994 to join the new studio), MGM, Warner Bros. and Fox, the Disney studio itself was once more the king of movie animation. If *Toy Story* succeeded with audiences, it would be another string to the company's bow (and allow Jobs to take Pixar public), while if it failed it could be an ignominious stain on an otherwise successful run of films from a newly energized company.

Upon release, *Toy Story* grossed over $360 million worldwide and was a huge critical hit. *Variety* praised the high-tech movie's 'razzle-dazzle technique and unusual look. The camera loops and zooms in a dizzying fashion', while Disney fan Roger Ebert wrote in the *Chicago Sun-Times* that *Toy Story* compared with Disney's own *Who Framed Roger Rabbit* in that 'both movies take apart the universe of cinematic visuals and put it back together again, allowing us to see in a new way'. According to *Entertainment Weekly*, *Toy Story* displayed 'the purity, the ecstatic freedom of imagination, that's the hallmark of the greatest children's films. It also has the kind of spring-loaded allusive prankishness that, at times, will tickle adults even more than it does kids.' John Lasseter received a Special Achievement Oscar for *Toy Story*, again emulating Walt Disney who was awarded two, one for creating Mickey Mouse and another for *Snow White and the Seven Dwarfs*.

For the decade following *Toy Story*, Pixar was on a creative high with hit animated film after hit animated film, all released through Disney until 2004. As well as two *Toy Story* sequels in 1999 and 2010, the company tackled insects in *A Bug's Life* (1998, curiously similar to the Katzenberg-DreamWorks film *Antz*, 1998), scary-but-loveable creatures in *Monsters, Inc.* (2001), fish in *Finding Nemo* (2003, and the 2016 sequel *Finding Dory*), comic superheroes in *The Incredibles* (2004, with a sequel in development) and sentient vehicles in *Cars* (2006, followed by sequels and other vehicular spin-offs).'I always equate it to having a child and then raising it,' said Lasseter of Pixar's movies. 'At a certain point, your son or daughter graduates from high school and goes to college. You give them to the world and hope that you did okay. That's very much like these movies. When we get to the release date, we realize that the movie doesn't belong to us any more. It belongs to the world and you just hope that you did okay.'

* * *

Although they had come to rely on each other over the years, Disney and Pixar always had an uncomfortable relationship. Those in charge at Disney, it seemed, were annoyed that they'd missed out on 'owning' the digital revolution in animation by firing Lasseter. The people at Pixar were none too happy about having to be in partnership with Disney in order to get their films released, especially when executives at the larger company insisted on things like making the sequel to *Toy Story* a straight-to-DVD project. 'There was a business model for Disney, following *Aladdin*, of straight-to-DVD sequels but I always felt that if it was done right, *Toy Story 2* should be a theatrical release,' said Lasseter. Pixar had a three-film agreement with Disney initially, so the *Toy Story* sequel would fall outside that agreement if released to DVD. Even when the film was upgraded to a theatrical release at Lasseter's insistence, Disney still refused to include it in the terms of the original deal, an issue that irked Pixar for many years.

The fight over the *Toy Story* sequel was the first of many cracks in the relationship between the two companies that would contribute to the parting of the ways by 2004. The biggest issue between them was Disney's insistence on retaining the sequel and character rights to all the movies created under the arrangement. In anticipation of the end of the original contract, Pixar attempted to negotiate new terms with Disney that would mean the older studio functioned as a distributor only, taking 10–15 per cent of the box office as a fee. Pixar would retain everything else, including ownership of characters and concepts in their movies, sequel rights and full creative control over their properties.

Feeling they were in the strongest position, Pixar walked away from a new deal with Disney when the company was unable or unwilling to agree to their new terms. They shopped their new slate of movies to other studios in the hope of finding a distribution partnership with Time Warner, Sony or Viacom. Pixar's first five films – *Toy Story*, *A Bug's Life*, *Toy Story 2*,

Monsters, Inc. and *Finding Nemo* – had taken $2.5 billion at the worldwide box office, making the company a very attractive partner for any studio. The stumbling block at Disney appeared to be the ever-stubborn Michael Eisner.

The Pixar situation in 2004–5 became part of the attack on Eisner by Roy E. Disney and Stanley Gold, who by that point had left the Disney board in protest. They issued a statement: 'More than a year ago, we warned the Disney board that we believed Michael Eisner was mismanaging the Pixar partnership and expressed our concern that the relationship was in jeopardy.' A personal clash between Pixar's Steve Jobs and Eisner contributed to the breakdown in talks between the two companies, even though all involved appeared to believe that a continued partnership of some description was in the interests of them all. 'After 10 months of trying to strike a deal with Disney, we're moving on,' Jobs said in January 2004. 'We've had a great run together – one of the most successful in Hollywood history – and it's a shame that Disney won't be participating in Pixar's future successes.'

While any new Pixar movies would not go to Disney, the Disney studio retained control of all the characters in the five films to that date, as well as the right to produce sequels without Pixar's participation. Disney also attempted to lay claim to the two yet-to-be-completed Pixar movies then in production, *The Incredibles* and *Cars*. Eisner seemed content to accept the departure of Pixar from Disney: 'We have had a fantastic partnership with Pixar and wish Steve Jobs and the wonderfully creative team there, led by John Lasseter, much success in the future,' Eisner said in a statement. 'Although we would have enjoyed continuing our successful collaboration under mutually acceptable terms, Pixar understandably has chosen to go its own way to grow as an independent company.' According to James B. Stewart's chronicle of Eisner's reign at Disney, *Disney War*, Jobs contacted Roy Disney admitting that while Disney was the 'logical partner' for Pixar, he could not do a deal with Eisner. Roy was reported as having replied: 'When the Wicked Witch is dead, we'll be together again.'

It did take the eventual departure of Eisner from Disney, following a failed bid from Comcast to buy the company, in September 2005 and his replacement as CEO by Bob Iger for talks with Pixar to resume in a more conducive atmosphere. Iger seemed to realize how important Pixar was to Disney, as media commentators had dubbed the company and John Lasseter as continuing the original spirit of Walt Disney in the storytelling evident in their animated films. Many who worked creatively at Pixar had been the result of Walt's training programme at CalArts – they had a direct lineage, if not to Walt himself, at least to some of his 'nine old men' who had taught at CalArts or mentored students. Pixar was, to all intents and purposes, the continuation of Walt Disney's ethos in a more modern form. Unlike Eisner, Iger did not let his own ego get in the way of doing what was right for the company. The result was a deal in January 2006 in which Disney bought Pixar for $7.4 billion (albeit in share stock only), but which was in reality a reverse takeover of Disney by Pixar's creative talents. Holding just over 50 per cent of Pixar shares, Steve Jobs would join Disney's Board of Directors and become the company's biggest individual shareholder with 7 per cent of the stock (Jobs would die aged fifty-six in 2011).

More importantly, the deal also put John Lasseter in charge of Disney animation as Chief Creative Officer. He would report to Iger, but would have a creative free hand to produce both Pixar and Disney animated movies of all types, and he would additionally consult with Roy Disney (who would die in 2009, aged seventy-nine, the last member of the Disney family to be actively involved with the studio – the new animation building on the Disney lot was named after him in 2010). Lasseter would also take on the role of Principal Creative Adviser for Walt Disney Imagineering, the division responsible for the company's theme parks and attractions. Ed Catmull continued as President of Pixar, but also took on the position of President

of Walt Disney Animation Studios. The structure was finalized in May 2006.

Under Bob Iger and with Pixar firmly in the Disney fold,
the Walt Disney Company would soar to new heights, only
some of which Walt himself had ever dreamt of. The warring
egos of the Eisner–Katzenberg period had produced much that
was successful, but had also turned the boardroom of Disney
into the location of an ongoing finance-and-power soap opera.
Under Iger, things were a whole lot calmer following the Pixar
merger. The 'Mouse House', as *Variety* liked to call Disney,
was now on a far more even keel, and Iger's recipe for success
would be expansion through acquisition, following the success
with Pixar. On the screen, Pixar's *Cars* and Disney's *Pirates
of the Caribbean: Dead Man's Chest* resulted in record profits
for the company, with net income almost reaching $3.5 billion.

Jim Henson's anarchic puppets known as the Muppets had
enjoyed a varied history in film and television since he created
them in the mid-1950s. Kermit the Frog, Miss Piggy, Fozzie
Bear and company had become household names almost as well
known as Mickey Mouse and Donald Duck, so it seemed like a
marriage made in heaven (a belief also held by Henson himself)
when Disney acquired the Muppets characters and franchise
in 2004. However, for the first few years of their ownership, it
appeared that no one knew quite what to do with the Muppets.
The distractions of Eisner's departure and the ongoing negotiations with Pixar probably didn't help.

By 2008, Disney had engaged properly with plans to revive
the Muppet franchise, culminating in the film *The Muppets*
that was released in November 2011. An Oscar winner for Best
Original Song for 'Man or Muppet', written by Flight of the
Conchords's Bret McKenzie, *The Muppets* met with a positive critical reception and took $165 million at the box office
worldwide. A star on the Hollywood Walk of Fame for the
Muppets ensemble followed in 2012, and a sequel – *Muppets
Most Wanted* – was released in 2014.

Disney and Pixar continued to be successful as the end of the first decade of the twenty-first century approached. By 2009, Pixar had released *Ratatouille* (2007), a comedy about a 'foodie' rat and a young chief; *Wall-E* (2008), an inventive tale of the adventures of a waste-disposal robot on a post-apocalyptic earth; and *Up* (2009), the nuanced and moving tale of a pensioner (voiced by Ed Asner) who teams up with a young Wilderness Explorer on a voyage of exploration. Disney itself had released *Chicken Little* (2005), the company's first non-Pixar computer-animated movie; *Underdog* (2007), a live-action comedy about a heroic pooch; *Enchanted* (2007), a musical romantic comedy that mixed live action and animation while paying homage to Disney's classic animated features; and *Bolt* (2008), another non-Pixar computer-animated film about a dog who believes he has superpowers.

In August 2009, Disney announced the purchase of Marvel Entertainment for $4 billion, giving them ownership of that company's thousands of comic-book characters, including many superhero household names such as Spider-Man, the X-Men, Iron Man, Thor, Captain America and the Avengers. The company had a long and involved history, from its founding as Timely Publications in 1939, before becoming Marvel Comics in the 1960s under the creative leadership of editor Stan Lee. Various owners, including Cadence Industries and New World Pictures, had been custodians of the company's comic-book superheroes, but none had adequately managed to exploit their cinematic potential.

Investor Ron Perelman had purchased the company in 1989, noting, 'It is a mini-Disney in terms of intellectual property. Disney's got much more highly recognized characters and softer characters, whereas our characters are termed action heroes. But at Marvel we are now in the business of the creation and marketing of characters.' Despite that intention, Marvel's best characters featured in poor television series or – as in the case of Spider-Man – were trapped in 'development hell' as various filmmakers attempted to bring them to the big screen.

In 1997, a corporate battle over ownership and looming bankruptcy put Marvel in the hands of Toy Biz entrepreneur Avi Arad, and saw it rebranded as Marvel Entertainment. With the Disney acquisition, comic-book editor, writer and artist Joe Quesada became Marvel's Chief Creative Officer.

In Marvel, Disney had acquired a rich heritage of characters, although many would not be available immediately for exploitation in movies due to pre-existing rights arrangements. Columbia controlled Spider-Man and Ghost Rider, and Fox held the Fantastic Four and the X-Men, among other studios. That still left Disney with an attractive host of characters around which the company would build a series of interlocking superhero movies culminating in the 2012 blockbuster *The Avengers* (released as *Avengers Assemble* in the UK), which took over $1.5 billion at the box office worldwide, making it the third highest grossing movie of all time (behind James Cameron's double whammy of *Titanic*, 1997, and *Avatar*, 2009).

Iger called Marvel's characters a 'treasure trove' that 'transcends gender, age, culture and geographical barriers. There are so many opportunities to mine both characters that are known and characters that are not widely known.' Films such as *Iron Man 2* (2010), *Thor* (2011) and *Captain America: The First Avenger* (2011) built to the release of *The Avengers* in 2012, but the expansion of the Marvel screen universe continued into *Iron Man 3* and *Thor: The Dark World* (both 2013), *Captain America: The Winter Soldier* and *Guardians of the Galaxy* (both 2014), and right up to the sequel, *Avengers: Age of Ultron* in 2015. Each film would be a cinematic superhero blockbuster.

The second decade of the twenty-first century was a mixed period for Disney's live-action productions. While Tim Burton's *Alice in Wonderland* (2010) was a huge box-office hit (with a non-Burton sequel planned for 2016), and overdue sequel *Tron: Legacy* (2010) a middling success, films such as *John Carter* (2012) and *The Lone Ranger* (2013) were both critical and financial bombs, with the company making significant losses on them both. In 2013 Disney finally had a crack at L. Frank Baum's Oz universe in the successful *Oz the Great and Powerful* (which is set to spawn a sequel), while also looking back on the story of Walt's real-life tangles with P. L. Travers over the making of *Mary Poppins* in *Saving Mr Banks* (2013), which featured Tom Hanks as Walt Disney.

In Disney animation, the story was similar, with the traditional-yet-modern tale of *Tangled* (2010, the fiftieth animated feature released by the Walt Disney Company) succeeding in updating the 'feisty princess' character and setting the animation division on track for Oscar glory once more with *Frozen* (2013). However, the digital production *Mars Needs Moms* (2011) failed miserably. Even Pixar experienced mixed fortunes, with *Brave* (2012) meeting a turbulent welcome, and prequel *Monsters University* (2013) not living up to its predecessor. Computer-game based films, such as the live-action *Prince of Persia: The Sands of Time* (2010) and the computer-animated *Wreck-It Ralph* (2012), which was a celebration of gaming characters from the 1980s to the twenty-first century, suggested other new directions Disney could explore.

In 2011, Bob Iger was candid about Disney's modern strategy to 'buy either new characters or businesses that are capable of creating great characters and great stories'. It should have come as no surprise (except that it did) when at Halloween 2012 the Walt Disney Company announced the purchase of Lucasfilm for $4 billion. Filmmaker George Lucas had visited Walt Disney's Disneyland during its first year in 1955 when he was aged just eleven years old. Lucas had gone on to build an empire to rival Walt's with *Star Wars* (1977), its sequels and the lucrative spin-offs and merchandise it produced. Lucas had worked with Disney previously in the creation of the film and theme-park attraction *Captain EO* (1986) and in the two versions of the *Star Wars*-themed Star Tours ride (1987, 2013). Like Walt, Lucas had developed new filmmaking technologies and his computer-graphics division had become the basis for John Lasseter's Pixar. Like Lasseter himself, George Lucas had a potential claim to be the 'new' Walt Disney, with his creation of a galaxy of beloved characters that spanned generations. As with Pixar, the Muppets and Marvel, the symbiosis between Disney and Lucasfilm was obvious when the news was announced.

Along with the purchase of the company and all its assets came the announcement of a new trilogy of *Star Wars* movies, with the first due for release in December 2015, and a series of stand-alone spin-off movies. There would also be a new computer-generated television series, *Star Wars: Rebels*, on the Disney XD channel from 2014. A little later Disney also acquired the rights to the Indiana Jones film series, co-created by Lucas with Steven Spielberg and previously distributed through Paramount, suggesting a new series of movies based upon *Raiders of the Lost Ark* (1981) and its sequels could be forthcoming.

For his part, Lucas said: 'For the past 35 years, one of my greatest pleasures has been to see *Star Wars* passed from one generation to the next. I've always believed that *Star Wars* could live beyond me, and I thought it was important to set up the transition during my lifetime.' Conversations concerning a possible sale to Disney had been ongoing between Lucas and Bob Iger over a number of years before the deal was finally done. Film producer Kathleen Kennedy, appointed co-chairman of Lucasfilm shortly before the sale to Disney, would supervise the new *Star Wars* movies, the first of which would be directed by *Star Trek*'s (2009) J. J. Abrams. Lucas would remain attached to the property he created as a 'creative consultant'.

Where Pixar and the Muppets had given Disney new access to the children's and family film market, Marvel had brought the company an older action-movie audience with its regular superhero movies. Now with Lucasfilm and *Star Wars*, Disney had acquired a long-running, hugely successful franchise that held as much financial promise in its spin-off merchandising as it did creative challenges in reviving the series' big-screen fortunes. It would be up to Bob Iger and his teams handling each of these properties to protect them and ensure they enjoyed an extended life into the future. The Magic Kingdom created by Walt Disney looked set to expand forever . . .

CONCLUSION: WALT'S WORLD

In March 2014, the Disney studio won its first Oscar for Best Animated Feature Film with *Frozen* (2013, loosely based on Hans Christian Andersen's *The Snow Queen*), on the same day that the acclaimed movie's box-office gross passed the $1 billion mark worldwide. The Academy Award category for Best Animated Film had only been established in 2001, and for its first twelve years had been dominated by the output of John Lasseter's Pixar, with *Finding Nemo* (2003), *The Incredibles* (2004), *Ratatouille* (2007), *Wall-E* (2008), *Up* (2009), *Toy Story 3* (2010) and *Brave* (2012) all taking the prize.

This Oscar-winning streak recalled that of Walt Disney himself, who took a record-breaking twenty-two competitive Academy Awards during his lifetime. He won ten Oscars for Best Short Subject (Cartoon) between 1932 and 1943, as well as another ten Oscars for his True-Life Adventures wildlife films between 1949 and 1959. In 1954, Walt had regained the Best Short Subject (Cartoon) award for Ward Kimball's *Toot, Whistle, Plunk and Boom* (1953). Walt's final Oscar had been awarded posthumously in 1969 for *Winnie the Pooh and the Blustery Day*, rather fittingly once more in the Best Short

Subject (Cartoon) category in which he'd won his first award thirty-seven years before. Beyond those competitive awards, Walt had received a total of four special Oscars, the first two for the creation of Mickey Mouse (in 1932) and the creation of the first animated feature film, *Snow White and the Seven Dwarfs* (in 1939). His third honorary Oscar (1942) was as part of the team who developed Fantasound – a new theatrical sound system – for the release of *Fantasia*, and his fourth (also 1942) came in recognition of his lifetime of showmanship with the Irving G. Thalberg Award.

The next time the Disney studio would enjoy such a winning streak was during the Disney renaissance, comprising the creative decade from 1989 to 1999. Collectively, the films of the Disney renaissance had taken almost $3.5 billion at the global box office. Nine of the ten movies released during this period were nominated for Oscars (1990's *The Rescuers Down Under* was the only one to miss out). Of the twenty Oscar nominations made for the animated movies during that period, there were eleven wins, with two each for *The Little Mermaid* (1989), *Beauty and the Beast* (1991), *Aladdin* (1992), *The Lion King* (1994) and *Pocahontas* (1995), and a single win for *Tarzan* (1999) – many of the awards were for the songs by Howard Ashman and Alan Menken or the musical scores that marked out this 'Broadway' era of Disney theatrical animation.

In that respect, *Frozen* was right on target with its two Academy Awards. Not only did the film triumphantly reclaim the Best Animated Feature Oscar for the Disney studio, it also took the Best Original Song Oscar for 'Let It Go', sung by Idina Menzel. *Frozen* had been co-directed by 1978 CalArts graduate Chris Buck and Jennifer Lee, who co-wrote the screenplay for *Wreck-It Ralph* (2012) and was the first female director at Walt Disney Animation Studios. Back in 1943 Walt had considered producing a 'package movie' that would be a biography of Hans Christian Andersen and tell some of his stories, including *The Snow Queen*, in animated form. That movie was never made, and the 1954 Danny Kaye-starring *Hans Christian Andersen* saw the Disney studio shelve the idea.

The concept had been revived in the wake of the Disney renaissance, with Pixar even making an attempt to adapt it. It took the success of *Tangled* (2010) to bring new attention to *The Snow Queen*, with Chris Buck (who'd been working on it since 2008) teaming up with Lasseter as producer (who contributed heavily to story development, in the way Walt used to) and Lee as co-director. She brought a new angle to the story, and the strong involvement of songwriters Robert Lopez and Kristen Anderson-Lopez recalled the Disney successes of the past by the Sherman brothers and the Ashman–Menken collaborations. In many ways, with *Frozen*, the Walt Disney studio was back to doing what it has always done best – producing classic animated feature films.

Walt Disney had died almost fifty years before *Frozen* was released – a film that, although made by other hands, he would surely recognize as containing the core 'Disney' elements. In that time, the studio he and his brother Roy created had prospered as never before. Walt's life story and achievements seemed to have been spurred on by a desire to shape and control his world. That desire had been born of four key betrayals. The first and most poignant (maybe the one that cut the deepest) had been by his father, when he'd sold off the farm and animals in Marceline, Missouri, and moved the Disney family back to the city. Walt had said those four years on the farm were the happiest in his life, and their loss was traumatic and long remembered by him. Later, but early in his business life, Walt was betrayed by Pat Power, Charles Mintz and Ub Iwerks in turn. The last one, especially, was hurtful, but at least Walt and Iwerks were reconciled when the latter came back to work for the Disney studio in a technical capacity in the 1940s.

Born of these losses of control – where others had a dramatic effect on his life and business – Walt set about his lifelong project of not only constantly challenging himself to create something new and never before achieved, but to reshape the world in the way he wanted it, in a way he could control. His first theme park, Disneyland, was built around the counterfeit worlds of his imagination. He recreated Marceline's centre as Main Street USA – an idealized, sanitized version of his imaginative recall of the real thing. Walt's desire for total control over the experience the parks' attendees would have was, if not authoritarian, at least heavily paternalistic. In his fantasy 'perfect city' of EPCOT, Walt Disney echoed other would-be utopian projects, like Henry Ford's Fordlândia (built in the Amazon rainforest in 1928, coincidentally the year of Mickey Mouse's birth) or the later Brazilian capital, Brasília. Walt Disney built his own world and invited America to live in it.

Walt Disney was the twentieth century – the 'American century' – embodied in one man, with all its contradictions. After his death, the man and his legacy were attacked, notably in the late 1960s in Richard Schickel's *The Disney Version*, and in the 1990s in Marc Eliot's *Walt Disney: Hollywood's Dark Prince*. His legacy was large enough to withstand such attacks. Walt Disney was somehow able to encapsulate core American values and resell them to his countrymen, especially in times of difficulty or doubt, such as the Depression, during the Second World War or the troubled years of the Cold War. The America he showed on screen was idealized and reassuring, another of his many counterfeit worlds. There is no doubt that he was in tune with everyday Americans, and perhaps saw something of Davy Crockett, the archetypal 'country boy done good', in himself. Americans, for their part, largely welcomed his self-admitted 'corn' into their movie theatres, their homes through television, and their lives through toys and games and family trips to Disneyland, however manufactured it may have been.

Walt Disney's quest for 'personality' in his character animation, beginning with *Snow White*, was almost a quest to recreate life itself – a fitting endeavour for a 'creator'. The delays in producing *Bambi* were due to his dissatisfaction with

his animators' abilities to realistically depict the animals of the
forest, while *Snow White* had to wait until they mastered the
human form. His later fascination with 'animatronics', an artificial form of life that attempts to pass for human, was perhaps
the ultimate expression of this. His robotic Abraham Lincoln
– like Pinocchio, a marionette with no strings, a simulation of
life – would have been the ideal inhabitant of his highly regu-
lated, planned and controlled society of EPCOT. In 2014,
sixty-six year-old futurologist Ray Kurzweil – who was working with Google to develop real-world, human-like artificial
intelligence and robots – admitted to still wearing his thirty-
year-old Mickey Mouse watch. 'It's very important to hold on
to our whimsy – I think it's the highest level of our neocortex:
whimsy, humour,' he said, sentiments Walt would have agreed
with. However, in his hubris as a would-be world planner and
social engineer, Walt's ambition finally exceeded his reach and
he died before he could follow through his outlandish plan for
EPCOT. What did eventually result was a pale shadow of what
Walt had intended, and perhaps that was for the best.

Writing in *Life* magazine in 1964, professor of architec-
ture Vincent Scully said of Walt Disney that he 'so vulgarizes
everything he touches that facts lose all force, living things
their stature, and the "history of the world" its meaning.
Disney caters to the kind of phony reality – most horribly
exemplified by the moving and talking figure of Lincoln – that
we all too readily accept in place of the true. Mr Disney, I'm
afraid, has our number.' Additionally, French philosopher Jean
Baudrillard claimed: 'Disneyland is presented as imaginary in
order to make us believe that the rest is real, when in fact all
of Los Angeles and the America surrounding it are no longer
real, but of the order of the hyperreal and simulation.' If he
was nothing else, Walt Disney was America and America has
increasingly become more like Walt's Disneyland.

John Lasseter has often been called 'the new Walt Disney' –
it is a niche within the company that he now fills, whether

he likes the comparison or not. He knows what Walt Disney stood for, and what Disney films should be – for many years he and his teams at Pixar were out-Disneying the Disney studio itself, before their successful merger. 'I want kids to grow old remembering our films fondly so when they have kids, they're gonna want to bring them along to our movies,' said Lasseter of the kind of films 'his' Disney studio now produces. 'It was that way with Walt Disney's films. That's what you aim for.'

There is much more to come from the Disney studio, beyond Muppet movies, Marvel superheroes and a new series of *Star Wars* films. Forthcoming from Pixar is *Inside Out* (2015), set inside the head of a young girl tackling her troubled emotions, and *The Good Dinosaur* (2015), exploring a world in which dinosaurs did not become extinct. The belated *Finding Nemo* sequel, *Finding Dory*, should arrive in 2016, and more Pixar movies are set to follow regularly.

For Disney animation, the immediate future beyond *Frozen* holds *Big Hero 6* (2014), based upon a Marvel comics team, and *Zootopia* (2016), about a fox who goes on the run in an animal kingdom when he's framed for a crime he didn't commit. In live action (or animated/live-action combination) Disney seems intent on exploring its back catalogue, with Angelina Jolie as the 'mistress of all evil' in *Maleficent* (2014) – a process arguably begun with the Nicolas Cage-starring *The Sorcerer's Apprentice* in 2010. Live-action versions of Disney stand-bys like *Cinderella*, *The Jungle Book* and the Brad Bird-directed science-fiction mystery *Tomorrowland* (named after a section of Disneyland) should follow in 2015 – other films based on the Disney characters of Cruella de Vil, Beauty and the Beast and Donald Duck's antagonists Chip 'n' Dale are in development. Additionally, the *Pirates of the Caribbean* franchise looked set to continue sailing the seven seas for years to come – fifth instalment *Dead Men Tell No Tales* comes ashore in 2016. Some years further off are modern remakes of *Flight of the Navigator* and *Pete's Dragon*; it was only a matter of time until someone got around to redoing the ill-fated *The Black*

Hole, and *Prometheus* (2012) writer John Spaihts was working on a screenplay in 2014.

When addressing the team behind the successful Oscar-winning, box-office-conquering *Frozen* (now the international highest grossing animated film of all time), Lasseter summed up what the legacy of Walt Disney meant to him. 'Aim higher than you think you can possibly go,' he told the hundreds-strong creative team, 'because Walt Disney's name will be on our films. We have got to make films worthy of that name. There is something special that Walt Disney created, that unique entertainment that no one in the history of the world has ever been able to reproduce. To me, the world needs that kind of entertainment.'

In 2005, the John Lasseter-directed *Toy Story* was selected for inclusion in the National Film Registry of 'culturally historical, or aesthetically significant films', alongside Walt Disney's *Steamboat Willie* (1928) and *Snow White and the Seven Dwarfs* (1937). Somewhere beyond *Sleeping Beauty*'s castle that appears before every Disney movie, Walt Disney himself may have been watching with a degree of justified pride.

ACKNOWLEDGEMENTS AND SOURCES

Acknowledgements
Thanks, as always, to Brigid Cherry and Paul Simpson for their patience, tolerance and guidance. Thanks also to Duncan Proudfoot for commissioning the work, Louise Cullen for steering the book through the publication process, Howard Watson for his meticulous copyediting, and all at Constable & Robinson and Running Press.

Sources
Magazine and newspaper articles on the past, present and future of the Disney studio consulted during research include those published by *Vanity Fair*, *Entertainment Weekly*, *Variety*, *Hollywood Reporter* and the *Guardian* and websites slate.com, Cartoon Brew and michaelbarrier.com, among others.

BIBLIOGRAPHY

Barrier, Michael, *The Animated Man: A Life of Walt Disney* (Los Angeles: University of California Press, 2007).

Barrier, Michael, *Hollywood Cartoons: American Animation in its Golden Age* (London: Oxford University Press, 1999).

Beck, Jerry (ed.), *The 50 Greatest Cartoons* (Atlanta: Turner Publishing Inc., 1994).

Behlmer, Rudy, *Behind the Scenes* (Hollywood: Samuel French, 1990).

Blitz, Marcia, *Donald Duck* (London: New English Library, 1979).

Canemaker, John, *Winsor McCay: His Life and Art* (New York: Harry N. Abrams, Inc., 2005).

Cavalier, Steven, *The World History of Animation* (London: Aurum Press, 2011).

Crafton, Donald, *Before Mickey: The Animated Film, 1898–1928* (Chicago: University of Chicago Press, 1993).

Eliot, Marc, *Walt Disney: Hollywood's Dark Prince* (London: Andre Deutsch, 1994).

Fleischer, Richard, *Out of the Inkwell: Max Fleischer and the Animation Revolution* (Lexington: University Press of Kentucky, 2005).

Gabler, Neal, *Walt Disney: The Triumph of the American Imagination* (New York: Random House, 2006).

Girveau, Bruno, *Once Upon a Time: Walt Disney – The Sources of Inspiration for the Disney Studio* (Munich: Prestel, 2006).

Holliss, Richard and Brian Sibley, *The Disney Studio Story* (London: Octopus, 1988).

Iwerks, Leslie and John Kenworthy, *The Hand Behind the Mouse* (New York: Disney Editions, 2001).

Jackson, Kathy Merlock (ed.), *Walt Disney: Conversations* (Jackson: University of Mississippi, 2006).

Kaufman, J. B., *Snow White and the Seven Dwarfs: The Art and Creation of Walt Disney's Classic Animated Film* (San Francisco: Walt Disney Family Museum, 2012).

Klein, Norman M., *7 Minutes: The Life and Death of the American Animated Cartoon* (New York: Verso, 1993).

Lenburg, Jeff, *The Great Cartoon Directors* (New York: Da Capo Press, 1993).

Maltin, Leonard, *Of Mice and Magic: A History of American Animated Cartoons* (New York: Penguin, 1987).

Mosley, Leonard, *Disney's World: A Biography* (Lanham: Scarborough House, 1992).

Schickel, Richard, *The Disney Version: The Life, Times, Art and Commerce of Walt Disney* (Chicago: Elephant/Ivan R. Dee, 1997).

Smith, Dave and Steven Clark, *Disney: The First 100 Years* (New York: Hyperion, 1999).

Smoodin, Eric (ed.), *Disney Discourse: Producing the Magic Kingdom* (New York: Routledge, 1994).

Stewart, James, *Disney War* (New York: Simon & Schuster, 2006).

Susanin, Timothy S., *Walt Before Mickey: Disney's Early Years, 1919–1928* (Jackson: University of Mississippi, 2011).

Thomas, Bob, *Walt Disney: An American Original* (New York: Disney Editions, 1994).

Watts, Steven, *The Magic Kingdom: Walt Disney and the American Way of Life* (Columbia: University of Missouri Press, 1997).